Thomas A. Kamla

Confrontation with Exile:
Studies in the German Novel

# Europäische Hochschulschriften

*Publications Universitaires Européennes*

*European University Papers*

## Series I

## German language and literature

Reihe I        Série I

Deutsche Literatur und Germanistik
Langue et littérature allemandes

**Vol./Bd./ 137**

Thomas A. Kamla

Confrontation with Exile:
Studies in the German Novel

Herbert Lang Bern
Peter Lang Frankfurt/M.
1975

Thomas A. Kamla

# Confrontation with Exile:
# Studies in the German Novel

Herbert Lang Bern
Peter Lang Frankfurt/M.
1975

ISBN 3 261 01843 7

©

Peter Lang GmbH, Frankfurt/M. (BRD)
Herbert Lang & Cie AG, Bern (Schweiz)
1975. Alle Rechte vorbehalten.

Druck: fotokop wilhelm weihert KG, Darmstadt

# TABLE OF CONTENTS

Introduction     7

Chapter I. Klaus Mann: Flucht in den Norden
The Problem of the Decadent Revolutionary     19

Chapter II. Klaus Mann: Der Vulkan
Reality, Geist, and Metaphysical Synthesis     27

Chapter III. Konrad Merz: Ein Mensch fällt aus Deutschland
The "Inner" and "Outer" Exile of Youth     35

Chapter IV. Hans Habe: Drei über die Grenze
The Waiting Room and the Political Left     45

Chapter V. Lion Feuchtwanger: Exil
Narrative Detachment and Self-Portraiture     57

Chapter VI. Bruno Frank: Der Reisepass
The Exile as an Aristocrat of Humanity     67

Chapter VII. Erich Maria Remarque: Liebe Deinen Nächsten
Asylum on the Border     77

Chapter VIII. Erich Maria Remarque: Arc de Triomphe
Escape from Exile     87

Chapter IX. Irmgard Keun: Kind aller Länder
The Writer in Exile     93

Chapter X. Renée Brand: Niemandsland
Political Captivity and Esthetic Freedom     101

Chapter XI. Walter Hasenclever: Die Rechtlosen
The Internment Camp and the Freedom of Captivity     111

Chapter XII. Ernst Neubach: Flugsand
The Orthodox versus the Western Jew: Exile as an Extension of
the Diaspora or a Preparation for Assimilation?     117

Chapter XIII. Robert Groetzsch: Wir suchen ein Land
Inner Emigration in Exile     125

Chapter XIV. Fritz Erpenbeck: Emigranten
Programmed Left-Sectarianism in Early Exile     135

Chapter XV.  Friedrich Wolf: Zwei an der Grenze
    The Frustrated Revolutionary in Exile                145

Chapter XVI.  Anna Seghers: Transit
    A Reassessment                                       155

Footnotes                                                163

Selected Bibliography                                    177

# INTRODUCTION

## A. Origins of the Exile Novel

German emigrant authors wrote countless novels in exile from which only a scattered few can be described as novels of exile. The novel of exile (or exile novel) forms a category of prose deserving of special attention by virtue of a condition common to all writers forced from their homeland -- the phenomenon of exile itself. That so few artists of established repute (Lion Feuchtwanger, Klaus Mann, Bruno Frank, Erich Maria Remarque, Friedrich Wolf, Walter Hasenclever, Anna Seghers) turned to the exile scene for their subject matter perhaps accounts for the present lack of a study of the kind to be undertaken here. Half of the fourteen authors to be treated either knew only a brief interlude of popularity prior to exile (Irmgard Keun, Fritz Erpenbeck, Robert Groetzsch) or did not take up writing until after their escape from Nazi Germany (Konrad Merz, Renée Brand) and Austria (Hans Habe, Ernst Neubach). Scholars in exile literature who limit their research to authors of artistic merit will understandably tend to pass over these obscure names in an attempt to restore the more renowned exiled writers to their proper place in German literature. For our purposes, however, the lesser known authors deserve to be included as an integral part of the body of writers addressing itself to the exile predicament in the novel. Although genuine artistic quality is not readily apparent in some cases, these authors nevertheless depict a problematical situation in the way they confront the political consequences resulting from their flight into exile. Indeed, their treatment of the exile condition is at times even more thought-provoking than the situations presented by some of the celebrated artists. In this respect, the literary beginners have just as much "originality" to offer as the professionally established. The emigration was perpetrated by adverse political conditions within the Third Reich, and the composite reactions to this situation must be considered if a total perspective is to be achieved. If we were to restrict our study to those exile novels produced by the more "worthy" authors, then the resultant dearth of material would hardly warrant their treatment as a special category of prose. The inclusion of the lesser known works in this group, however, lends an added depth to the novel of exile which justifies its evaluation within the framework of literature as a select body of prose.

Needless to say, a total of sixteen novels is still unimpressive when one recalls the wealth of novels portraying nonexile themes (e. g. , universal problems of man, history, class exploitation in Nazi Germany, the conflict in Spain). One could rightly ask what had prevented more writers from treating such a pervasive condition as exile in their works. The scarcity of a particular kind of novel whose essential aspects are representative of the emigration as a whole begs clarification.

Although critics have noted this peculiarity, few have really attempted to explain it. Walter A. Berendsohn comments: "Es widerspricht völlig der landläufigen vorgefassten Meinung, aber ist doch eine merkwürdige Tatsache, dass nur so wenige der emigrierten Schriftsteller das Emigranten-Dasein selbst zum Gegenstand wählen." (1) Berendsohn reiterates his bewilderment in yet another publication: "Das Emigranten-Dasein und die neue Umwelt nehmen wider Erwarten in der Zeit 1933-39 nur wenig Raum ein in der Emigrantenliteratur." (2) Matthias Wegner makes a similar observation: "Das Schicksal des Emigranten ist nicht nur das Erlebnis eines einzelnen; der grösste Teil der deutschen Schriftsteller teilte in den zwölf Jahren der NS-Diktatur dieses Schicksal, und folglich stand auch die Auseinandersetzung damit vielfach im Mittelpunkt ihres Denkens. Natürlich hat nicht jeder Schriftsteller der Emigration die Exil-Problematik in seinem literarischen Werk beschrieben." (3) Wegner goes on to cite some of the famous authors in this connection (e.g., Thomas Mann, Robert Musil), but fails to explain why it was "natural" that most writers turned to other themes in their works.

Karl O. Paetel's more penetrating assessment sheds historical light on the situation:

> Der Begriff der Emigrantenliteratur oder die Bezeichnung 'Literatur im Exil' umschreiben keineswegs in erster Linie Publikationen, die die deutsche Emigration der Hitlerzeit zum Thema haben. Relativ selten findet sich in den bis zum Zusammenbruch des Dritten Reiches im deutschen Exil veröffentlichten Büchern (auf deutsch oder auch in andern Sprachen!) Problematik, Erlebniswelt oder Lebensform des 'Anderen Deutschland' autobiographisch, sei es in Form von Tagebuchzeichnungen, Lebensgeschichten, politischen Memoiren oder auch Romanen, ausgewertet. Von Ausnahmen abgesehen haben deutsche emigrierte Autoren oft erst nach dem Sturz Hitlers nach ihrer Heimkehr nach Deutschland oder nachdem sie endgültig in einem andern Land Wurzeln geschlagen haben, sich Rechenschaft über die Zeit des Exils abzugeben versucht. (4)

Paetel touches on a point here that explains one reason for the meager sum of exile novels produced during the emigration. The exile scene, based largely on the personal situation of the author to begin with, was in most cases less an esthetic experience as it was a factual, or purely empirical, one. Rather than confront the immediate situation in artistic terms, which for most liberal writers would have restricted their freedom of expression, countless authors dealt with nonrelated themes that precluded the possibility of such a compromise arising. Instead, they reserved their account of the exile for other such nonliterary genres as the autobiography, memoirs, and diaries. In our text analyses it will become apparent that documentation and factual narrative are basic structural characteristics of the exile novel. Reality is not prescribed, but rooted in direct experience. Therefore, the treatment of life in exile predominantly in the form of autobiography, etc., rather than in creative fiction, was a more appropriate medium for relating a highly eventful set of circumstances.

Besides the apparent preference for autobiographical accounts of the exile years, another factor could have explained the sporadic output of the novel. The emigrant author had to consider the kind of audience for whom he was writing. In order to market his books within the German-speaking guest nations, he could not afford to overlook the element of appeal. The salability of a product could only have been jeopardized if an author had in mind to portray the distressing manifestations of exiled life in a foreign country. The writer depicting a milieu which critically reflected the bureaucratic injustice of the guest nation and the daily hardships suffered by the emigration as a direct or indirect outcome of this predicament could hardly expect to fare favorably in the particular country forming the setting of his work. The German-speaking readers, many of whom were taken in by the extreme nationalism of Nazi ideology, (5) were suffering similar hardships produced by the world economic crisis, and it is unlikely that they would have been openly receptive to a novel portraying an unwanted emigration that aggravated already existing economic and social problems. The Marxist writer, on the other hand, could turn to the ideological homeland in the Soviet Union for a more favorable reading audience inasmuch as the problems described in his exile novel arose only in n o n - C o m m u n i s t countries. In the Soviet Union he could often rely on local publishing firms to translate his work into the vernacular. Two novels in question -- Fritz Erpenbeck's E m i g r a n t e n and Friedrich Wolf's Z w e i  a n  d e r  G r e n z e -- appeared in Russian editions before ever reaching the German exile press. That only three of the fourteen writers in this study are Marxists shows that the artistic confrontation with exile was largely a bourgeois phenomenon. If a Marxist author did sense a conflict related to his exile experience (and some certainly did during the People's Front era), it usually tied in with his ideological loyalty to the Soviet Union, a problem he was not about to admit openly in his writings.


## B. The Exile Novel as a Topic of Scholarly Inquiry

Systematic research in the area of the exile novel is about as scanty as the production figures of the genre itself. To date, only one scholarly attempt has been made to view this novel as a select category of prose. In his analysis of four of the novels included in this study, Matthias Wegner (6) has shown the necessity of further investigation into a field of exile literature which has been overlooked thus far. Most other evaluations have been undertaken on an individual basis and usually from a position that tends to discount the more obvious exile dilemma as it relates to the author's political and artistic outlook  Besides Wegner, the only other critic, himself a former exile, who offers any kind of valuable insight into the body of exile novels as they reflect the political, psychological, and existential manifestations of the emigration is Hans Mayer. (7) These critics will be treated in greater detail as the introductory discussion progresses.


Investigations before 1945

To avoid repeated cross-reference, specific comments on the reactions of exiled writers to the novels of their colleagues will be reserved for the individual chapters. The intent at this point is to give a general synopsis of the artistic and political opinions advanced by bourgeois and Marxist writers in their reviews of certain exile novels at the time. If one could arrive at a unifying characteristic that would describe the attitudes of various writers towards the exile novel, it would have to lie in their failure to regard it as an exile novel  According to the approach displayed, each reviewer, whether from the liberal or Marxist camp, extracts from the work those artistic precepts which conform to preconceived standards. Thus, when the liberal Klaus Mann (8) talks about Bruno Frank's Der Reisepass or the Marxist Heinrich Werth (9) treats Friedrich Wolf's Zwei an der Grenze, a tendency arises on their part to evade the problematic issues in an effort to cast the author in question in a light favorable to their particular way of viewing things. Where the liberals do not seem concerned with the fact that one of their own might betray an artistic dilemma produced by the political demands of exile, the Marxists are unwilling to admit that their revolutionary ideology might have encountered certain obstacles stemming from immediate conditions. Admittedly, these reviewers do acknowledge the presence of the emigration scene in their discussions. Invariably, however, they overlook any conflict between the artist and his environment. What we are left with, in most cases, is an interesting plot summary with personal remarks interjected by the reviewer that correspond to the artistic norms he has already established for himself.

Ludwig Marcuse (10) and Lion Feuchtwanger (11) (who, during the People's Front period, sided closely with the Marxists) have joined Mann and Werth, respectively, in their praise of Der Reisepass and Zwei an der Grenze. In dealing with these novels both ideological camps, the liberal-humanistic and the revolutionary, render an interpretation that suggests all is well with the world. Mann and Marcuse see Frank's hero as the model of noble humanity, an ideal figure who has weathered the turmoil of the times without compromising the great cultural and moral values that had traditionally elevated humanity and Geist above the distasteful reality of political engagement. Feuchtwanger and Werth perceive Wolf's novel in simple terms of the class struggle against Fascist oppression at home and abroad. The dissatisfaction of the Bohemian workers with the ruthless conditions of employment and the hero's secret political missions on the border are an expression of an undaunted revolutionary spirit that will one day culminate in the dissolution of "capitalist" tyranny. Neither group confronts the representative exile issues in these novels. The liberals fail to see Frank's retreat to an abstract ivory tower as an escape from the political demands forming an inextricable part of the Nazi-perpetrated emigration. Their intrinsic assessment of Der Reisepass transcends the problem of art and politics that had characterized a sizable segment of the liberal literary emigration. They seem to find solace in the knowledge that an esthetic humanism can still be perpetuated in spite of the exile.

The Marxist side, in contrast to the individualistic reactions of its liberal colleagues, displays a traditional propensity for viewing social struggle in revolutionary literature that admits of no ideological dilemma on the part of the author. Feuchtwanger and Werth express an interest only in that part of Wolf's novel portraying collective action. Either through oversight or for strategic reasons they refrain from discussing the crucial chapter "Einsamkeit," which not only forms the ideological basis for the representative exile experience of those leftist writers torn between exile and the homeland, but also sheds questionable light on the source of revolutionary theory, namely, the Soviet Union. Feuchtwanger and

Werth make no mention of the exiled Marxist's loyalties being split between the Soviet Union as the ideological home and the true homeland, a conflict which is unmistakably present in Wolf's novel, however concealed in tone. Exile for the Marxists became somewhat problematic when the revolutionary homeland had compromised the spirit of the People's Front through its "cleansing" program of 1936-37. Wolf's novel, a product of this era, shows that the revolutionary struggle of a people undergoes a redefinition in light of the specific circumstances prevailing. The two reviewers miss the obvious point of the work, and in doing so they skirt the problems experienced by German Marxists in exile in much the same way that the liberal reviewers evade the crucial issue of the bourgeois humanist caught up in the predicament between an abstract preservation of art and the historical necessity of actualizing his craft in the service of a political commitment.

The novel treating the emigrant scene apparently exerted little influence on the general body of exiled literati. In addition to the novels just mentioned, I cite two more that came up for discussion in exile journals: Klaus Mann's D e r  V u l k a n and Irmgard Keun's K i n d  a l l e r  L ä n d e r. The intellectuals reviewing these works manifest the same uncritical tendencies as the foregoing. (12)

These observations would seem to point to one conclusion: the isolated works treated by emigrant authors are discussed only peripherally as exile novels. The exile themes, if acknowledged at all, are usually summarized and then distorted to fit either pre-established concepts of artistic production or a dogmatic ideology that presumes to be flawless. That so few exile novels enjoyed the privilege of widespread reviews (13) suggests that the psychological and ideological problems they reveal were not of especial interest to writers in terms of artistic content. Authors apparently did not care to be reminded of the realities plaguing their daily lives, at least not through the creative medium. The tendency of reviewers to evade or purposely overlook the pressing issues stemming from the novels mentioned above would seem to bear this out. Rather it is the novel dealing with less confining and more artistically appropriate themes that receive the greatest attention in such prominent emigrant newspapers and journals as D i e  S a m m l u n g, D a s  N e u e  T a g e b u c h, M a s s  u n d  W e r t, D i e  N e u e  W e l t b ü h n e, D a s W o r t, and I n t e r n a t i o n a l e  L i t e r a t u r.


## Investigations after 1945

The first literary impulses pointing to the existence of such a category of prose as the exile novel appear in the form of surveys and handbooks. Walter A. Berendsohn's D i e  h u m a n i s t i s c h e  F r o n t (14) and F.C. Weiskopf's U n t e r f r e m d e n  H i m m e l n (15) were instrumental in enabling me to gather the small amount of primary material now at my disposal. Without the aid of these histories the present study very likely would never have been undertaken. These texts extend beyond the presentation of the more celebrated authors who wrote exile novels, including lesser known and obscure ones as well. Berendsohn's and Weiskopf's broad surveys of the literature in exile do not presume to initiate a critical study into the individual works at hand. For my purposes rather, their service to the field of the exile novel rests with the classification of emigrant literature into thematic groupings. By organizing the wealth of writing, both belletristic and factual, into meaningful categories, they have performed a welcome service to scholarship in this untapped area of German exile studies.

The two bio-bibliographies that appeared subsequent to the above surveys provide added information about the lives and works of exiled authors. Wilhelm Sternfeld's and Eva Tiedemann's Deutsche Exil-Literatur 1933-1945 (16) was useful insofar as I could readily acquire biographical data through an alphabetical listing. When one has only the novel itself to draw on in an analysis (as in the case of the obscure writers), one is grateful for any amount of biographical information, however skeletal it may be. Werner Berthold's catalogue Exil-Literatur 1933-1945 (17) was also helpful in that it categorizes, like Berendsohn's and Weiskopf's works, the literature in exile according to groups. Berthold's handbook provides thorough biographical descriptions and text summaries, however, on only a limited number of exile novels.

Actual scholarly criticism of the exile novel, beginning in the late 1950's and continuing to the present, has produced only scattered insights into the matters concerning us here. When one considers that a mere six of the sixteen novels occupying our attention have received scholarly treatment after 1945, then it becomes plain that the exile novel as a collective body of prose still needs to be investigated. For the most part critics have dealt with the exile novel on an individual basis, producing thereby an isolated impression of this genre. Furthermore, the majority of scholars treating these novels are Marxists. This implies two things: the works written by exiled revolutionaries had produced a substantial amount of socialist literature showing a historical continuity with post-war Eastern Europe; liberal critics, on the other hand, seem to be less prepared to make a similar acknowledgment. Until the appearance of Matthias Wegner's Exil und Literatur in 1967, West German criticism has undertaken practically no detailed studies of the exile novel. Lion Feuchtwanger's Exil, Erich Maria Remarque's Liebe deinen Nächsten and Arc de Triomphe, and Klaus Mann's Der Vulkan -- all novels by bourgeois writers -- have captured mainly the interest of Eastern critics. The Communist writer Anna Seghers has enjoyed a degree of popularity in the West with her novel Transit, but the majority of critical acclaim has originated in the Communist countries.

The question as to what is to be classified as true German literature and what is not seems to account partly for the relative lack of concern in the West for exile literature in general, of which the exile novel is but a small part. Matthias Wegner has disclosed the historical causes leading up to this segregation:

In der DDR verlief die Konfrontation von Exil-Literatur und Gegenwarts-Literatur einigermassen nahtlos: von den marxistischen Emigranten, die nach dem Zweiten Weltkrieg in den östlichen Teil Deutschlands zurückkehrten, führt eine konsequente Linie zur dortigen Gegenwarts-Literatur schon insofern, als sich die kulturpolitischen Dogmen des Marxismus dort kaum verändert haben und der 'sozialistische Realismus' formal gesehen an die bürgerliche Erzähltradition des 19. Jahrhunderts unmittelbar anschliesst und somit einen Rückgriff auf altbewährte Dichtungskategorien bezeichnet. Dadurch, dass die Nachkriegsliteratur der Bundesrepublik von Anfang an das Zeichen des Neubeginns in sich trug, und damit für viele Emigranten einen enttäuschenden Verlauf nahm, musste auch oft der Eindruck entstehen, als zeige sich der westliche Teil Deutschlands den Emigranten gegenüber sehr viel feindseliger als sein östlicher Nachbar. (18)

Relating this historical gap to the "Versäumnis der deutschen Literaturwissenschaft gegenüber der Exil-Literatur," (19) Wegner goes on to say:

Ein Blick in unsere Literaturgeschichte zeigt, dass das Stichwort Exil-Literatur dort entweder gar nicht oder bestenfalls am Rande auftaucht. Ein Grund dafür, dass Literaturwissenschaft und -kritik eine umfassendere Analyse der Exil-Literatur in ihrer Gesamtheit bisher versäumt haben, liegt wohl in der häufig vertretenen Ansicht, die deutsche Literatur im Exil könne nicht den Anspruch erheben, als eine eigene literaturgeschichtliche Kategorie behandelt zu werden. So berechtigt ein solcher Einwand sein mag, so verbergen sich dahinter doch oft nur unausgesprochene und schwer zu beseitigende Ressentiments gegen den Emigranten an sich; zudem fehlt es oft einfach an den nötigen Einblicken in das Text- und Dokumentations-Material der Exil-Literatur. Die Tatsache, dass wohl der grösste Teil der deutschen Schriftsteller von Rang Deutschland zu Beginn des Jahres 1933 verlassen musste, ist für diese Literatur doch folgenreicher gewesen, als es auf den ersten Blick scheinen möchte. Selbstverständlich ändert das nichts an der Tatsache, dass die Exil-Literatur zum Gesamtbereich der deutschen Literatur gerechnet werden muss. (20)

That a thorough investigation into the literature in exile has been sorely neglected in Western Germanistik only serves to point out that such a "disagreeable" genre as the exile novel has failed to receive any criticism to speak of. Such names as Konrad Merz, Robert Groetzsch, Renée Brand, and Ernst Neubach -- even Friedrich Wolf and Walter Hasenclever, whose primary dramatic medium would understandably draw more critical interest than their prose writings -- can hardly be expected to emerge as subjects of literary study when the overall literature in exile is still attempting to secure its rightful place in German literary history.

In view of these circumstances, the isolated number of exile novels which do appear as topics of literary scholarship after 1945 do not constitute a systematic overview of the genre, but are restricted to individual interpretations over which debate would be superfluous in an introduction. The specific comments of these critics will be incorporated in the chapters to follow.


C. The Exile Novel Defined
_____

In the closing chapter of Exil und Literatur, Matthias Wegner introduces the novel that embodies the exile experience as a literary theme. About the selection of novels examined (Lion Feuchtwanger's Exil, Anna Seghers' Transit, Klaus Mann's Der Vulkan, and Walter Hasenclever's Die Rechtlosen), Wegner remarks: "In den hier behandelten Romanen liefert das Exil nicht nur den

Hintergrund für eine Handlung, die auch unabhängig von der Exil-Situation vor-
stellbar wäre. Die vier Romane beziehen ihren Stoff ausschliesslich aus der Pro-
blematik des aus seinem Land vertriebenen Emigranten." (21) Wegner makes it
clear that he is dealing with a certain kind of novel in exile, one in which the exile
scene provides the artistic stimulus (in contrast to the autobiography) for the work
at hand.

In line with this description those novels will be excluded that only allude to
the exile situation or deal with it peripherally. (22) Prose works written for the
express purpose of enlightening society about the brutal oppression of the Nazi
regime, whether in the form of historical novels, novels about life in concentration camps, or novels of class struggle and revolution, will not fall within the
scope of this study. Although works of this kind are definitely products of the exile
period, they portray an arena other than that of exile from which they launch their
anti-fascist polemic. The political stance of the author is of significance only in
its relationship to the exile condition itself. To illustrate, I mention briefly two
of the Marxist novels under consideration: Fritz Erpenbeck's E m i g r a n t e n and
Friedrich Wolf's Z w e i  a n  d e r  G r e n z e. In that the political unification of the
working class and the propagation of a revolutionary ideology are themes functional
to the works of Communist writers as a whole, they normally would belong to the
category of proletarian K a m p f l i t e r a t u r, and not necessarily to that of the
exile novel. Yet the exile scene has a direct bearing on the political behavior of
the revolutionaries in these novels, and it is for this reason that they are included
in this study.

Perhaps the most outstanding characteristic of the exile novel is its topicality,
which presupposes that the action, setting, and motivations of the figures evince an
illusion of historical authenticity. Concomitantly, a conspicuous structural peculiarity of most exile novels is that of adventure, whereby documentary material
and stirring personal experiences directly influence the author's choice of material. The degree to which factual phenomena are adhered to varies from one writer
to another so that, at times, the dividing line between art and nonfiction is not always readily apparent. Ernst Neubach labels F l u g s a n d a documentary novel, in
which the events in themselves become so hectic as to suggest an illusion of action-
packed fiction. At the opposite extreme lies Klaus Mann's D e r  V u l k a n, a novel
whose erotic interludes, metaphysical digressions, and individual estheticism are
so pervasive that the reality of exile momentarily eludes the critic.

In those instances where the author deals in intimate character analysis or
transcends the realm of empirical reality, we must see how such apparent digressions relate to the exile situation. Contrary to Hans Mayer's assessment of the
exile novel (to be discussed in the following section), one could defend the position
that such "poetic" episodes would not necessarily have arisen in a nonexile
environment. They do not constitute an end in themselves. Then one would be
dealing primarily with love stories, utopian dream worlds, and timeless existential
predicaments -- themes that conceivably c o u l d be removed from the exile experience but, as the analyses will try to show, are not.

The artistic merits of the body of exile novels occupy a wide spectrum.
Each novel must be examined in light of the way an individual author assesses the
political and material demands imposed on him in exile. Intimate character study

may reveal a tendency to escape from the distressing realities of exile (D e r
V u l k a n); it may, on the other hand, heighten the misery felt by uprootedness
(E x i l). Retreat to the "nonexile" realm of symbol may serve to place a historical
imprint on the exile period, indicating a dynamic struggle between the forces of
progress and retrogression, of enlightenment and obscurantism (Konrad Merz's
E i n  M e n s c h  f ä l l t  a u s  D e u t s c h l a n d). This retreat may also spring
merely from an author's predilection for envisioning the exile years leading up to
the holocaust of 1939 to 1945 as a manifestation of cosmic determinism (Walter
Hasenclever's D i e  R e c h t l o s e n).

In Merz's case, the author's attempt to come to terms with exile reflects a
dialectic progression in the form of an idea, one erupting from a world pervaded
by futility, senselessness, and despair. In the discussions of the novels to follow,
the credibility of this kind of portrayal will be examined. Briefly, Feuchtwanger
copes with this problem in  E x i l  when the ominous realities of the day (politics
and M a c h t) clash with their timeless opposites (art and G e i s t). In D e r  R e i -
s e p a s s  Bruno Frank imparts a transforming quality to the exile experience
when he envisages a humane Germany built upon the noble values upheld by those
who had left it. Merz undertakes a similar task, but in a set of metaphors that at
first seem to defy the logic of historical progress. Again, other novels viewing
the exile in historical, philosophical, or metaphysical terms (Hasenclever's D i e
R e c h t l o s e n, Mann's D e r  V u l k a n, Habe's D r e i  ü b e r  d i e  G r e n z e)
fail to achieve any sort of dialectic confrontation and remain dangling in archetypal
categories that appear just as irrational as the chaos of reality underlying them.
Such a failure does not necessarily remove them from the category of the exile
novel, however. The author may alter his reality at times, mold it to his wishes
in order to escape it, elevate it into symbolic spheres. But these artistic devices
only illustrate the way he reacts to the problematic state of exile, which always
constitutes his starting point.


D. The Writer in Exile
_____

In D r e i  ü b e r  d i e  G r e n z e  Hans Habe devotes an extra chapter to an
analysis of the historical background of the German emigration. From this analysis
one will readily conclude that the heterogenous nature of the literary emigration
merely reflected the diverse character of the emigrant population as a whole. In
one passage Habe perceptively notes a certain incongruity in the emigration of
1933. Although the experience of exile was common to all, the reactions to it were
multifarious:

> Auf Hunderten von Landstrassen strömte ein Volk von Tausenden hinaus aus
> der Heimat, das Einzige zurücklassend, das gemeinsam gewesen war:
> Deutschland. Auf Hunderten von Landstrassen vollzog sich gemeinsames
> Schicksal ohne Gemeinsamkeit, Tausende wanderten, nebeneinander, aber
> nicht miteinander. Auf Hunderten von Eisenbahnschienen jagte tausend-
> fältige Hoffnungslosigkeit hinaus aus dem geliebten verfluchten Land, Hoff-
> nungslosigkeit erster Klasse, zweiter Klasse, dritter Klasse, Hoffnungs-

losigkeit im Schlafwagen und auf der Holzpritsche, Hoffnungslosigkeit, die sich nicht verstand. In Hunderten von Städten begegneten sich dann die Verbannten, die kein Zeichen trugen, das sie einander erkennen liess. In kleinen und grossen Hotels, auf dem Zwischendeck und in der Salonkajüte, vor dem Bezirksrichter, und in der vornehmen Anwaltskanzlei, in der Gefängniszelle und auf dem Konsulat erlebten sie, was sie auf der Landstrasse erlebt hatten: Die Gemeinsamkeit ohne Gemeinschaft, die Parallelität, die sich nie, oder nur im Unendlichen schneidet. Millionen gleichlaufende Schienen, Ewig-Einander-Sehen -- aber nie Zueinanderkönnen. (23)

The distressing reality of exile was shared by all; yet the reactions were divided. Grouped together by a common fate but segregated by conflicting attitudes, beliefs, and ideologies, the emigration of 1933 exhibited a variety of individual actions and motivations that became typical through the experience of identical hardships and misery. Throughout the majority of novels there appears the perpetual fugitive who lacks official identity and is always hounded by bureaucratic agents; there are the resigned and despairing, the uprooted languishing in nostalgia; there are the politically defiant whose anti-Nazi protests are motivated out of contempt, a sense of democratic humanism, or a collective ideology; there are the hopeful whose brief and delusive optimism is sustained by love and a selfless readiness to give; and there are the esthetes and anarchistic revolutionaries who denounce all forms of society, whether totalitarian or democratic.

This typology, as well as our definition of the exile novel, could appear unconvincing to scholars who postulate a different set of criteria for establishing this genre as a distinct category of prose. The former emigrant and literary critic Hans Mayer has addressed himself to the very issues that concern us here. (24) In his investigation of the novel taking as its theme the material and political manifestations of the German exile, he arrives at some conclusions that would appear to make questionable any scholarly inquiry into the genre. Mayer contends it is not possible for contemporary critics to grasp the real meaning of exile in belletristic prose because the majority of novels had failed to present a true picture of the situation. He bases this argument on the premise that most emigrant writers had traditionally fostered an "unkritische Konzeption des literarischen Realismus." (25) Accordingly, he sees their artistic presentation of the prevailing scene as transcending common experience and resulting in a fabricated portrayal ("Fiktion" (26)) that could have been written at most any time in history. Mayer cites, as examples, such works as Bruno Frank's Der Reisepass, Klaus Mann's Der Vulkan, Lion Feuchtwanger's Exil, and Erich Maria Remarque's Liebe deinen Nächsten and Arc de Trimphe. Only with Anna Seghers' Transit does he make an exception. He describes her work in terms of "Wahrheit der Kunstwerke" (27) because of its realistic depiction of the exile. Mayer then cautions critics to beware of other works treating the exile scene. As an antipode to "Wahrheit" he refers to "gestaltetes Erleben," (28) which, in his opinion, any imaginative author could have created irrespective of direct experience. Implicit in Mayer's criticism is an attack on the tradition of individualism and its preoccupation with the supremacy of the independent intellect over social and political phenomena which tend to restrict autonomous creation. He thus sees a discrepancy between the political demands and harsh realities of exile and their artistic treatment "in der erlernten und ... bewährten Arbeitsweise." (29) Taking Mayer's line of argument as a methodological approach to the exile novel, we would have to exclude the majority of works in this study as well as drastically revise our definition.

Yet the analyses of the novels included here are predicated on the assumption that these works would, in fact, have appeared in a different form had they been written during another period. With the exception of Erich Maria Remarque's two novels, the others emerged as products of a chaotic environment of which the writer was an integral part. The liberal author who resorts to a "traditional" mode of portrayal in the exile novel reveals a narrative posture which does not distort the W a h r h e i t of historical reality, but which creates a conflict with respect to it. In other words a quasinaturalistic portrayal of the emigrant condition does not constitute the criterion for determining the credibility of the exile novel; rather it is the way the liberal writer confronts the W a h r h e i t , or reality, of exile that lends to the works at hand a definite credence.

I cannot share Mayer's partiality to T r a n s i t when I speak of the liberal writer. The Communist novelist Anna Seghers fosters a creative method in which art and social reality had traditionally served a mutual function. The liberal authors, many of whom represent an ideology in which individual freedom had transcended the dictates of political programs and social action, must be considered critically within the scope of their own artistic premises.

Mayer correctly observes the lack of a "gemeinsamer Erlebniszusammenhang" (30) in the exile novel. He goes on to say: "Man wird von einem bestürzenden Misserfolg all dieser Bemühungen sprechen müssen. Die Exilliteratur hat vor dem Phänomen des Exils weit stärker versagt als vor nahezu jeder anderen Realitätsparzelle." (31) Mayer's criticism is based on the premise that the exile condition ought to have brought about an artistic posture that accurately reflected the political and social foundations of a homeless "other Germany." Since, in his opinion, a discrepancy emerged between the experience of a common reality and its nonrepresentational artistic portrayal, one cannot rightfully speak of the exile novel as a valid body of prose.

It is arguable, however, that a nonsocialist-oriented writer cannot be expected to adapt his traditional style that readily to an abruptly changed situation. The way he had previously conceptualized reality in his works will continue, in a variety of forms, to influence his writing in exile. Admittedly, problems invariably arise when these writers turn to a theme in which political and social conditions, thus far largely divorced from their artistic concept of freedom, constitute the main subject matter. But then such problems are to be anticipated. Thus an absence of a "gemeinsamer Erlebniszusammenhang" really ought to induce one to further investigation. (32)

# CHAPTER I

## KLAUS MANN: FLUCHT IN DEN NORDEN

### The Problem of the Decadent Revolutionary

Like most literary spokesmen for the "other Germany," Klaus Mann had
left his native land in defiance of the intellectual Ungeist molded by Hitler's
cultural politics. His physical move into exile did not alter his material existence
appreciably; nor was the psychological break with the German people an especially
uprooting experience for him. A frequent traveler outside Germany, Mann had re-
sided in France, Switzerland, and the United States prior to the Nazi rise to power.
More often away than at home, he was able to acclimate himself to his foreign
surroundings without serious difficulty when he found himself in France again in
1933. In Escape to Life he remarks that he had never felt homeless, for he
could never lose his native country as a "spiritual possession," (1) albeit he never
regarded Germany as his only home.

Yet the departure in 1933 was precipitated by a political crisis which, even
to a cosmopolitan esthete, demanded a critical assessment of a Weltanschauung based on liberal humanism and intellectual freedom. (2) "The relentless strain
of those days," Mann recalls in his autobiography, "compelled the sensitive and
creative minds everywhere to revise a philosophy of laissez-faire and individualism
to which all of us had adhered more or less openly, in various ways and degrees."
(3) Mann quickly rose to the occasion. One of the most prolific and versatile
essayists of the early emigration, he unrelentingly set his pen to the task of exposing the duplicity of the new German government and of revealing to other nations
the fallacy of an attitude that fails to distinguish the German people from their
leaders. (4) He, like other literary exiles, had naturally entertained the hope that
the reign of Nazism would be shortlived once the major Western powers recognized
its imperialistic designs and responded firmly to the urgency of the situation: "But
I took it for granted that the Nazi farce wouldn't last. No doubt, the powerful democracies would know how to cope with the primitive rascals. It could hardly be
difficult for France, Great Britain, and the United States to do away with a handful
of morbid imposters. All that seemed necessary was one stern and impressive
gesture on the part of those governments, the recall of their diplomatic representatives or the severance of trade relations with a Nazified Reich." (5) Needless to
say, Mann was to learn differently. The democracies remained aloof from the
internal affairs of Nazi Germany, a policy which often led other Europeans to believe that the exiles had performed a disservice to their country by deserting it,
regardless of the party in power. (6)

A general attitude of fear and noninvolvement in Europe, the preferential
treatment afforded Germany as a potential counterthreat to Bolshevism, and the
presence of nationalist factions identifying with the Nazi regime underline the foreboding political climate that was beginning to loom over the Continent when, during

the early months of 1934, Mann decided to deal with the exile scene in his novel Flucht in den Norden. The democracies had proved to be an ineffective deterrent to Nazism in the early thirties. Yet the Soviet Union, the antipode of that democratic individualism professed by Mann himself, was mustering its forces in a united front effort that was sorely lacking among noncommunist nations.

In dealing with the exile theme in his novel, Mann could hardly overlook the issues which were descending upon the international political scene at the time. But he gives form to these issues in a manner most unexpected for a writer whose artistic predilection was to keep creative expression free of any sociological content, especially if it smacks of "vulgar materialism." (7) In Flucht in den Norden he makes a rather radical swing to the left when he develops a theme centering on the experiences of a communist exiled in Finland. Since the democracies were politically panicstricken and the Soviet Union was not, it is understandable that Mann, in a nonliterary role, would be willing, at least, to cooperate with the one nation that did pose a viable counterthreat to the spread of fascist tyranny. (8) It is another matter when he attempts to radicalize this cooperative spirit through an artistic posture that is anything but socialistic.

Mann's portrayal of a revolutionary as his heroine immediately elicits some ideological assumptions which must be considered in a critical approach to the work. Does the author's exposure of both the right-wing political and cosmopolitan, liberal attitudes evinced by the secondary characters anticipate, by the emergence of a communist as leading character, a revolutionary solution to the present crisis? Concomitantly, does the heroine's dedication to the class struggle stem from an attitude that dialectically engages the forces of progress against those of reaction and apolitical individualism, and is it based on a critical insight into Hitler's "socialism" as a ruthless capitalist undertaking? As we deal with these issues, it will become apparent that the author's manner of treating his revolutionary figure gives rise to definite problems relating to structure and content.

At first glance it would indeed appear that the heroine Johanna had converted to communism on the conviction that the society into which she was born, and which was now building Hitler's military state, could no longer exist in its present form ("Natürlich ist die ganze Schicht, zu der ich meine Eltern rechnen muss, zum Untergang verurteilt"; "die Sache, das heisst einfach: die Zukunft, und die kann nur der Sozialismus sein" (9). About her past we discover:

> Johanna entwickelte ... eine immer entschlossenere, mutigere und radikalere Aktivität auf einem Gebiete, an dem sie bis dahin nur aufs allgemeinste und durchaus dilettantisch interessiert gewesen war: auf dem politischen. Sie trat in eine kommunistische Studentengruppe ein, arbeitete progagandistisch, redete in Versammlungen. Das hing nicht nur mit inneren Entwicklungen und intellektuellen Erkenntnissen zusammen, sondern vor allem mit der neuen und heftigen Beziehung, die sie einem der Freunde ihres älteren Bruders Georg verband. Sie hatte sich dem radikalen und unduldsamen Kreise, der um ihren Bruder ... gruppiert war, bis dahin fern gehalten. Dem Reporter, Versammlungsredner und Sportsmann Bruno war sie zunächst ausserhalb dieses politischen Zirkels begegnet. Ihre Freundschaft mit ihm brachte sie auch seinen Genossen und dadurch ihrem Bruder näher. Nach

einigen Wochen gehörte sie ganz zu diesen. Sie nahm energisch, von Tag zu Tag hingebungsvoller, Anteil an ihrer Arbeit. (15-16)

The image we receive of Johanna as the story unfolds, however, stands in decided contrast to the one Mann describes out of the past. At no point (with the exception of the end) does she reveal to her hosts the political nature of her exile. Only Karin, an intimate acquaintance from her student days in Berlin, learns that the heroine's motives for leaving Germany go beyond a mere moral rejection of a barbaric regime. It is in private conversations with her apolitical, lesbian confidant that Johanna feels free to speak about her political background. In this type of relationship there exists little possibility for an ideological confrontation. As Johanna recounts her harrowing experiences as an enemy of the Third Reich, Karin merely interjects with a consoling "War es sehr schlimm?" (14). Unlike the other members of the family, such a politically harmless figure as Karin cannot possibly rationalize the revolutionary implications of Johanna's forced exile. And when the bisexual Johanna finally discards Karin for her brother Ragnar, she remains true to character by sublimating the pain of her unrequited love in "Wohltätigkeit" and "innere Ablenkungen" (101).

The transition from antecedent action to present narrative becomes even more problematical on those occasions when Johanna is directly confronted with grave political issues to which -- so it would seem -- she ought to have responded in a manner consistent with her revolutionary convictions. Instead, she either evades the issue or disagrees purely on emotional impulse. At one point, for example, the impassioned nationalist Jens remarks: "Ein sehr schönes Land, sehr achtenswert; romantisch und dabei sehr achtenswert. Ja, ich bin sehr für Deutschland. Ragnar ist ja immer gegen Deutschland gewesen. ... Jedenfalls ... alles, was in Deutschland geschieht, muss doch einen gewissen Sinn haben. In Deutschland geschieht doch sicher nichts ohne Sinn und Verstand" (20). Although Johanna is visibly angered by this outburst, Mann lets the matter rest: "[Es] widerstand ... ihr, sich ... auf eine Diskussion einzulassen" (20). A later statement by Jens constitutes a direct affront to the origin of Johanna's political belief: "Ich weiss auch nicht, ob in Deutschland die Gefahr des Bolschewismus so nah war, wie hier. Wir sind hier nur ein paar Stunden von Petersburg entfernt -- von Leningrad, wie sie es jetzt nennen. Wir haben den Feind an der Grenze" (26). This time Johanna finds the provocation to be actually humorous and thus has no desire "sich auf eine Diskussion einzulassen" (26). Mann promptly dismisses this ticklish issue with the comment: "Uebrigens merkte sie auch schon etwas von der Wirkung des Alkohols. Ihr war ein wenig benommen im Kopf" (27).

Jens' mother is no less reactionary in her views. Although lacking the extreme fervor of her son, she too favors any political system in Germany as long as it opposes the classless one existing in the Soviet Union: "Deutschland, ja, ja, ein sehr schönes Land, ein sehr nobles Land. ... Ein sehr ordentliches Land, das muss jeder zugeben. Freilich, in letzter Zeit hat es auch dort manchmal Durcheinander gegeben, aber doch kein derartiges wie in Russland" (51). In this scene Mann does allow Johanna a retort -- "Es ist keine Revolution, obwohl es etwas ganz abscheulich Unordentliches ist" (52) -- but then abruptly leads his characters into an unrelated topic.

In these dialogues Mann is holding up to certain right-wing elements of "democratic" society a mirror of their own stupidity. That the author does not have any one nation in mind as the object of his polemic is evidenced by his omission of a geographical designation. Although we can infer from Jens' reference to Leningrad that the country in question is Finland, Mann still avoids a specific designation of the setting ("Man war in einem sehr entfernten Lande, irgendwo hoch im Norden," 29). The multilingual characterization of the family (Swedish, Finnish, German, French, English) suggests that the author is assigning an extranational physiognomy to his figures to show his exposure of a certain European political mentality. This critical portrayal has a basis in reality when one considers that France, Austria, and the Sudetenland had their share of rightists and fascist sympathizers in the thirties. That these countries, including England, harbored a general anti-Soviet sentiment goes without saying. Thus the statements uttered by Jens and his mother typify currents of extreme and moderate reaction prevalent in Europe at the time.

The existence of such tendencies among free nations at a time when fascism was threatening to dominate Europe explains, in part, why a united anti-Nazi front of the democracies never really materialized. In light of Mann's shattered hopes that the liberal nations would promptly stifle Nazi Germany's imperialistic designs, and in view of his portrayal of a revolutionary who acts as a symbolic stabilizing element to this situation, the above dialogues logically elicit an argument in favor of a nation politically sound enough to resist the forces of tyranny, namely, the Soviet Union. But here the author reaches an impasse. His liberal tradition precludes his following through systematically with the creation of a revolutionary who actively functions as an ideological foil to the figures exposed. Mann is caught up in the predicament of the defiant liberal writer who, at this unstable time in history, appears to envisage a counterthreat to fascism through a mobilization from the left, but who is unable to develop the social implications of this view in the actions of his heroine.

In the most dramatic scene of the novel, where Johanna cannot avoid becoming involved in a heated argument provoked by the two brothers, the heroine is at a loss to advance a counterargument that would lend credibility to the role in which we see her in retrospect. Jens, the militant nationalist, and Ragnar, the cosmopolitan pacifist, both identify Hitler with the whole of Germany, but from opposite viewpoints. After Jens has declared Nazism to be a popular movement of the people, Johanna issues a vehement protest which would have made her political position clear had it disclosed the revolutionary implications of the word Volksbewegung, in contradistinction to Jens' reactionary interpretation of it. As it stands, her response is noncommittal, which intimates a reluctance on her part to engage Jens' rightist position from the left: "Wissen Sie denn, wovon Sie reden?! ... Wissen Sie denn, was in Deutschland geschehen ist und täglich geschieht?! Ahnen Sie denn, zu was für Katastrophen das führen muss -- führen muss, verstehen Sie mich?! -- Volksbewegung! ... Der schamloseste Betrug, ausgeübt von einer verantwortungslosen Bande an einem verzweifelten Volk ..." (174). Mann refrains from taking the next step toward bringing Johanna's retort into historical perspective. Proceeding from the social and ideological premise he ascribes to his communist figure, one would expect Johanna to debunk the myth of Volk and Führer in typical revolutionary terms establishing the Volk not as submissive victims of the Führer, but as his destined vanquisher. Needless to say, the confrontation turns into a stalemate. Johanna is moved by emotion just as strongly as Jens. No rational counterdebate ensues which would expose the malicious fallacy of the "blood and soil" ideology espoused by the brother.

Equally untenable is Ragnar's position. He likewise associates Volk with Führer and justifies this identification in terms of mass psychology. To him the German nation had always been barbaric, crude, and militant. It is only natural then that the herd instincts of this uncultivated people should culminate in a society of Nordic warmongers. Unlike Jens, Ragnar can only feel disgust for what he considers to be an amorphous mass of nonentities in Germany. He is the egotistic, overcultured individualist, the escapist from reality who regards any kind of collective alignment, be it from the right or left, as inimical to his bourgeois sensibilities. Ironically, Johanna represents a following diametrically opposed to Ragnar's extreme individualism. Uninformed of his lover's past, however, he naturally assumes Johanna shares in his decadent life style and accordingly views her state of exile as a reflection of her nonidentity with the German people ("Johanna hat gar nichts Deutsches an sich. Sie ist nicht typisch," 172). He sees her flight from Germany as an attempt to preserve her individuality before the onslaught of mass brutality: "Tatsache ist, dass kein Land so wenig von seinen Eliten repräsentiert wird wie Deutschland. Die deutschen Eliten haben ja wohl immer gegen Deutschland gelebt, nie mit ihm; sie haben niemals einen Einfluss auf ihm [sic] gehabt, und wahrscheinlich haben sie es immer eher gehasst!" (172).

Much of this assertion is valid. Mann could conceivably be leveling subtle criticism against those intellectuals of pre-Nazi Germany who thought it below their dignity to mix culture with politics. But, once again, the heroine offers no argument that would refute Ragnar's apolitical impression of her flight into exile. It is understandable that Mann would have reservations about countering Ragnar's individualistic position with a collectivistic one. After all, he too belongs to a tradition of liberal intellectualism. If Johanna were to respond to Ragnar's views in a manner consistent with her revolutionary past, this tradition -- which Klaus Mann could never totally reject -- would be rendered questionable. While in Germany, Johanna had presumably shed all remnants of individualism when she dedicated herself to a movement that would ultimately work toward its elimination. As a member of a communist group (the image evoked of her in retrospect), she would have had to answer Ragnar's statement by denying any affinity with an elite class. Furthermore, it is partly because the intellectual elite had failed in its responsibility to Germany (10) that she aligned herself with a movement that proposed to effect change. A refutation on these grounds would have been congruent with the position the heroine had held in Germany. But Mann drops the matter altogether. Johanna replies to Ragnar's views with the feeble comment: "Ich glaube nicht, dass das ein Tischgespräch ist" (172).

The theme of the novel -- that of impassioned love and political engagement -- never turns into an open conflict because of Mann's predilection for intimate psychological study. (11) It is not just a coincidence that he should portray a member of the bourgeoisie as his revolutionary ideal, rather than one from the proletarian masses. Nor is it mere chance that he creates a setting divorced from the activities engaged in by Johanna's comrades in Paris. The bizarre world

into which he places his heroine ("sie war ganz verzaubert"; "diese magisch er-
hellten Tagnächte," 145) acts as an artistic justification for avoiding a direct
clash between the forces of progress and reaction. If Johanna embodies a conflict
at all, then it is internalized; the author does not allow it to influence the attitudes
of the other figures. While exposing the obscurantism of reaction in his depiction
of the secondary characters, Mann at the same time betrays an artistic penchant
for the morbid emotionalism underlying this retrogression in his treatment of the
voluptuous relationship between heroine and lover. The structural weakness of the
novel lies not so much in Johanna's experience of a conflict between inclination
and duty -- after all, revolutionaries are human too -- but in her repression of
it. Mann's description of her emotional involvement as "Gesetze, die den Tag bestimmen" (144) almost sounds like an apologia of bourgeois refinement. The
other "Gesetze," those placing Johanna in a social context, lack the integration
that would illuminate the problem of a personal relationship divided by class
interests.

Only at the very end of the novel do we view a dramatic confrontation between opposing positions. Having exhausted the various possibilities of sexual
aberration, psychological intimacy, character eccentricity, and nature myth, the
author is ready to restore his heroine to the role in which she is introduced. For
the first time Johanna finds herself in a situation where she must choose between
private indulgence and political responsibility. Her collective obligation in exile
now becomes her main preoccupation, to the degree that it takes priority over
her intoxicating passion for Ragnar.

But even here Mann is at a loss to make concrete the revolutionary implications of Johanna's exile. That her decision finally to join her comrades in Paris
does not arise from a rational insight into her political function is evidenced by her
state of mind leading up to the dispute with Ragnar: "Verzeih mir, mein strenger
und kluger Bruder Georg, dass ich das denke und so fühle. ... Ihr werdet siegen,
auch ohne mich. Ich will nicht dabei sein. ... Ich will sterben. Ich möchte den
Tod. Ich will mich nicht mehr beteiligen an den Dingen, die herankommen. ...
Ragnar, lieber Ragnar, mein Leben ist in deiner Hand, warum wirfst du es denn
nicht fort? ... Warum sollten wir nun nicht noch tiefer fahren und sinken zusammen?" (302). The stimulus releasing Johanna from this morbid state is a telegram announcing the execution of her comrade Bruno in Germany. Now she suddenly feels she no longer has the right to die. Bruno had accomplished that for
her. Instead, she must perpetuate his heroism because S c h i c k s a l so wills it.

This reference at the end to a metaphysical force that will enable Johanna
to carry out her political mission bears little resemblance to her earlier portrait
as an activist whose conversion to the left was based on "inneren Entwicklungen
und intellektuellen Erkenntnissen." Johanna's political change of heart is just as
fickle as her involvement with Ragnar. The schooled revolutionary of the past is
now viewed as a spiritual martyr for humanity -- a "leftist" synthesis which could
only be valid in individual-aesthetic, and not in Marxist terms. The image of a
communist realistically evoked in retrospect becomes atypical the moment Mann,
as a writer bent on individual character analysis, treats such a figure creatively:
"Johanna, das Jünglingsmädchen, das lieber sterben wollte, aber sie muss das
akzeptieren, was sie heute noch erhobenen Hauptes ihr Schicksal nennt -- was

wird es sein? -- Johanna mit dem erhobenen Haupte, was wird es sein, dieses Schicksal, um dessentwillen du nun alles opfern musst, so dass dein arg verwundetes Herz nie mehr, niemals mehr wird heilen können?" (317).

Klaus Mann perceived the necessity of taking a political stand in exile as keenly as any other liberal anti-fascist writer. But the spirit of political alignment and its literary expression are not one and the same. It becomes apparent that Mann was unable to bridge the gap between ideological premise and artistic praxis. That he takes an extreme position by creating a revolutionary as his leading character is explained by his sympathy -- more emotional than rational -- for the Soviet Union at a time when the democracies were displaying an irresolute political posture toward the Third Reich. Mann's early attraction to the cultural policy of the Soviet Union culminated in his attendance at the First Congress of Soviet Writers in the summer of 1934, just following the completion of Flucht in den Norden. The situation of the bourgeois writer vacillating between the extremes of collectivism and individual freedom highlights Mann's impressions of this convention (12) and provides us with a revealing statement of the problems ineluctably emerging from the novel.

# CHAPTER II

## KLAUS MANN: DER VULKAN

## Reality, Geist, and Metaphysical Synthesis

In view of the five years separating the publication of Flucht in den Norden (1934) and Der Vulkan (1939), one might ask whether Klaus Mann, by the late thirties, had finally came to terms artistically with the political manifestations of exile. One could speculate that the first novel marks the onset of a socially influenced esthetic which saw the author attempting to bridge the gap between individual freedom and collective responsibility. Such a speculation would, at first glance, seem cogent in light of Mann's confrontation with Soviet cultural politics at the writers' convention in Moscow in 1934. When he began writing Der Vulkan in 1938, however, he appears to have overcome the problem of "Ergriffenheit" and "Widerspruch" that had characterized his reaction to socialist realism in "Notizen in Moskau." (1) Mann's sympathy with the collective unity of the Soviet people, because it was more emotionally inspired than politically induced, was bound to conflict with a rational esthetic predicated on a dispassionate, objective portrayal of human conflict. Mann's ambivalent position already emerges in Flucht in den Norden where he treats Johanna, the communist heroine, as a marginal figure restricted to flashbacks and Johanna, the sensitive lover, as the visible protagonist of the story.

Marxism's rejection of creative autonomy and metaphysical exploration, as Mann had understood it in the uncertainties raised in "Notizen in Moskau," ultimately was to prompt his rejection of a leftist political function in art. In his autobiography he states that he had always been disenchanted with the "shallow and erroneous doctrine of dialectic materialism," (2) and that he could never visualize the salvation of the human race in economic terms: "I reject a philosophy which banishes and defames all metaphysical thought as a capitalistic contrivance to distract the proletariat attention from the only matter that counts, namely the class struggle. I do not believe that religion is the opium of the people (although I realize that religious ideas have been often abused to paralyze the human will to progress)." (3) Here we see an esthetic justification for the creation of the ethereal figure Kikjou in Der Vulkan. An attempt will be made later on to establish a closer identity on the part of the author to this character rather than to Marion von Kammer, who is commonly believed to be Mann's artistic persona. (4)

Throughout his exile Mann had addressed himself on several occasions to the function of the writer in society. In Escape to Life he admits to never having undergone a political transformation to the extent that art was to serve only a tendentious purpose: "We are charged not only to unmask and denounce evil, but to practise good as far as in us lies. Our inner life would wither if we were to confine ourselves to an endless repetition of: Hitler is abominable, Hitler is deplorable. We have other things to do. The values and traditions we wish to protect from the

clutches of Fascism must be c r e a t i v e l y [italics mine] upheld. " (5) In an essay
entitled "Die Wirkung Frankreichs," Mann expresses certain views which are
highly relevant to the present analysis since they coincide in time with the writing
of D e r   V u l k a n : "Die französischen Schriftsteller zeigen mir nicht vor allem,
was wir zu verändern und mit welcher Taktik wir zu verändern haben, als viel-
mehr: was es für uns zu b e w a h r e n gilt: den europäischen Geist, in all seiner
komplexen Zusammengesetztheit, mit all seinen Fragwürdigkeiten, seinen Reizen;
mit seinem dialektischen Spiel zwischen 'Romantik' und 'Klassik', zwischen
Mysterium und Vernunft, mit seiner Melancholie und seiner Zuversicht, seiner
Grazie und seinem Ernst." (6) Instead of viewing art as a vehicle for influencing
social change, Mann regards it foremost as an expression of the autonomous
intellect. In this vein he is concerned with experiencing, in the creative process,
the various manifestations of G e i s t e s g e s c h i c h t e in their total complexity.
In the work under discussion, we shall try to determine just how the author proposes to deal with this "dialektisches Spiel," for it is in this area that the key to
an understanding of Mann's artistic intent lies.

Of course, one might raise the objection that a direct relationship between
artistic theory and practice simply does not hold true for all writers, and that to
proceed deductively, as our critical method suggests, could lead to false conclusions
In deference to this objection, therefore, we should first test the applicability of
Mann's creative views.

The above citations would seem to prompt the following questions: How does
Mann's theoretical predilection for extricating G e i s t from socio-political exigencies hold true for his artistic product? When applied to D e r   V u l k a n , do
these views imply an ahistoric perpetuation of a l ' a r t   p o u r   l ' a r t attitude, or
do they have historical relevance to the period at hand? Is the dichotomy between
creative freedom and political conscience, which Matthias Wegner sees as typical
for Mann's situation as well as for the bourgeois intellectuals as a whole, (7)
really an artistic dilemma in D e r   V u l k a n , or does the problem lie elsewhere --
in the political lethargy of the West, for example?

To be sure, Mann does depart from the main thrust of his theoretical premises just do develop this latter point in the novel. In the figure of Marion von
Kammer, he proceeds to show the ineffectiveness of political art among liberal
societies unwilling to stand up to the threat of fascism. That Marion's recitations
are unable to inspire a spirit of defiance is not due to her art, but to an unresponsive public. Thus I fail to see any conflict between G e i s t and political reality in
Mann's creation of his artist-heroine. These poles are not sensed as incompatible
by Marion. On the contrary, they are quite dramatically interfused. It is not the
artist's fault if the message goes unheeded.

In the discussion between Benjamin Abel and Marion following her recitation
at an American university, the reader is left with little doubt that Marion's prose
and verse selections from classical and modern authors are meant to have a tendentious effect. Abel criticizes Marion for profaning the works of timeless artists
by turning them into a political weapon. He calls her an agitator and interprets
her polemic as a manipulative tactic that is no better than the K u n s t p o l i t i k
propagated by Nazi Germany: "Der Geist als ein Propaganda-Instrument der
Tyrannis --: dies ist seine letzte Entwürdigung. Machen wir uns nicht mitschuldig

an ihrer Vorbereitung, wenn wir unsererseits die geistigen Werte rhetorisch 'benutzen', in der Auseinandersetzung des Tages -- anstatt sie zu lieben, gerade weil sie dem Tage entrückt sind, und das Unvergängliche, Unverlierbare, das schöne Menschliche repräsentieren?" (8)

Marion's retort below would not appear to reflect Wegner's contention that she and Abel repeatedly lose themselves "in idealistischem Pathos." (9) Where Wegner regards the two positions as essentially the same, Mann portrays them as contrasting. Even after their marriage, Marion desires to continue her political activities, while Abel persists in upholding an abstract ideal of humanity. In the scene just referred to, the heroine promptly silences her challenger with the argument:

'Das schöne Menschliche' -- hübsch und poetisch formuliert! Fraglich scheint nur, ob wir es auch 'das Unvergängliche' und 'das Unverlierbare' nennen dürfen. Gerade jetzt sieht es doch ziemlich bedroht und gefährdet aus; in Deutschland, zum Beispiel -- wo es so besonders zu Hause schien -- hat man es zur Zeit ganz verloren. Der Faschismus und 'das schöne Menschliche' vertragen sich nicht. -- Sie haben es selber betont, Herr Professor! Deshalb bekämpfen wir den Faschismus. Mann sollte nicht gar zu wählerisch sein in kriegerischen Zeiten; die Dinge vereinfachen sich. 's ist Krieg, 's ist leider Krieg --: um noch einen deutschen Dichter zu zitieren, den frommen Matthias Claudius. Hoffentlich finden Sie nicht, dass ich ihn 'demagogisch benutze' und 'entwürdige'. ... Entwürdige ich die Grossen, wenn ich sie als Zeugen anrufe für unseren Zorn und für unsere Hoffnung? Wenn ich ihre Worte klingen lasse, zur Verteidigung des 'schönen Menschlichen'? (341)

A more concrete impression is conveyed of the kind of results Marion is striving for when she discusses her recitations with the British writer during her sojoun at Mallorca. The writer's apprehensive reaction to Marion's address, when viewed on a broader political scale, is really symptomatic of the general conciliatory attitude of the West, from which arose the hope that Nazi Germany would vent its wrath upon an even more ominous threat -- the Soviet Union: "In Ihrem Vortrag hat etwas mich schockiert. Sie haben manchmal einen kriegerischen Ton -- als wollten Sie zur Schlacht rufen. Das beunruhigt mich. Gewalt wird schon genug gepredigt und angewendet -- von den anderen. Wir sollen friedlich sein. Nicht Rache, nicht Kampf -- Versöhnung sei unsere Absicht" (201). In the ensuing confrontation Marion is quite adamant about the purpose of her recitations; they are intended to instill in her audiences a sense of political, even military, urgency. To the writer's question as to whether she is for an anti-fascist war, Marion replies: "Die faschistischen Staaten würden ihn nicht führen können. Diese aufgeblasenen Monstren sind innerlich hohl. Aber es sollte kein Zweifel darüber bestehen, dass die Demokratien bereit und gerüstet sind; dann würden die Aggressoren es mit der Angst bekommen" (202).

Unfortunately, it is the democracies themselves that betray A n g s t , with the result that Marion's political art can never achieve the desired effect. The disturbing quality of her talks becomes only too clear when she commences her European tour. If her addresses had amounted to nothing but idealized pathos or meaningless chatter, then the various governments would hardly have taken notice

of her appearances. Needless to say, they find her verses to be somewhat too pro-
vocative. And so we hear: "In Wien durfte sie nicht auftreten, weil die österreichi-
sche Regierung auf die Empfindlichkeit des Dritten Reiches Rücksicht nahm. ...
Nicht nur in der Schweiz, auch in der Tschechoslowakei und in Holland interessier-
ten sich nun die Behörden für die Auswahl der Verse, die sie sprechen wollte.
Ueberall vermied man womöglich Unannehmlichkeiten mit den reizbaren deutschen
Gesandtschaften oder Konsulaten" (177). Nor was the situation any different in
France and England. In the United States it was, in some ways, more frustrating
yet. There the majority of Marion's audiences were totally ignorant about conditions in Europe and first had to be enlightened about the very existence of fascist
terror.

Der Vulkan sheds light on the problem of the exiled liberal artist
especially in those scenes showing a direct relationship between current reality
and a progressive, humanistic tradition in German literature. Here a figure
emerges who is able to adapt a literary-cultural heritage to the difficulties of the
time. The heroine has achieved a balance between political commitment and art;
still, this achievement is destined for failure. The problem of art and reality
derives not from a discrepancy between form and content, (10) but from the aura
of political irresoluteness prevailing at the moment. An exiled artist's failure to
receive public resonance for his attempts to influence change does not necessarily
indicate that he is laboring under a conflict between socio-political topicality and
the timeless values of a humanistic literary tradition. The artist-intellectual, as
evidenced in Marion's case, is quite conscious of the political demands of exile
when he can relate his literary past to the exigencies of the period.

It becomes apparent in his characterization of Marion that Klaus Mann can
relate Geist to empirical reality if he wants to. Yet, as noted earlier in "Die
Wirkung Frankreichs," his attitude toward artistic creation eschews this kind of
dialectic. Such a confrontation, rather, remains confined to the realm of Geist
alone. In his creation of Marion, Mann suspends this Hegelian esthetic in the
realistic sections of the novel so as to demonstrate the ineffectiveness of political
art among nations who prefer peace at all costs, despite all obvious indications to
the contrary. In a sense, then, his predilection for artistic autonomy, which is
only Geist-oriented, is justified in view of the "apolitical" international scene
forming the backdrop of the novel.

Returning to our deductive method of analysis, we infer from Mann's
theoretical postulates that it is not Marion who reveals the author's creative
intention, but rather Kikjou, an erotic-mystical figure whose background obligates
him neither to politics nor art. (11) He neither functions as an artist in the novel
(Kikjou only plans to complete Martin's and Marcel's novel at the end); nor is he
a German emigrant, but a Brazilian whose Bohemian existence in Paris had
emerged apart from the Hitler exile. Thus the politics-art issue plays no direct
role in the development of this character. (12)

Another phenomenon does, however. Mann had always entertained an
esthetic interest in man as a composition of opposites. The spiritual and corporeal,
embodied in such oxymora as erotic mysticism, metaphysical sensuality, realistic
phantasy, phantastic reality, were in a perpetual state of antagonism and could
be resolved only in death or God. In Kikjou ("den von Lastern und Visionen Ver-

zückten, das suspekte Lieblingskind Gottes," (392), Mann sets out to portray aspects of this dualism from a psychological as well as spiritual standpoint. (13) Kikjou emerges as a delicate, almost ethereal figure who instinctively indulges in abusive excesses. Homosexuality, sodomy, and drugs determine the pattern of his life, and he senses these disruptive drives as the antipode to the idealistic side of his nature. The transcendental scenes depicting Kikjou in the company of the angel serve a symbolic function inasmuch as they neutralize (a u f h e b e n) the essential dichotomy of man. (14) Thus contradiction resolves itself into synthesis.

If we examine the other dominant characters of the novel in terms of a "dialektisches Spiel zwischen 'Romantik' und 'Klassik'," we find that the leading currents of thought that had influenced European culture since the eighteenth century are reflected in the following attitudes: bourgeois individualism and the ideal of humanity (Abel); conflicting views towards progress and history implicit in the Goethean concepts of N e p t u n i s m u s (Abel) and V u l k a n i s m u s (Marion, Marcel); Schopenhauer's pessimism with its preoccupation with man as an embodiment of irrational, blind forces (Martin, Tilly, Kikjou); expressionist anarchy with its penchant for sacrifice and death (Marcel, Tullio); and the Nietzschean concept of man who lacks the will to give irrational drives a positive direction (Nazi Germany and the middle-class mentality of submission to power, e. g. , Martin's parants).

In the final analysis the main bearers of European intellectual thought are narrowed down to Marion, (15) Abel, and Kikjou, who represent differing historical perspectives towards the exile period. In the confrontations between Abel and Marion, the author weighs one W e l t a n s c h a u u n g against the other; but neither Abel's evolutionary outlook (idealized nature) nor Marion's revolutionary world view (disruptive nature) can be said to reflect Mann's own attitude towards the time. Where the one view tends to preserve out of passive distance, the other interprets the period in terms of dynamic upheaval. To resolve this antithesis, Mann creates Kikjou who, elevated to the celestial realm, represents a synthesis of conflicting philosophies in which the pure idea of a defiant humanity can be fostered. Mann himself considered the kingdom of heaven to be revolutionary. (16) The transcendental scenes enable him to envisage the noble and anarchistic forces of existence in a kind of c o i n c i d e n t i a   o p p o s i t o r u m (symbolized through Kikjou) whereby Marion's active, but irrational world view fuses with Abel's humane, but passive one.

To elucidate the above assumptions we must first examine the most conspicuous leitmotif of the novel: the volcano metaphor conjured up by Marion on a number of occasions. In a literal sense the image means a violent eruption of nature, a dynamic, revolutionary metamorphosis of existing elements. The unbridled, anarchistic force behind this eruption anticipates chaos and destruction, a total upheaval of everything that had existed beforehand. Related metaphorically to the wave of Nazi terror, this image suggests an unleashing of man's destructive instincts, a mass overthrow and the annihilation of a continent about to be devoured by the holocaust. Mann frequently refers to Marion as a seer who perceives the fate of the exiles in just these terms: "Man lässt das Scheussliche rasen, zerstören, sich austoben -- als wäre es eine Naturkatastrophe! Als lebten wir auf einem Vulkan, der Feuer speit!" (387). Apocalyptic visions of an "Abgrund" and a "Krater eines Vulkans" (129, 323), of "Chaos" (320), "das Böse" (324), and the "Auflösung der Zivilisation" (319) elevate Nazism to the realm of myth, whose participants symbolize a perversion of nature and the impending transformation of civilization into barbarism after humanity has been wiped out.

In contrast to Marion's eschatological world view, Abel takes the position that nature will follow a course of logical development. This Goethean figure, a "Repräsentant klassischer deutscher Traditionen" (84) who has achieved a balance between "besitzen" and "verzichten" (389), embraces a stoical optimism that sees the noble and good in man as ultimately winning out. The island of humanity he has created for himself in the United States ("Welcher Friede! Wie weit entrückt waren Qual und Aufruhr!" (386) enables him to nurture the ideal of "Schönheit" (386-87) unhindered by the foreboding realities threatening this ideal across the ocean. Abel is not prepared to attribute a revolutionary significance to the barbarism plaguing Europe. Unlike Marion, he does not interpret this force as being apocalyptic or universally destructive. The wave of fascist tyranny constitutes merely a retarding element in nature rather than the ultimate direction it is to take. He is of the opinion that the laws of nature will take care of themselves ("Dem Gesetz dieses Lebens gehorsam. Geduldig und gehorsam sollen wir sein," 390); thus it is senseless, in his estimation, to involve oneself as Marion has done:

> Ueberstehen ist siegen! ... Wer Geduld hat, wer aushält -- der siegt. Alles geht langsam, alles dauert lang. Wir überschätzen die Ereignisse des Tages, der Stunde; wir stilisieren sie apokalyptisch, geben ihnen gewaltige Namen: Historische Wende, oder Weltuntergang. Das ist Irrtum und Eitelkeit. Soll unsere Epoche alles verändern und unterbrechen -- nur weil es gerade unsere Epoche ist? Der Prozess geht weiter -- zäh und langsam, sehr langsam. ... Es gibt Störungen, Rückschläge: dergleichen erleben wir jetzt. Lassen wir uns doch nicht gar zu sehr erschüttern und verwirren! Lasse dich doch nicht wirr und kopflos machen, liebes Herz, durch die Störungen und die Rückschläge! Vertraue doch: es geht weiter! Glaube mir doch: in den grossen Zusammenhängen rechnet dies alles so wenig, und wird einst ruhiger und kälter beurteilt werden, als wir's heute vermuten. (390)

This "classical" assessment of the situation recalls a certain philosophical view held by Goethe which advanced the idea of progress towards fulfillment (entelechy). "Rückschläge" and "Störungen" do not hinder, but promote this striving towards an ideal end. Accordingly, Abel assumes an attitude of detachment so as to preserve a vision of a "Welt-Republik" harboring "die totale Wiederherstellung, die totale Erneuerung, die Steigerung und Erhöhung der Menschenwürde" (345).

Is this how we are to understand the author's interpretation of the exile years? As a transitional period of waiting, of noninvolvement, of upholding that which is noble so that it can one day become a universal reality? The difficulty in analyzing Mann's intent lies in his metaphysical symbolism at the end, where he creates a vision even more remote from reality than Abel's. On the one hand Mann seems to pit Marion's activist stance against Abel's idealistic one to show the tenuity of the latter's position; on the other he oversteps the limits of Abel's ideal of humanity by withdrawing to a sphere that has transformed reality into pure spirit. The conflicting world outlooks fostered by Marion and Abel initially form the esthetic extremes of Mann's preoccupation with the "dialektisches Spiel zwischen 'Romantik' und 'Klassik'," extremes which are ultimately resolved in a transcendental realm. Mann identifies fully neither with Marion's disruptive outlook nor with Abel's harmonious one; yet aspects of both form a part of his own esthetic-philosophical predicament. The very title of the novel suggests a certain agreement with Marion's apocalyptic interpretation of events to come. And certainly Mann does not find Abel's esthetic view of humanity to be disagreeable in principle. The irrational forces of nature, culminating above all in the spread of barbaric Nazism but also postulated as a condition of man's dichotomy, and their idealistic opposite are dualistically portrayed in Kikjou (whose nature is both anarchistic and sublime) and reconciled in providential terms. In this context Christ too was both spirit and sensuality, enduring (Abel's idealistic view) and subject to human impulse (Marion's irrational one), (17) before His reunion with the Father, that is, before He "transcended" the dichotomy of existence.

In an analagous sense Kikjou symbolizes a synthesis of this dichotomy when he ascends into the celestial sphere where, acting as overseer and spokesman for the Almighty, he subsumes the destinies of the exiles under a divine master plan. The historical significance of the exile condition is thus eclipsed by the metaphysical interpretation it receives at the end. (18) Exile from the homeland means separation from one's spiritual kingdom. The limitations of the imperfect reality inherent in this existential exile are gradually overcome in the course of one's struggle to return home. Thus the sufferings, passions, and weaknesses of the homeless are perceived (in Hebbel's language) as a "Heils-Prozess" (416), during which the contradictions of existence strive, of necessity, towards the negation of the irrational and the resultant goal of a harmonious existence: "Hat Er euch nicht Seinen Sohn geschickt, damit es nur weitergehe, und der Prozess eurer Selbsterlösung nicht stocke?" (415).

The artistic merit of Der Vulkan, in contrast to the many scenes Mann describes more as an objective chronicler, lies in the myriad of conflicting views espoused by the central figures. Mann's fascination for the psychologically problematic character and, in particular, his treatment of the exile scene in terms of the history of ideas are a reflection of his esthetic preoccupation with "europäischen Geist, in all seiner komplexen Zusammengesetztheit." In "Die Wirkung Frankreichs" he states: "Es ist merkwürdig: Im Mittelpunkt meines Lebens steht der Kampf gegen die widerwärtige Pest des Fascismus, gegen den brutalen sozialen Rückschritt in all seinen Formen. ... -- und wenn ich an all die Kostbarkeiten, all das Unvergessliche denke, was ich der neuen französischen Literatur zu verdanken habe, so fallen mir nicht zunächst jene Schriftsteller ein, deren Pathos vor allem das soziale ist. ..." (19) Only the "ästhetische und moralische Werte" of his literary mentors were of paramount interest to Mann as a creative writer. (20) The historical scenes chronicled throughout the novel are an outgrowth of Mann's noncreative role as an essayist. The objective narrative style he employs in rendering a concrete account of the exile scene emanates from this role. In "Die Wirkung Frankreichs" Mann admits to being a "politisch linksorientierter junger Deutscher," (21) but prefers, as demonstrated in the failure of Marion's politicized art to inspire action, to keep this aspect of his intellectual responsibility in exile apart from his creative function.

The novel's subtitle "Roman unter Emigranten" is more applicable to those episodes describing the activities and adventures of the homeless within the actual exile environment. The detailed psychological and religio-philosophical scenes, a product of Mann's artist pen, take on somewhat atypical characteristics with respect to the period at hand. (22) They reflect a narrative attitude that receives its creative impulse not so much from immediate social and political conditions, but more from European literary masters who had regarded the autonomous intellect to be the molder of one's own reality.

## CHAPTER III

## KONRAD MERZ: EIN MENSCH FAELLT AUS DEUTSCHLAND

### The "Inner" and "Outer" Exile of Youth

Konrad Merz numbers among the younger writers who made their literary debut in exile. Written shortly after his flight to Holland in 1934, Ein Mensch fällt aus Deutschland (1936), an epistolary novel, describes the traumatic experiences of the uprooted emigrant who attempts to find some purpose to his new existence. The semi-integrated status in which Merz portrays his autobiographical hero at the end anticipates his own situation after 1945. Merz never returned to Germany to take up the law practice for which he had studied prior to his exile. A brief visit to Berlin after the war was such a depressing experience for him that it apparently made him feel more alienated than the condition of exile itself. (1) Since the end of the war he has been employed as a masseur in a hospital near Amsterdam. Merz's second and last novel to come out of his exile, Generation ohne Väter (1938), unfortunately was never published. No doubt it would have shed valuable light on the author's treatment of the youth issue in the work at hand.

Born in 1908, Merz belongs to a generation of youth caught up in the wave of political extremism in the 1920's. The problem of the youth vacillating between the poles of radicalism and liberal humanism is new to the category of novel presently under study. Ein Mensch fällt aus Deutschland gives such unusual expression to this problem that one is tempted to write it off as a simple lamentation of an existential predicament followed by an irrational, dirt-throwing denunciation of the regime responsible for putting the hero Winter into this dilemma. It is not surprising that Merz's name remained a virtual nonentity among the population of exiled literati. Certainly the more established humanistic writers would have envisioned little meaningful protest arising from a novel employing images of excrement and festering limbs as an expression of defiance towards Nazi Germany. The representative spokesmen of the established "other Germany" could only have looked with repugnance upon such "vile anarchy." Even Klaus Mann, a fellow younger writer always ready to promote new talent in Die Sammlung, would probably have drawn the line with Konrad Merz.

Despite this unfortunate nonrecognition, Merz is still very much a part of the exiled "other Germany" which sought to defend humanity against its barbaric abuse at home. But the astonishing way he approaches the dilemma of youth, seen in the dualistic position of Winter as both representative and defier of traditional humanism, undoubtedly accounts for this author's isolation among his contemporaries. Neither young nor old could have sympathized with a form of protest, emanating especially from the second half of the novel, that is divested of all reason -- so it would seem. A critical glance at this highly problematic work is, therefore, long overdue.

As the novel opens we find Winter hiding out with his former classmate Heini, a left-wing anarchist wanted by the Nazis. Winter does not share his friend's radicalism; his alignment with this political fugitive is rather a sign of general protest felt by a betrayed youth. Essential to an assessment of Merz's intent is an understanding of Winter's historical insight into Hitler's rise to power. The protagonist does not seek to cancel out tradition through anarchistic revolt, as Heini and his clique of followers do, but recapitulates critically the developments leading up to and explaining the desperation expressed by his generation: "Weg mit dem Kaiser, her mit der Republik; her mit der Inflation, weg mit dem letzten Wohlstand. Dann die Scheinblüte, und dann blühten die Stempelämter. An jeder Haltestelle ein neuer Betrug. So war unser ganzes Leben: ein Fahrstuhl nach unten -- und mit uns fiel auch unser Gott den Fahrstuhl hinunter. Dann kam Hitler: Erdgeschoss, aussteigen!" (2) We will see that Winter does not attempt to totally reject the past, but takes a position whereby he interacts dialectically with it. Merz regards him as a historical person, as one who criticizes the past but who also is a product of it. Winter emerges as a figure who must settle accounts with the old in order to bring about the new. Later in the novel he exclaims: "Dürfen wir auch deine Fehler lieben, Deutschland? Wir dürfen nicht: wir müssen" (77). Only by overcoming the mistakes of the past can a realistic future be envisioned, and the realization of a solution to the future will depend on the type of youth portrayed by Winter.

The dilemma confronting Winter in Germany is representative for those youth who did not seek to establish an identity in the late twenties and early thirties by taking extreme positions to the left or right: "Der Boden von Deutschland brennt. Schon fast ein Jahr lang wanken und fallen alle Balken in unserem Lande, und ich sollte so tun können, als ginge mich das wenig an? Oder ich sollte gar die Hacken zusammenschlagen, weil irgendein Stiernacken es befiehlt, mich bücken, ein krummer Hund werden, weil ich meine Dreigroschenhoffnung, mein ranzigge-wordenes Glück in Sicherheit bringen wollte?" (20-21). Dietrich, another school-mate of Winter's, typifies the dissatisfied youth who embarked on this reactionary path. Heini, the other comrade, has chosen the opposite road. The one will per-petuate the corrupt elements of society; the other, by the task assigned him to eliminate Hitler, will seek to eradicate these elements and, by committing this act, compromise the decency in man. The justification given this deed by Heini's anarchistic group recalls the revolutionary fervor of the expressionist generation (with which Merz felt an affinity): "Ein einziger Mensch müsse weg, damit Millio-nen leben können. Diese Tat sei nicht Mord, nicht Töten, sie sei Gebären, Leben-schaffen. Endlich sei es an uns, zu vollbringen, an der Jugend. Das Gesetz, darum ginge es, und das Gesetz seien wir" (15). Winter, an innocent bystander to this plot, interjects defiantly: "Eben um das Gesetzliche geht es. ... Ihr kommt mir vor wie ein Verein für Selbstentleibung" (16). Still, Winter is linked by association to the conspiracy, and when the attempted assassination fails, he is forced into exile.

From a documentary standpoint, E i n M e n s c h f ä l l t a u s D e u t s c h -l a n d sets the tone for the typical material problems of exile. An opponent of the Nazi regime must flee Germany to avoid imprisonment. Unable to make prepara-tions for his exodus, he finds himself in exile without finances or passport. Since work permits are not issued to foreigners, especially to those who have crossed borders illegally, life in exile becomes a constant struggle for survival. Without identification papers the newly arrived refugee must avoid any confrontation with legal authorities; at the same time he is dependent upon the generosity of the guest country for his material existence. As so often happens, he must resort to peddling to earn a livelihood, an occupation which offers little assurance·of continued survival.

In approximately the first half of the novel -- before Winter sustains a leg injury and meets the Dutch physician Coy, the two incidents spurring him to defiant protest -- the hero occupies an apolitical role not unlike that of certain other figures in the exile novel. The everyday problems of exile take precedence over a direct concern for the political oppression existing at home. The recurrent motif of "Durchhalten" in Merz's novel exemplifies a passive attitude emerging in other works, where numerous emigrants optimistically endure their misfortune in the knowledge that they will prevail if the Germany they once knew is to survive. In the initial stages of his exile Winter is portrayed in much the same way. A sense of responsibility towards the disgrace that has befallen Germany has not yet crystallized into open conflict. Winter psychologically withdraws from the present Germany by nostalgically seeking refuge in the past: "Deutschland. Ilse. Mutter. Aber nicht jenes Deutschland, ans Hakenkreuz geschlagen!" (62). (Ilse, the girl Winter left behind, eventually becomes an enthusiastic supporter of the brown-shirts.)

Merz's disjointed style initially reflects the personal conflicts related to the alienating experience of exile. Winter's flight from Germany is symbolic of a loss of identity. His experiences as an emigrant consist of repeated attempts to restore this identity, to establish roots in an antagonistic environment. His conversations, often internalized, serve the purpose of discovering whether he is who he is: "Ich sitze mir gegenüber" (36); "Ich sehe garnichts. Ich will ja nur ... ja was will ich! Ich bin hierher gefallen ... ich muss nun ... ja was muss ich! Ich werde jetzt endlich ... ja was werde ich!" (31). He finds himself in a perpetual state of movement, without direction or goal: "Da steht ein Baum. In der ganzen Strasse steht nur ein einziger Baum. Und nicht einmal dick. Er steht rechts, also muss ich nach links ... nach links ... nur nicht ... bumm! In der ganzen Strasse steht nur ein einziger Baum, und gerade gegen den muss ich ... ein richtiger Rad-fahrer würde ihn vielleicht garnicht treffen ..." (39-40). Winter's inability to orient himself, to establish a self-identity, takes on the appearance of a timeless, universal uprootedness. Even repossession of his passport fails to alter his situation appreciably: "'Staatsangehörigkeit 'Preussen'. Ist das wahr? 'Gestalt: leider vorhanden'. 'Beruf: Ausländer'. 'Farbe der Augen: verboten'. 'Gesicht: unangenehm'. 'Besondere Kennzeichen: Hat mächtigen Hunger'. 'Wohnort: auf der Erde, postlagernd'" (76).

Merz's later departure from a treatment of an exile experience that is quasi-existentialistic to one that is violently polemic seems, at first glance, to lack structural continuity. We know from the pre-exile scenes in Germany that Winter is an active opponent of the Nazis, a fact born out by his association, however indirect, with an anarchist left-wing group. Why then should Merz delay the polemic aspect of the novel by spending so much time on his hero's personal encounters in Holland? Surely not for the purpose of leveling criticism against the red tape of a foreign bureaucracy. This aspect certainly presents itself, but there appears to be a more critical reason, one that ties in with Winter's experiences in Germany.

It would seem that Winter had been an exile figure from the very start, the result being that his actual exile status forms the physical extension of a spiritual uprootedness that had already existed at home. His search for identity already had its inception in Germany. Thus one form of exile, the inner, complements the other, the outer.

One might question the credibility of such a comparison by calling to mind the active political impression conveyed of Winter in Germany, an image hardly resembling that of an uprooted isolationist. Yet what Merz does is characterize Winter as a political opponent without a following. Winter's alignment with Heini signifies the spiritual bond of one youth to another, a bond which Heini vitiates, however, by his bloodthirsty anarchy: "Und ... wenn ich kein Genosse bin von Heini, so ist er doch mein Freund, mein Bruder, ein Stück von mir: ich weiss in dieser Sekunde nicht einmal genau, wo er aufhört und wo ich beginne" (21). Winter's isolation is evidenced by his futile desire to champion a form of political opposition based on reason, on G e s e t z , an undertaking naturally lacking aspirants in a period governed by irrationality and extremism. Winter's political stance, however noble it may be, was virtually outmoded at a time when the majority of German youth had swung to the left or right. In the second half of the novel the problem of Winter's dual exile experience assumes highly dramatic proportions, crystallizing in the conflict between the hero and both his radical peers in Germany as well as the humanistic "other Germany" whose idealistic tradition had indirectly brought on the disillusionment and resultant extremism of his generation in the 1920's.

That Winter includes himself as a member of a dissatisfied youth movement becomes clear in the one scene where he recalls the inspirational leadership of his fascist classmate Dietrich. Winter's relationship to Dietrich in school was marked by an ambivalence which in the present action of the novel helps to illuminate his conflict. On the one hand he identifies with Dietrich's rebellious pathos as an expression of freedom from the constraints of an unsympathetic system: "Er war der Apostel einer neuen Bewegung, die Deutschland Ehre und Kraft zurückbringen werde und Befreiung. Und danach suchten wir. Er steckte uns an, denn er war der Stärkste von uns" (143); yet he also recognizes the potential dangers erupting from a revolutionary fervor rooted in militancy and power: "Dann gingen wir mit ihm, Heini und ich. Und an diesem Tage wurden wir Feinde. Denn wo er Blut fühlte, fühlten wir Schminke, und wo er Taten sah, hörten wir Worte" (143). We know the path that Heini was soon to take. However extreme and irrational the political poles represented by Dietrich and Heini were, they still insured the group identity for which the youth of Germany had been searching. Ironically, Winter was forced into isolation because he foresaw the disastrous consequences. Idealism on the part of German youth was distorted into the partisan loyalties of communism and fascism. Winter stands, therefore, in opposition to the present as well as the past that had spawned it.

Merz characterizes this opposition by placing his figure in a double dilemma.

On the one hand, Winter's insistence on reason and Gesetz implies a respect for the best of German tradition. This is revealed in his admiration for Goethe: "Man hasst ein ganzes Land und meint doch nur seine Krankheit. Und manchmal werde ich selbst irre daran, darum und darum soll es über mir sein, wenn ich mich abstaube, und wenn ich die Knöpfe an meine Hosen nähe, über mir sein, wenn ich meine Muskeln zurückschleppe in den Abend zu mir: das Bild von Goethe" (162). On the other hand, Winter literally profanes the machtgeschützte Innerlichkeit (Thomas Mann) of the recent German past for its failure to incorporate into reality the lofty ideals of its rich tradition. Merz leaves no doubt as to his polemic intent when, in a later episode, Winter assumes the duties of a "Kuhstallknecht" for a herd of cattle, one of which symbolizes the innocuousness of Germany's intellectual heritage: "Die Kuh Idealismus ist kurzsichtig, wir werden ihr eine Brille kaufen müssen, dieser abgemagerten Vergangenheit. Aber es lohnt sich nicht, sie gibt so unverschämt wenig Milch, sie wird wohl abgeschlachtet werden" (173). In this invective Merz is exposing a politically unconcerned society's ineptitude for dealing with the social realities of the day. Winter's admiration for Goethe and the travesty of idealism illustrated here are not to be construed, however, as contradictory. He is really opposing a regression to tradition, not its realistic application in society. It is an abstract idealism he makes a mockery of, one whose adherents had not put into practice the humane principles implied therein.

The other side of Winter's dilemma rests with his own generation. He is both one and at odds with the youth of his day. Whereas he identifies with his peers in their disillusionment over a politically inept Weimar Republic, many of whose constituents were descendants of the "rising" bourgeoisie under the monarchy, he cannot share the extremism underlying their desire to change things. Thus, when Dietrich is suspended from school for undisciplined behavior, Winter's reaction is one of both approval and rejection: "Wir wurden die besten Feinde" (144).

Merz goes so far as to idealize his main character by setting him up as a model of youth in Nazi Germany, but he also stains him with the guilt incurred by many members of his generation as they gathered in force to support the fascist movement. The last half of the novel shows Winter violently erupting from the twofold nature of his isolation. In the most loathsome of metaphors he proceeds to vent his wrath against a Germany for whose barbaric tyranny he expresses both guilt and rejection. Whether an "idea" workable for the future can be reconstructed from this extreme confrontation remains to be seen.

Werner Vordtriede has discussed various images and tones employed in the poetry of exile which can be partly exemplified in this novel, whose subjective, highly stylized language has a lyrical quality about it to begin with. Vordtriede refers to the emigrant lyricist who departs from a traditional art form by resorting to unesthetic metaphors. The artistic medium for conveying this iconoclastic imagery is the parody: "Dialektisch verbunden mit dieser schweren Traditionstreue ist die Exilparodie. Sie ist kein spassiges Randwerk, sie gehört zum Hauptwerk, ist Waffe gegen die Traditionsverderber zu Hause und zugleich ein Eigenkorrektiv." (3) Merz employs his language along similar lines whereby the polemic intent is to expose the inhumanity of Nazism through the evocation of dehumanized imagery. Vordtriede goes on to mention "Hassdichtung" as one of the extreme forms of parody in exile: "Der Exilierte ist zunächst selber nichts als ein Opfer des Hasses, er will nicht hassen, nur als Gehasster wird er zum Hasser." (4) This hate frequently takes on the form of animal comparisons: "Das Hassgedicht hat aber die Fähigkeit, das Scheusslichste, den Kot, den Dreck, dichterisch möglich zu machen." (5) And so we see Merz executing such language as a vehicle of protest and satire against the animalism of a soulless regime:

Jeder Fusstritt hat seinen Sinn, jede Blutsstrieme auf meinem Rücken hat ihren Wert. Saat unterm Schnee. Und sie wird aufgehen in jenem Sommer. Dafür bluten wir. Für jenen Sommer. Den wir vielleicht niemals erleben werden. Schon drei andere Säcke über dem Allerwertesten. Ob wir nun draussen bluten oder im Lande. Jeder Tropfen soll Saat sein. Wird Saat sein. Wir glauben es. Wir sind Dünger. Nur Dünger. Aber das sind wir! (127)

. . . . . . . . . . . . . . . . . . . . . . . . . . . . . . . . . . . . . . . .
Mein linkes Bein ist heiss. Es glüht wieder. Fieber. Dieser hündische Oberschenkel, der mich trägt. Und nicht tragen will. ... Er will mich quälen, er will nach Berlin. Der Oberschenkel gehört mir. (128)

. . . . . . . . . . . . . . . . . . . . . . . . . . . . . . . . . . . . . . . .
Jetzt bin ich also Kuhstallknecht. Habe morgens und abends den werten Kühen den Strunk unter ihren Hinterausgängen wegzuschaufeln und abzufahren. Der wird dann draussen aufgeschichtet zu einem Denkmal. Die Kühe erkundigten sich erst, ob ich auch die Universitätsreife hätte, und nachdem ich ihnen das beweisen konnte, liessen sie mich, sichtbar befriedigt, an ihre Allerwertesten. (167)

. . . . . . . . . . . . . . . . . . . . . . . . . . . . . . . . . . . . . . . .
Immer wieder stampfte ich mit den beiden Dreckeimern an den Pfuhl und zog das Gestinke an den Tag. Es wurde nur langsam weniger, denn die Kühe legten immer noch mehr dazu, aus persönlicher Niederträchtigkeit; das floss durch die Rinne immer wieder in den Pfuhl. ... Mein Körper war schwer wie selbst voll Kuhmist. ... Ich möchte jedem, der mir in die Quere kommt, eins in die Schnauze hauen oder ihn abküssen. Bis zum letzten Vorrat. (171-72)

. . . . . . . . . . . . . . . . . . . . . . . . . . . . . . . . . . . . . . . .
Die Löcher an meinen Händen eiterten. (174)

. . . . . . . . . . . . . . . . . . . . . . . . . . . . . . . . . . . . . . . .
Als ich heute früh unserer werten Kuh Bügelfalte den Rücken säubern musste, schlug sie mir mit dem Schwanz ins Gesicht. Ich wollte ihr in den Hintern treten vor Wut, konnte es aber nicht, ich darf mich hier ja nicht mit Politik bemühen. Für Ausländer verboten. (184)

Two related events incite Winter to action. Hospitalized with an injured leg as a result of an automobile accident, he comes under the care of a Dutch physician named Coy, whose German husband is languishing in a Nazi concentration camp. Winter's festering leg refuses to heal and he associates this rotting limb with Germany's sickness: "Die Krankheit Deutschland tut mir mehr weh als mein Bein" (87). His sense of guilt prevents him from reciprocating Coy's affections and he escapes from the clinic. Finding work on a peasant's farm, he wallows in self-chastisement, associating his malady with dung as a symbol of Germany's corruption: "Hier riecht es doch nach Kuhdung, nach Pferdeäpfeln, nach Dreck, hier riecht es doch nach mir. Ich bin aus Deutschland geflohen, geflohen, ich Hund ... ich Hund. Ich will bezahlen" (110). On the farm Winter attempts, through self-inflicted pain, to overcome his affiliation with a diseased country. Dehumanized images of decay, rot, filth, excrement are evoked as an indication of his desire to remove his burden of guilt. He wishes to atone for Nazi Germany's bestiality by self-degradation, by writhing in pain as a martyr for the transgressions of a barbaric regime.

Merz does not depict these indignities as an end in themselves. Winter is no masochist. However grotesque the metaphors may seem, they demonstrate a definite polemic function. Merz is exposing a barbaric ideology by employing images appropriate to the situation. His hero's conflict evolves from a desire to overcome, to supercede, the fascist path his generation had taken: "Das 'Dritte Reich' ist nicht D e u t s c h l a n d. Man sieht nur die Pickel und nicht das Gesicht dahinter" (162).

The author does not set off the real Germany from the false one, but views them dialectically. "Wir sind dort und hier," Winter states, "weil wir zu schwach waren, darum dort und darum hier" (149). That this antagonism does not stagnate, but symbolizes a dynamic struggle that begs for a historical solution is evidenced by frequent references to the future: "Was mir heute wehtut, das muss in Schweiss eingelegt werden für künftige Zeiten" (115); "wir werden zurückfinden nur, wenn wir überwunden haben" (149). The comparison between Winter's festering leg and a barbaric regime has a deeper level of meaning. By symbolically relegating Nazism to the level of decay and filth, Merz in effect strips his lampoon of all human qualities, thereby enabling Winter to overcome, and thus render nonexistent, any element of guilt -- also a human quality.

This dialectical turnabout crystallizes in Winter's application of his festering limb -- symbolic of his link with fascist Germany -- to constructive action. A dynamic process associating past with future passes before our eyes in Winter's figurative working of the soil on the farm:

Und dann kommt der gute Morgen.
Der beginnt mit Unkrautrausziehen. Unkrautrausziehen, ... das müsste jeder Mensch lernen, das müsste sehr zeitgemäss sein. ... Das müsste man heute über die ganze alte Erde tun. Das wäre endlich ein Anfang.
Oder ich muss Stangenbohnenpflanzen an die Stange binden. Damit sie aufrecht werden. Immer mit dem Köpfchen an die Stange. ... Auch das müsste man über die ganze alte Erde tun. Gleich nach dem Unkrautrausziehen.
Du siehst, ... ich arbeite nicht nur für meinen Bauch, die Arbeit geht in kommende Jahrzehnte.
Und dann das Pflücken. Auch das will gelernt sein. Zum Beispiel die Erdbeeren ..., die müssen mit festem Griff abgezogen werden. Aber das Pflücken, soweit sind wir auf der alten Erde noch längst nicht.
Darum muss ich jetzt auch meistens nur Unkrautrausziehen. (117-118)

The incisive critical tone of this passage reveals itself once again in Merz's use of dehumanized images as a means of exposing the inhumanity of Nazism. The complexity of politico-social ideas erupting from this symbolic process of nature is significant in that it underlines the basic structural character of the novel: by employing a negative form of protest (festering leg, "Unkraut") Merz unmasks the debasement of a barbaric regime, also a negative condition. He does not oppose the inhumanity of Nazi tyranny by depicting his hero as a model of decency. Fascist Germany had viewed humanity as a weakness to begin with; only the irrational and instinctual in man counted. Accordingly, Merz engages in an invective that the Nazis would understand. At the same time he imparts a dynamic aspect to Winter's criticism, one which develops beyond this purely negative stand by virtue of the positive qualities he possesses. In the metaphoric scene just described Merz does not predict a utopian society after the corrupt, objectionable elements have been "weeded" out. Rather his optimism is matched by a critical awareness of the constant reappearance of these elements. The kind of society on which a future Germany must build -- typified in the figure of Winter -- is one that must also realistically contend with and eradicate those reactionary elements that thrive anew ("Unkraut") even after they have been uprooted (the situation prevailing in Germany in the early thirties).

This interpretation is not as outlandish as it may first seem. In the scene which shows Winter reflecting on his school days with Dietrich in the twenties, reference is made to the type of apolitical bourgeois intellectual who ignores the blunders of the Republic and reminisces instead on the "good old days" of the Wilhelminian era: "In der Aula, vorne, über dem Pult, war ein Stehkragen, er erzählte etwas von Vernunft, und wir verstanden ihn nicht, er sprach gar von guten Zeiten und konnte wohl nur seine Gehaltstüte meinen, und dann pries er zaudernd und verlegen eine Republik, die nicht bestand" (143). These so-called pillars of society who had expelled the impudent Dietrich for crying "Deutschland erwache!" (144) were the same ones who eventually re-echoed this call by bowing to Hitler: "Jetzt sind wieder die dran, die mich damals aus der Schule geworfen haben, genau dieselben, sie haben sich nur mein Abzeichen angesteckt und andere Vorsitzende gewählt" (144). Looking to the future, after Nazi Germany ("Unkraut") has been "eradicated," Merz is quite perceptive in recognizing that the ills of society will not have been cured overnight. He envisions a future in which reactionary attitudes will continue to spread, but he also envisions a youth coming to maturity which, having suffered and learned from the past, will represent an enlightened, democratic segment of society that will retard the growth of reaction ("Unkrautausziehen"), thus enabling the positive forces of society to grow ("Stangenbohnen," "Erdbeeren").

The most problematic area of the novel lies in Winter's sense of guilt over the wrongdoings of a movement he had denounced from the very start. Why should he bear the guilt of Nazi Germany's disgrace if he was not responsible for its emergence? The answer seems to lie in Merz's conception of youth in Nazi Germany. Winter acts as both heir of the old and harbinger of the new. As spokesman for the new he, by virtue of his own youth, must count himself amont the future leaders of Germany. Yet the new, the current moving force of history, has retrogressed to barbarism, a retarding state, and a part of Winter has fallen with it. The redeeming factor enabling Winter to transcend this backward state reveals itself in his humanity, that part of the "other Germany" that respects reason, justice, "Gesetz," which draws on and realistically applies the humane principles of Goethean tradition. The struggle against Nazi tyranny is still being waged ("Un-krautrausziehen"), but Merz does not allow his polemic to stagnate into mere opposition. Very likely he was of the opinion at the time that the fascist hegemony would appear as a brief phase of history, that the forces of corruption would soon induce their own dissolution. Thus the images of degeneration, decay, putrefaction. Merz looks beyond this phase of barbaric tyranny, anticipating a future that will be better because of its critical assessment of the past.

One might still be inclined, however, to question the credibility of a figure like Winter in his relationship to the future. Is he not, in the last analysis, still an isolated type without a following? Does not Merz characterize merely a dynamic struggle of ideas that lacks realistic backing? Where is there an indication of a presence of social forces during this period that would lend credence to the type that Merz draws? Such questions are not without foundation. If the other types representing the majority of youth -- the Dietrichs and Heinis -- ended in extre-mism, then there is not much left to recruit from. Merz makes it quite clear that Winter's political opposition was nonpartisan. It would seem then that he does create an isolated figure lacking representation in reality.

But youths are impressionable. It was not they who concocted the truculent theories of Germanic supremacy, racial purity, blood and soil, Volk and Führer. The credulous youths of the twenties were understandably intimidated by a political program that promised to restore social stability and national esteem. And a typical enthusiast of the new movement was Winter's "best enemy," Sturmführer Dietrich von Winterstein.

The relationship in this contradiction is not one-sided. The reverse side comes into play as well: that Winter is also Dietrich's "best enemy," suggesting that a reciprocal attraction of the two exists and that Merz is not condemning the rest of youth while singling out Winter as the exception. Rather he envisages in youth as a whole a redeeming quality quite absent in the totally corrupt fascist leadership. Winter indeed becomes Dietrich's "best enemy" when the latter joins him in exile!

Dietrich's presence in Holland is self-imposed. Other functionaries of the SA had relegated him to a lower position and, infuriated over this indignity, he comes to his political enemy and school friend for advice. His behavior is decidedly ambivalent at first. He is still the dedicated Nazi who clicks his heels, dons his SA cap, and flaunts his title, but who, behind this facade, is also looking for a rational meaning to the movement he has joined. It is Winter who tips the scale from the false to the real Germany for Dietrich. In a grotesque boxing match, where Winter literally beats Dietrich to his senses, Merz constructs a violent ritual symbolizing the struggle between the forces of reason and tyranny. Winter's victory has synthesized the "best-enemy" dualism of youth in the novel. His friend's trans-formation, his "cleansing," is not without psychological motivation, however. Prior to the confrontation Dietrich had exhibited an attitude towards humanity that directly refutes one of the main tenets of fascist ideology, namely, Jewish racial inferiority: "Du weisst, ich habe diese Seite niemals gedeckt. Ich habe denn doch zu grosse Achtung vor uns Deutschen, man hat mir niemals einreden können, dass sich 99 Deutsche von einem einzigen betrügen oder gar 'unglücklich' machen las-sen. ... Ich bin selbst aus zu reinem Geschlecht, als dass ich Judenhasser sein könnte. Diese habe ich jetzt kennengelernt. Davon gibt es im ganzen nur drei Sorten, sage ich dir: neidische Schwächlinge, perverse Schweine, und die dritten sind selber ehemalige Juden" (163). After a short stay in Holland, Dietrich returns to Germany on a humane mission whose failure is really envisioned as a victory. While attempting to free Coy's husband from a concentration camp, he is caught and imprisoned. Winter's optimistic reaction to Dietrich's incarceration reflects the victorious expression of a generation's united opposition to tyranny: "Dietrich im Konzentrationslager ... Das Schicksal ist doch grösser als unser grösster Wunsch! Was ich nicht konnte, das wird dort ... er wird dort ... er wird dort vielleicht erwachen!" (195). The implication of this optimistic outcry is that many youths who had initially regarded Hitler as a symbol of Germany's future would soon realize their mistake and join together in opposition. Despite his incapacitation through imprisonment, Dietrich nevertheless symbolizes the will of youth to resist. The satiric polemic still carried on by the exiled Winter in his role as a "Kuhstallknecht" reflects the spirit of the resistance to be undertaken in Germany.

At this early stage of exile such an optimism was not so ill-founded. Merz was not the only writer who believed that the anti-fascist opposition of the "other Germany" was the verbal counterpart of the real battle being waged at home. Many exiled writers had entertained the belief that Hitler's hegemony would crumble once the German people had come to their senses. If Merz had written his novel at a later period, one would be justified in viewing his confidence in a defiant youth as politically untenable. For, as time went on, it became evident that Hitler's most enthusiastic following came from these very ranks. Merz's premises seem to have been sound at the time he wrote the work. Unfortunately, the remaining years until 1945 did not bear them out.

## CHAPTER IV

## HANS HABE: DREI UEBER DIE GRENZE

### The Waiting Room and the Political Left

When Hans Habe wrote his exile novel D r e i ü b e r d i e G r e n z e (1937) while in Geneva, his native Austria had not yet capitulated to the Nazi Regime. Since 1935 he had been assigned to the League of Nations as a correspondent for a leading Viennese newspaper, and his foreign status in Geneva was not that of a stateless refugee, but of a bona fide Austrian citizen. In view of these circumstances one might question the reason for treating an exile novel by an author whose interest in the subject matter would seem to be no more than casual. After all, our main concern in this study is to examine how e x i l e writers deal with their new existence.

In Habe's case, however, citizenship does not necessarily mean agreement with the political management of the homeland. While it is true that the candid journalist was not forced to leave Austria in 1935, it is also true that his presence as a newsman who persisted in printing the truth was not welcome either. As chief editor of the most liberal newspaper in Vienna at the time, D e r M o r g e n, Habe had published photographs and articles which came off as sounding somewhat too democratic. The truthful intentions of his newspaper abruptly clashed with the equivocal ones of Schuschnigg's government, and steps were promptly taken to silence the editor. Habe's journalistic operations were crippled when the 10-G r o s c h e n -B l a t t, a subsidiary newspaper providing D e r M o r g e n with its financial backing, was confiscated by Austrian authorities. In the meantime Habe had been vacationing in Geneva and was informed in so many words that it would be best if he stayed there. His description of these events in his autobiography reveals the threatening tone behind what appears to be a harmless reassignment: "There was no ill feeling against him personally; indeed, he would be welcome to take up a post of 'unofficial Press attaché' in Geneva. There was no hurry; he could have four weeks to wind up his affairs in Vienna." (1)

Habe did not return to Austria. After two years of reporting on the diplomatic sessions of the League, which never got anywhere, he switched to belletristic writing. His interest in the German emigration was really not so unusual, for this phenomenon was the harbinger of what was soon to come in Austria. Already there appeared in the author's reaction to the emigration a certain sympathy with those who had fled fascist oppression, however detached it might have been at the time: "Although I was no refugee myself, at least not in the literal meaning of the word, I had been profoundly stirred by what I had seen of escape from Hitlerism, and T h r e e o v e r t h e F r o n t i e r thus became the first German emigration novel." (2) (The last statement, of course, is entirely unfounded. It merely shows that Habe, as a journalist, was unaware of the earlier exile novels written by Germans.)

It was simply a matter of time before Habe's unofficial estrangement from Austria took on a "literal meaning." Following Germany's annexation of Austria in March of 1938, he was forthwith declared a political undesirable and deprived of his citizenship.

In the short period of three months Habe wrote his somewhat bulky novel. His diffuse, sentimental style indicates that he was just as concerned with indulging his emotions as he was with the disclosure of the problems surrounding the German emigration. Even he was surprised at the novel's overwhelming popularity: "During 1937 and 1938 it appeared in eighteen languages, including Russian and Chinese. It was an undeserved success, and I find it difficult to understand it to-day. Only the topicality of the subject-matter, the frivolous ease with which it was treated, and the skill with which journalism had been turned into fiction can explain and justify its effect." (3) A rather succinct personal appraisal. For with the critical eye of a journalist and the impulsiveness of an amateur literary writer we see in D r e i ü b e r  d i e  G r e n z e a fusion of both historical insight and subjective trivia replete with platitudes and erotic overtones.

The title would seem to imply that Habe is more interested in drawing individual portraits than group experiences. The novel concentrates, for the most part, on the interrelationships of three figures of varied backgrounds who flee to Prague for racial and political reasons following Hitler's assumption of power. Heinz Kiesler, an unscrupulous textile manufacturer, Nora Geldern, a promiscuous society-lady, and Richard Sergius, a proletarian revolutionary, come together in exile and occupy the central action of the novel. Sergius, an ex-worker in Kiesler's factory, is smuggled across the Czech border by his communist comrades after having slain his fascist foreman in self-defense. Of the leading and secondary characters, Sergius is the one exile, of course, who assesses his situation in terms of a political commitment. While awaiting further instructions from the resistance movement as to the proper time for his return, he attempts, in the meantime, to collect funds for the support of the anti-Nazi struggle. These finances are supposed to be donated by Kiesler himself, Sergius' former capitalist boss and ideological opponent. That Kiesler is willing to lend assistance to a movement which threatens everything he had stood for is not indicative, on his part, of any kind of political alignment in exile. His motives are entirely selfish, stemming from a request made by Nora which he is powerless to refuse in his mad passion to possess her. Her intercession results, in turn, from her love for Sergius, not from a direct identification with his cause. Attracted to Sergius as a person but alienated from him as a communist, Nora continues to indulge in her old ways, becoming at first Kiesler's mistress and then the wife of the Englishman Vernon McCallum. Kiesler's agreement to support Sergius' movement fails to materialize due to the impracticality of a patent which the industrialist had sold to an English firm. Kiesler suffers bankruptcy, is deported from England, and returns to Germany in a desperate attempt to revive his capital investments by selling Dutch securities. There he is captured by the Nazis and imprisoned. Nora voluntarily renounces her citizenship by divorcing McCallum in order to free herself for marrying the stateless Sergius. After Sergius' return from a perilous assignment across the border, the two are seen together in the end prophesying in a mixture of pagan and Christian metaphors the resurrection of a new Germany.

46

Habe sets out to develop in two of his three leading characters certain attitudes and prejudices typical for the emigration as a whole. He loses himself repeatedly in subjective digression when treating these figures. Still, they are not totally isolated from the panoramic cross section presented of the exiles in 1933, for they are seen in their relationship with other emigrants as well, thus implying that their private interests and concerns stand out as exemplifying a certain psychological disposition of the emigration. Consequently, Habe's predilection for delving into individual problems (evidenced by the frequent use of internal monologue) does not evade the exile issue, but has a historical function.

On two separate occasions the author breaks the continuity of the story for the purpose of describing the personal and factual circumstances surrounding the emigration, which in turn sheds light on how he is to proceed critically in the novel. On the one occasion Habe draws a distinction between those exiles who had merely departed and those who had actually fled Germany: "Die Abreisenden, nicht die politischen Emigranten, machten die grosse Masse der Emigration aus." (4) The identifying characteristic of the former is a certain unchanging attitude, that of the latter a political awareness. Habe does not discount the fact that the element of forced flight is applicable to those who had to depart for racial reasons. Because this act was negative in character, however, ("Sie hatten nichts miteinander gemein als den Fluch ihres Judentums. Der Fluch konnte sie nicht einen," (104), Habe includes the majority of Jewish emigrants among the "Abreisenden" who remain fractionalized through their inability to unite under a common cause: "Die deutsche Emigration formte kein Weltbild ..., aber sie formte das Weltbild tausender Menschen. Sie änderte das Leben nicht ..., aber sie änderte Tausende von Menschenleben" (314). Habe addresses himself to this heterogeneity by drawing types resembling the masses in a waiting room: "Die deutsche Emigration wusste um diese Zeit, im Frühjahr 1933, noch nicht, wo sie sich niederlassen sollte. Auch andere Emigrationen fanden keine Heimat in der Fremde, aber ihre Mitglieder warteten wenigstens in einem gemeinsamen Wartesaal. Die deutsche Emigration fand nicht einmal diesen gemeinsamen Wartesaal. Uneinheitlich wie der Ort war sie selbst" (99-100).

The value of Habe's novel as a critical assessment of the early emigration is revealed, in part, by his treatment of certain secondary figures in this waiting room metaphor. Casting them in a social context, he reveals the prejudices, political and philosophical differences, religious disputes and artistic arrogance typifying the heterogenous character of the exile. Having grown up in the aftermath of the Austro-Hungarian monarchy, Habe was well aware of the social standards resulting from class regimentation. It becomes apparent in the novel that he views the members of the waiting room from this perspective. The major obstacle to a unification of the exiles lies in their persistent clinging to class distinction. The appearance-reality antithesis so prevalent in Austria's literary tradition comes into play in Habe's criticism. With the exception of Sergius, the refugees (all middle class or of aristocratic lineage) prefer to evade the reality of their situation, finding the term "emigrant" to be distasteful because of the leveling, equalizing connotation it carries.

A first impression of the novel is not a final one. Passing over the enigmatic conclusion for the time being, one could easily judge the work in terms of popular taste by virtue of its frequent pre-occupation with subjective trivialities. Bearing in mind Habe's discontent with the general disunity of the German emigration, however, we should regard his subjective character study as an illustration of a group bent on private indulgence. Habe's psychic dissection, therefore, need not constitute an end in itself but can take on historical significance when applied to the overall waiting room imagery. Almost without exception the secondary characters are depicted exactly in this context. They are repelled by being classified as emigrants and attempt to avoid this stigma by individual isolation, regression to the past, or by acting as if nothing had really changed through their departure. At one point Habe exemplifies this attitude in the former police magistrate who deludes himself into believing that his French colleague will continue to treat him as an equal despite his newly acquired status.

The case of Heinz Kiesler serves to present a large segment of the emigration with a mirror of its own actions. That he is an important textile manufacturer, a wealthy industrialist with sizable capital holdings, is not the major point of contention in Habe's character analysis. One could conceivably make the mistake of interpreting Drei über die Grenze as an illustration of the class struggle between business and labor. Such an evaluation would seem justified in view of the role played by Sergius, the factory worker formerly employed by Kiesler himself. To say that Kiesler's bankruptcy and downfall and Sergius' unwavering collective spirit show the inner contradictions of bourgeois capitalism as opposed to the unrelenting solidarity of the working class would be to misconstrue Habe's purpose. As a bourgeois intellectual he never committed himself to the revolutionary philosophy of Marxism. Like Klaus Mann in Flucht in den Norden, he introduces a proletarian revolutionary more out of emotional identity with a cause that can stand up to Nazism than with the hegemonic demands it makes as a system of politics.

It is Kiesler's individualistic manner of approaching things after his "transfer" to exile which Habe purports to debunk. Kiesler refuses to acknowledge any identity or association with other refugees. He persists in viewing himself as a businessman whose sojourns in Prague and London are undertaken for the express purpose of expanding his industry. Even though his factory in Germany was confiscated by the Nazis, much of his wealth and capital investments remained intact after 1933. Kiesler displays only repugnance towards other emigrants, and it gives him almost physical pain to think that he should have to share their company: "Dr. Heinz Kiesler empfand kein Mitleid mit diesen Menschen, es war ihm fast körperlich peinlich, dass ihn Leute im Kaffeehaus gegrüsst hatten, und er beschloss, nie mehr herzukommen" (110).

Professional status, wealth, intellectualism, racial heritage, noble birth, indifference -- these factors, portrayed in a multitude of the figures occupying the various waiting rooms, account for the class consciousness and accompanying isolationism Habe sees as characterizing the physiognomy of the German emigration. In a Viennese cafe the writer Minz views the emigration in terms of a select, elitist group and expresses his discontent over some of the riffraff that has drifted into exile. When a former tavern owner from Berlin has the audacity to join the other emigrants in the restaurant, Minz betrays the prejudice and intolerance exemplary for many members of the waiting room: "Sowas darf sich auch

Emigrant nennen. ... Sehen Sie, früher, da hatte jede Emigration was Aristokra-
tisches, man war gewissermassen geadelt durch Heimatlosigkeit. Man hat die Aus-
lese der Leute selbst getroffen, mit denen man ins Exil ging. Aber die drüben, die
in Deutschland, die haben uns den ganzen Mist nachgeschmissen, damit wir nur
recht schmutzig werden. Jede Emigration ist eine Emigration wider Willen. Aber
in unserer Emigration gibt es sogar Emigranten gegen unseren Willen" (188).

The sophisticated Parisian brothel operated by Madame La Pipe, a former
"house mother" from Berlin, is a popular entertainment club for emigrants of
every rank and class. Since a waiting room makes no distinction in social status,
the prestigious emigrants are forced to put up with the presence of the more inferior patrons:

> Der Polizeipräsident und der Landtagsabgeordnete kamen zuerst. Die Arri-
> vierten -- jene, wohlverstanden, die in Berlin arriviert waren -- hielten
> sich immer noch abseits von der übrigen Emigration. Den Polizeipräsidenten
> Schinkopp hatte noch nie jemand mit einem anderen Emigranten gesehen als
> mit dem Landtagsabgeordneten Degen oder mit dem Professor der National-
> ökonomie Dr. Herder. Zwar besuchte auch der Polizeipräsident die Lokale
> der Flüchtlinge auf dem Montparnasse, er kam am Abend in Rotonde, ins
> Dôme oder in die Coupole, später zur Dusika [La Pipe] ... aber er grüsste
> nur steif und abgemessen zu den Emigranten-Tischen hinüber und er sah
> sich die Leute durch sein Monokel mit einer Miene an, als wäre er nicht
> ganz sicher, ob er sich nicht eines Tages einen dieser Leute aus dem Arrest
> vorführen lassen müsste; es wäre dann unangenehm an eine Tischgenossen-
> schaft bei der Dame La Pipe erinnert zu werden. (257)

Habe does not restrict himself to critical exposure alone, to giving a merely
dismal, static impression of the emigration without suggesting a counterproposal.
He repeatedly opposes the passive, dissolute atmosphere of the waiting room with
a corrective argument. Although he turns to the German emigrant scene as it
existed in its initial stages, a sense of political urgency emanating from the time
of the novel's inception pervades the work. This sense of urgency is seen in the
introduction of a revolutionary who acts as a unifying contrast figure to the dis-
cordant emigrant group. By late 1937 the threat of militant fascism had left its
mark on Spain and Habe's identification with Sergius (5) is an indication of his own
awareness of the necessity for a united ideological stand against Nazi Germany.
Implicit in his exposure of the snobbish superiority contributing to the disunity of
the emigration is a corresponding warning to the exiles to suppress their private,
separatist attitudes and band together as a group. Even in the scenes where Sergius
is physically absent, Habe makes his presence known. Usually it is Nora who
yearns for Sergius when he is away. And it should be noted that her attraction to
the revolutionary is not based solely on passion. Invariably, she recalls the image
of the lover-communist as a contrast figure to the waiting room crowd with whom
she herself becomes rapidly disillusioned. In the Viennese cafe, where the writer
and other emigrants have congregated, Nora, bored with the pointless conversa-
tion being carried on, interjects unexpectedly with the question: "Kennen Sie
Richard Sergius ?" (192). Her remark elicits a response which, by its negative
character, points out the bigotry that hinders collective solidarity among the

exiles: "Fanatiker .... Dürfte im Konzentrationslager sitzen oder auf der Flucht erschossen worden sein" (192).

The ideological gap between the members of the waiting room and the non-member Sergius is further developed in the brief episode in a Parisian cafe describing the emigration in terms of this metaphor:

'Das Ganze ist ein grosser Wartesaal,' sagt einer ... 'Keiner kennt keinen. Und doch werden sie alle mit dem gleichen Zug reisen. Sie warten alle auf das Gleiche.'
'Unser Professor philosophiert schon wieder. Banalitäten ...,' höhnt eine dünne Stimme.
'Mit dem gleichen Zug,' setzt der erste fort. 'Dem gleichen Schicksal entgegen. Mit Unfällen und Zusammenstössen und nächtlichen Entgleisungen.'
'Warum nicht auch mit prächtiger Aussicht und Fahrt durch den Frühling?' quietscht die dünne Stimme.
Keiner beachtet sie.
Plötzlich sagt einer:
'Ich weiss einen Zug der entgleist ist. Heute. Ihr habt ihn alle gekannt, zumindest aus den Versammlungen.'
'Wer hat sich schon wieder umgebracht?' meint der Philosoph, gelangweilt.
'Niemand,' sagt der andere. 'Verhaftet wurde er. In Prag. Der Richard Sergius.'
Aber es scheint niemand zu interessieren. (233-34)

Here and in other scenes Habe frequently engages in name-dropping as a way of defining his own position and admonishing the emigration for its political indifference. The gulf between passivism and activism seems to be widened even more by the fact that certain emigrants are aware of Sergius' anti-Nazi activities, but remain oblivious to their significance. The reason many of these emigrants do not learn from Sergius' example lies in their status as "Abreisenden," whose presence in exile is not motivated out of any political alignment or ideological conviction. Habe illustrates this situation at Count Richemont's castle in Geneva, where Sergius is granted refuge for a brief period. The Countess, "mother of the German emigration," has generously offered her castle as a haven for homeless exiles. While the other emigrants parasitically enjoy her hospitality for want of anything better to do, Sergius' stay stands to be interrupted at any moment through directives from Germany regarding the political effort. His presence in exile is portrayed in direct connection with his obligation to the anti-fascist struggle. His exile is a constant reminder to the apathetic that their homelessness has a political function inasmuch as its very emergence was a political phenomenon.

In effect, Habe is presenting a prelude to the People's Front movement which was officially under way at the time he wrote the novel. More specifically, his portrayal of the early exile shows how difficult it was for all elements of the emigration to forget social and ideological differences and unite in a mutual effort to fight a common enemy. This problem takes on form especially in regard to those emigrants who express an openly anti-Nazi attitude for definite ideological reasons. These are the political exiles whom Habe had set apart from other "Abreisenden" because their flight was based on convictions which clashed sharply with fascist ideology. They indeed were compelled to flee or else face imprisonment as political undesirables. If anyone could be rallied to an anti-Nazi cause, then it ought to have been this group of emigrants, which was overtly antagonistic towards the Third Reich from the very start. Yet division was pronounced even among the defiant opposition. In his historical sketch Habe also draws attention to this fact:

> Dazu kam noch, dass selbst die enge politische Emigration nicht einheitlich war. Es war ja nicht ein Regime abgetreten; nicht ein politisches System, eine Partei, eine Weltanschauung hatte dem anderen System, der anderen Partei, der anderen Weltanschauung Platz gemacht. Die neuen Herren hatten es sich zum Ziele gesetzt mit der ganzen Vergangenheit aufzuräumen, was gewesen war, war schlecht. Die Vertreter des deutschen Sozialismus flohen, aber es flohen auch die Vertreter des deutschen Katholizismus, es flohen Kommunisten und Priester, demokratische Bürger und radikale Arbeiter. (102-03)

That Habe includes the communists here, but in the novel detaches Sergius from this group, reveals an apparent contradiction which will be clarified as we go along.

With the more politically defiant exiles one receives an insight into Sergius' function in the novel. It would appear that Habe is probing the issue of an anti-fascist front even at this early stage of the emigration. In the figure of his revolutionary we shall see how he proposes to deal with this problem. The two episodes showing the difficulties underlying the establishment of a collective front take place in Prague and London, where communists and Social Democrats, along with former officials of the Weimar Republic, are assembled. These thought-provoking scenes highlight the tendentious aspects of the novel in that they reveal the great ideological divergencies that had characterized the early political emigration. Heated philosophical and religious debates are carried on in an attempt to come to terms with the past. People who earlier had opposed one another now are forced to bring their differences to the forefront in the face of a common threat. The ideal unifying impulse for an anti-fascist front is Sergius himself, who is present at both meetings.

The perplexing thing about the conduct of these debates is Sergius' noncommittal behavior. For the most part, he allows the various representatives to speak their piece without taking a turn himself. In Prague, a Social Democrat and a communist confront each other and a discussion ensues as to how the masses are to be regarded -- as part of a classless or class society. In London, an ex-naval officer and Deputy, a former Catholic Minister of the Interior, an ex-major of the Reichswehr, and a count -- all "Zentrumsleute" and "Deutschnationale" (356) and bitter political opponents of Sergius -- gather in Nora's hotel room and analyze Hitler's rise to power as an outcome of protestant lower middle class nationalism whose origin is traced to Martin Luther, the "Erfinder des National-sozialismus" (360). Only two spokesmen stand out in these scenes. In Prague, the Social Democratic union leader Gottlieb dominates the floor and, in London, the Catholic minister Walter presides over the debate. In neither case does Sergius become involved or offer any kind of rebuttal.

Habe's motives for creating an undogmatic communist are both personal and critical. He himself could never submit to the rigid authoritarianism of a revolutionary doctrine. In his autobiography he states: "I soon discovered that there exists an unbridgeable gulf between Marxism and the Muses: the Communists see in anything poetic -- or, indeed in anything human -- a threat to their principles." (6) This would explain the personal reasons underlying the creation of an undogmatic, humanitarian revolutionary. The historical explanation for such a creation must be viewed in the context of a unified opposition. If Sergius had asserted an authoritarian position in the aforementioned episodes, the ideological gap among the various political exponents would have been strained even more. Particularly in the scenes depicting Sergius with his liberal opponents -- class conscious bourgeois and aristocratic nationalists but decidedly anti-Hitler -- we see how sensitive this polarity could be. Through Sergius, Habe expresses the necessity of allaying political and philosophical differences in a period that calls for undivided unity:

> Die Grenzen sind verschwommen, seit die Schöpfer des neuen Reiches, drüben, die Herrschaft an sich gerissen haben. Verschwommen sind die Grenzen, meint Richard, und doch hat man den Mut noch nicht, einander die Hände zu reichen. Man wird ihn wohl auch kaum finden, noch lange nicht, den Mut der Gemeinsamkeit. Dass man sich nicht finden könnte, im Negieren, im Nullen, im Verneinen dessen, was dort drüben vorgeht -- das sei eine Phrase, sagt Sergius. Es ist eine Redensart, dass nur das Positive einen kann. Was ist übrigens positiv? Ist es nicht mindestens ebenso positiv die Bedrückung nicht zu wollen, den Freiheitsraub zu verneinen, den Terror zu hassen, den Mord zu ächten, dem Totschlag sich zu widersetzen und sich zu wehren gegen die Lüge: ist es nicht ebenso positiv, wie alles, was man aufbauend nennt? Es könnte einen, auch dieses scheinbar nur Verneinende -- aber noch ist es nicht soweit. (365-66)

That Habe makes a Christianized Marxist out of his revolutionary is a further illustration of his attempt to combine personal motives with an undogmatic front, whose unifying element is a defiant humanism that transcends particular differences. Habe is not concerned with the class struggle and dialectical materialism of Marxist philosophy, but with the collective, humanistic spirit implicit therein. When Sergius and Kiesler meet face to face, the revolutionary does not try to convert his capitalist opponent to the goals of a classless society. Rather, he wishes to instill in the industrialist an awareness of human suffering and oppression. Kiesler is such an unprincipled egotist that to expect his sympathy in matters concerning social equality would be unthinkable. He must first become cognizant of the fact that a unified commitment to anti-fascism does not mean a compromise or loss of one's private business interests, only their postponement. Sergius hopes to impress this upon him by combining the human individual (Jesus Christ) with the idea of humanity (collectivism): "Ich habe versucht den Widerspruch aufzulösen zwischen Menschheit und Mensch. Ich bin bei diesen Bemühungen dahinter gekommen, dass der Widerspruch künstlich ist, konstruiert. Damit will ich nicht sagen, dass ich neue Wege gehe. Keineswegs. Das ist ja das Grosse, das Nicht-Erreichte des ersten Kommunisten, dass er zu den Menschen sprach und die Menschheit meinte" (339-40). In Sergius' following statement, the undogmatic principle of humanitarian communism comes to the fore: "Die Genossen sind weniger doktrinär, als man gemeiniglich annimmt. Im übrigen sprach ich weder von Christus als göttlicher Erscheinung, noch vom Christentum als Glaubensbekenntnis. Ich sprach lediglich von dem ersten kommunistischen Agitator, der nicht übertroffen ist. ... er wirkte durch den Menschen auf die Menschheit; später erst durch die Menschheit auf den Menschen" (340).

Implicit in the above scenes is a clash of attitudes and ideas that reveal the novel's historical function. The extremes of these attitudes, as seen in Kiesler's egotism and Sergius' selfless, collective spirit, are representative in varying degrees of how the emigrant mentality was split and how it could be corrected. By holding up to the early emigrant public, through the figure of Kiesler, a reflection of its own apathy, passivity, and discord, Habe produces a kind of prose that was still topical in the year 1937 when he wrote D r e i   ü b e r   d i e   G r e n z e . He apparently sought to expose this continuing disparity and then offer a proposal for effective action through Sergius' efforts to mold a fighting spirit along the lines of a popular front, although this is not made explicit in the work. Assuming Habe employs the revolutionary Sergius as a stimulus for solidifying the divisions of the emigration, then we must visualize these efforts in their early imperfect stages. The kinds of opposition Sergius encounters are historically credible inasmuch as the change from bourgeois individualism and subjectivism to a unified, active commitment must be seen as a process. Thus we observe some emigrants who are totally pre-occupied with prejudices, anxieties, and sentimentality, and some who possess a spark of defiance but lack the collective spirit which would lend it direction. That a united anti-Nazi front can come about only gradually is evidenced by the fact that its would-be exponent represents a decided minority. Habe is not so much concerned with the dogmatic superiority of the Communist Party in matters governing political unification. He is concerned with imparting to the majority the spirit of solidarity found in communism. It is therefore significant that Sergius confronts other emigrants in this way. It is known to those with whom he comes in contact that he is a Bolshewik taking orders from comrades in Germany. And those emigrants, most of whom were bitter opponents of communism in the Weimar Republic, would be intolerant of a doctrinaire attitude originating from such a source. We receive then a fairly accurate picture of a political revolutionary who must deal delicately with other exiled "comrades" in trying to initiate a collective spirit.

Such a process transpires in Sergius' relationship with Nora. These characters stand at opposite poles ideologically; yet Sergius' example of selflessness and concern for the fate of the German people awakens in her a corresponding sense of duty to others. That she risks being implicated in communist activities by delivering to Sergius the secret papers given her by her brother Peter already hints at a certain sympathy for their cause, however much she had denied any direct affinity with it. This dormant collective sympathy was observed earlier in her ambivalent feelings towards Sergius when she set out to persuade Kiesler to lend his financial support.

In a sense Nora acts as a model for others in completing the process from extreme individualism to collective identification. It is, in fact, because Sergius devotes himself to a cause at the risk of personal danger that she falls in love with him. He provides the motivation for bringing about this realization in her. Habe demonstrates, in this pair, that ideological divisions need not pose an obstacle to a united effort when the emigration as a body is faced with a common threat. By divorcing McCallum and thereby nullifying her English citizenship in order to marry Sergius, she accepts the added hardships emerging from her relationship with a political enemy of Nazi Germany. Had Habe terminated his novel at this point, he would have produced a rather effective work dealing with the problems involved in solidifying a basically heterogenous group of exiles during the initial days of the Hitler emigration. That such a consolidation of disparate elements involves a slow process is clearly revealed by the multifarious groups of emigrants who remain set in their ways throughout the novel. In effect, the situation as Habe shows it in 1933 did not differ greatly from the actual time in which the novel was written. Its relevance and accompanying demand for change -- seen in Sergius and the process Nora goes through -- point to the ideological differences and private animosities that still persisted in 1937 when the necessity for united political action was all the more urgent.

Habe's indictment against a perpetuation of individual interests in exile culminates in his characterization of Kiesler. Refusing to recognize his newly acquired status as an emigrant, he continues to promote his business interests in foreign enterprises, subscribing to the rationale that wealth will obliterate the stigma of exile. But he is a poor financial risk from the very beginning, and the moment he becomes caught in a predicament involving other currencies, he is deported as an undesirable alien. His re-entry into Germany is not motivated out of a sudden commitment to a cause, but out of personal greed in an attempt to regain part of his financial loss. Habe shows what can become of a refugee who tries to escape the reality of exile by viewing his new existence as a mere transfer of interests from one physical location to another.

When we reach the end of the novel, however, we wonder if Habe might not have inadvertently inserted the conclusion of a totally different manuscript he was working on. In the closing pages his critical portrayal falls completely apart. The satiric tone directed against a number of the characters, the tendentious note urging a confrontation with the immediate crisis, the unmasking of bourgeois complacency and individualism as a self-criticism designed to stir the emigration into an awareness of its passivity towards the present threat, the allusions to a possible People's Front as a process to be realized only when the fractionalized emigration suppresses personal interests and political differences and bands together to combat a common enemy -- these themes undergo a drastic revision at the end where they completely lose touch with the issues at hand. The points just enumerated suddenly become less aktuell as Habe recedes to the realm of vision and prophesy, attributing to the reign of terror an apocalyptic necessity suggestive of a new man born of destruction:

> Die tiefe Notwendigkeit der Dinge hat sich erfüllt. Tiefe Notwendigkeit der Dinge, dass alles Vergangene unterging in diesem deutschen Chaos. Notwendigkeit auch, dass aus dem grossen Chaos die Ordnung geboren werde. Die deutsche Katastrophe hat den Weizen gesondert von der Spreu. Denn nur darauf kommt es an: auf die Sonderung von Spreu und Weizen. Noch herrscht das Chaos, das ist die Vermischung von Weizen und Spreu. Aber

schon naht die Ordnung, die Sonderung heisst. Und das heimkehrende
Deutschland bedeutet das grosse gesunde reine Weizenfeld. (470)

Habe veils the current turmoil in myth and symbolism in attempting to place
a stamp of order and harmony on man's destiny. Without any apparent logical
transition, he switches his earlier polemic tone to a totally uncritical one. Unexpectedly, we hear that something noble exists in the trials of waiting, whereby
the emigrants are to find solace in the knowledge that "der grosse Tag der Aufer-
stehung" (474) is at hand. All of a sudden it is no longer anti-Nazi unity or the
formation of a unified ideological stand that will combat the elements of political
corruption; these elements will be reckoned with by cosmic destiny. Habe becomes
absolutely ecstatic over the prospect of a new Germany erupting from chaos,
mythicizing the sacredness of German earth to the extent that one wonders just
where his loyalties lie:

> Eines Tages aber, da würden sie alle, die Deutschland verlassen hatten,
> sich zusammenfinden, zusammentragen die mitgenommene deutsche Erde
> und eine Macht würde entstehen vor der staunenden, erwachenden, aus
> ihrem Schlafe gescheuchten Welt, so gross und mächtig, dass der Wider-
> stand der falschen Cäsaren zusammenbrechen würde, versinken in Nichts,
> denn Erde zieht Erde, und liebevoll empfinge der geschändete deutsche
> Boden die befruchtend frische Kraft heimkehrender verwandter Erde, zu-
> rückflutete der Wald von Macbeth, sich brüderlich vereinigend mit dem
> verlassenen deutschen Wald. (474-75)

Habe's incessant repetition of the word "deutsch" has a spellbinding effect about
it that defies rationality:

> Aufbraust da das jauchzende Lied der Arbeit, aus Millionen Kehlen jubiliert
> das Dankgebet der Befreiung, aufstehen die Toten, den Tag zu künden, vor-
> an marschiert das Heer der Gefallenen, in gutem festem Schritt [not
> "ruhig festem Schritt?"], die Toten marschieren über Landstrassen, die
> Toten fahren auf Schienen, die Toten rasen durch die Luft ..., der grosse
> Tag der Auferstehung kommt und über deutsche Felder und deutsche Aecker,
> deutschen Wald und deutsche Flur, deutsche Städte und deutsche Stätten
> klingt und singt im Sonnenschein die Siegesmelodie des Landes, das seine
> Ketten abgeworfen. (474)

Such acclamations could have been uttered by Goebbels himself!

Hopefully, Habe was not conscious of the kind of ideology he is propagating
in these closing scenes, for they literally reek with primitive, demonic images
of a German nation erupting from a kind of fertility myth. In his autobiography
he confesses that fascism did appeal to him at one time as well as communism,
and that both lay behind him as he grew older. (7) In all probability, he elected
to bring the novel to a quick close either out of eagerness to submit it to the press
or in deference to its length. Its undisciplined tempo at the end certainly suggests
an unreflected, careless conclusion.

The fact still remains that the author's critical tone is decidedly vitiated by
this abrupt retreat to the realm of prophetic vision. His dilettantish employment

of Germanic myth and imagery could p e r h a p s be overlooked had it appeared at some other period, but, at the time, the power of suggestion conveyed by such irrational symbols had played a real role in bringing a whole nation to its knees. There was certainly nothing dilettantish about this kind of language after 1933.

# CHAPTER V

## LION FEUCHTWANGER: EXIL

### Narrative Detachment and Self-Portraiture

In his Nachwort to Exil, Lion Feuchtwanger envisages the exile condition portrayed in the novel as already "in sich abgeschlossen, übersehbar." (1) At the time of the novel's completion in August, 1939, however, Feuchtwanger belonged very much to the period he chooses to describe as terminated. In the chapter titled "Trübe Gäste," the author conveys the impression that the exile scene, observed in the year 1935, is a thing of the past, and that he himself is now living in a subsequent period of history, a factor enabling him to treat with greater objectivity a situation which at one time did involve him directly. Indeed, the reader uninformed about the German emigration or Feuchtwanger's life might be surprised to discover that the author of Exil was still in exile when it was written. He might then ask: "How could the author divorce himself from a condition which was still a current reality?" Of course, the question could readily be dismissed with the qualification that Feuchtwanger is foremost a historical novelist and that complete mastery over the subject matter is a concomitant of this genre. This explanation does not settle the issue at hand, though. The problem still exists whereby the author appears to historicize a segment of a contemporary setting. Feuchtwanger intends to show that he is writing about other exiles and creates the illusion of dissociation from the epoch of which he, in actuality, is still a part.

In dealing with this apparent enigma, we must first consider the relationship of Feuchtwanger's narrative perspective to time. The autobiographical elements embodied in the main character Sepp Trautwein reflect Feuchtwanger's conflict between art and politics in a capitalist society before his trip to Moscow in 1937. After his return to France the same year, his political Weltanschauung had moved so far to the left that it would appear he had resolved this conflict. The problem of the bourgeois artist whose liberal, democratic heritage prevents him from reconciling creative expression to socio-political exigencies seems, at first glance, not to be applicable to the author's situation in 1938-39, the years that saw the completion of the major portion of the novel. (2) In Moskau 1937, Feuchtwanger assumes an ideological stance that no longer vacillates between the extremes of feeling and reason. These antithetical forces, which Trautwein must face unresolved, had characterized Feuchtwanger's own ambivalent position before he embarked for the Soviet Union. Subsequently, however, he renounced any further allegiance to a bourgeois tradition which continued to uphold the ideals of democracy and humanity at a time when Nazi Germany was manipulating such ideals to its own purpose. Feuchtwanger's discontent with the political ineptitude of capitalist society in Moskau 1937 illustrates, in capsule form, the motivation underlying his detached narrative posture in Exil: "Die Luft, die man im

Westen atmet, ist verbraucht und schlecht. Es gibt innerhalb der westlichen Zivilisation keine Klarheit und Entschiedenheit mehr. Man wagt nicht, sich gegen den andrängenden Barbarismus mit der Faust zu wehren oder auch nur mit starken Worten, man tut es mit halbem Herzen, mit vagen Gesten, und die Erklärungen der Verantwortlichen gegen den Faschismus sind verzuckert und verklausuliert. ... Man atmet auf, wenn man aus dieser drückenden Atmosphäre einer verfälschten Demokratie und eines heuchlerischen Humanismus in die strenge Luft der Sowjet-Union kommt." (3)

Liberal and Marxist critics have tended to view Trautwein's irresoluteness as an indication of the author's own position in 1939. Horst Hartmann speaks of Feuchtwanger's "Unbehagen an der Uebergangszeit" (4) and his "Zwiespalt ... zwischen theoretischer Einsicht und praktischer Schlussfolgerung," (5) relating Trautwein's ambivalent reaction to socialism to Feuchtwanger's situation per se. Matthias Wegner refers to Feuchtwanger's "unterschiedliches Verhalten in Theorie und Praxis," (6) and draws a parallel to Trautwein's classical statement: "Ich habe begriffen, dass eure Grundprinzipien richtig sind: aber ich habe es eben nur begriffen, mein Hirn sieht es ein, aber mein Gefühl geht nicht mit, mein Herz sagt nicht Ja" (875).

Yet Feuchtwanger had issued statements between 1937 and 1939 which would seem to refute such an identification. In M o s k a u 1937, it is unlikely that he consciously includes himself among the bourgeois intellectuals he reproves when he states: "Viele Intellektuelle nämlich, selbst solche, welche die Ablösung des kapitalistischen Systems durch das sozialistische für eine historische Notwendigkeit halten, haben Angst vor den Wirren der Uebergangszeit. Sie sehnen ehrlich den Weltsieg des Sozialismus herbei, aber sie haben Sorge für ihre eigene Zukunft während der Zeit, da die grosse sozialistische Umwälzung sich vollzieht. Ihr Herz verneint, was ihr Hirn bejaht. Theoretisch sind sie Sozialisten, praktisch unterstützt ihr Verhalten die kapitalistische Ordnung." (7) To say that this statement constitutes an admission of the author's own dilemma in E x i l would mean to underestimate the ideological significance of his visit to the Soviet Union. Whereas he had already passed through the "Uebergangszeit" after 1937, the figures in his novel were yet to experience it.

In another essay, "An meine Sowjetleser (1938)," Feuchtwanger regards his bourgeois past as a transitional phase surpassed by historical developments: "Diese beiden Erlebnisse [World War I and socialism] haben mir dazu verholfen, mich zu befreien von gewissen Vorurteilen der Klasse, inmitten deren ich geboren war und den grössten Teil meines Lebens verbrachte." (8) In a letter to the Second International Congress of Writers held in Valencia and Madrid in 1937, Feuchtwanger addresses himself specifically to the function of the writer in society:

Es ist heute im Lager gewisser Gegner viel die Rede von der Freiheit der Kunst und der Literatur, die nur durch Demokratie gewährleistet werde; aber so lange man unter Demokratie etwas rein Formales versteht, wird da, scheint mir, ein gefährliches Spiel mit Worten getrieben, von manchen übrigens in gutem Glauben. Die wahre Freiheit des Schriftstellers kann nur dort gedeihen, wo jene andere Freiheit, die wirtschaftliche der gesamten Gesellschaft, gewährleistet ist. Jede andere Freiheit bleibt zufällig.

Wo also um die wirtschaftliche und politische Unabhängigkeit vom Kapitalismus gekämpft wird, dort wird auch um die echte Freiheit des Schrifttums gekämpft, und dort hat der echte Schriftsteller seinen Mann zu stehen. (9)

This letter was written shortly after Feuchtwanger's return from Moscow and coexists with the resumption of his work on E x i l. It clearly shows his readiness to commit his pen to the socialist goals of a classless society. An analysis of this work presupposes, therefore, that we are dealing with a writer who lays claim to having completed the transition from the old to the new order of society. The G e i s t - M a c h t predicament with which Feuchtwanger had to struggle earlier in his W a r t e s a a l trilogy (10) was supposedly resolved after his return from Moscow, and it remains our task to determine if Feuchtwanger has attempted to actualize his views in the practice of his craft.

The established opinion that Sepp Trautwein's conflict directly mirrors the author's situation is an oversimplification and tends to ignore other textual characteristics. By arguing this way, one inevitably extricates the dilemma from the time frame of the novel and applies it to the later Feuchtwanger. Critics see the antagonism between Trautwein and his son as typical of the author's own problem when he wrote the work. Yet where Hanns was preparing to embark for the Soviet Union ("Sein Leben war nichts als ein Warten auf die Uebersiedlung in die Sowjet-Union," 797), Feuchtwanger had already returned. It seems improbable that Feuchtwanger would purposely transpose the conflict to 1935 when it was presumably a u f g e h o b e n by 1937. Furthermore, the creation of a musician as leading character reduces the likelihood of an intended autobiographical link. To establish such an intention, we must look elsewhere.

One figure emerges peripherally whose W e l t a n s c h a u u n g, attitude of detachment, and professional interests constitute, as Hans Mayer points out, "ein regelrechtes, wenig geschmeicheltes Selbstportrait" (11) of Feuchtwanger himself. This is the renowned writer Jacques Tüverlin. The physical description of Tüverlin would alone suffice to justify this connection: "Diesen rötlichblonden Schädel mit dem sonderbar nackten Gesicht, den grossen, festen Zähnen, den tiefliegenden, eiligen Augen über der scharfen Nase ..." (626). And in almost the same breath Feuchtwanger adds: "Man sprach von der Sowjet-Union, aus der Tüverlin vor nicht langer Zeit zurückgekehrt war" (626).

This scene, depicting Tüverlin's sole appearance in the novel, is highly revealing of Feuchtwanger's attitude of detachment from the heterogenous emigrant scene he is describing. Feuchtwanger is juxtaposing a figure from the post-1937 period with the events of the novel in 1935. The reference to André Gide, who visited Russia in 1936, is a further indication of the dual nature of time in the novel. Tüverlin, who in the first two parts of the W a r t e s a a l trilogy (12) was experiencing a dichotomy à la Sepp Trautwein, emerges in E x i l as a writer having achieved a synthesis through his conversion to Marxism. By transcending the immediate time frame of the novel, the year 1935, Feuchtwanger introduces through the socialist writer Tüverlin another historical perspective altogether. From Tüverlin-Feuchtwanger's viewpoint, this perspective is a reflection of the author's ideological leanings at the end of the decade. Tüverlin echoes his creator's sentiments when he opposes those who sympathize with André Gide's (13) displeasure

with a regime that suppresses individual freedom in favor of the collective body:
"In Millionen Fällen ... schliesse der Wille zur Errichtung des Sozialismus das
Mitleid des einzelnen zum einzelnen aus. ... Wer sich in politischen Entscheidun-
gen von privatem Mitleid lenken lasse, laufe Gefahr, unsozialistisch zu handeln und
die Interessen der Gesellschaft zugunsten einzelner preiszugeben" (626).

From the vantage point of one who has supposedly freed himself from the
individual inclinations of his past, Feuchtwanger proceeds to demonstrate in
E x i l why the ideology he (or Tüverlin) advocates presents the only effective
counterthreat to Nazi tyranny. The German emigration emerges as a product of
the capitalist system which, in Feuchtwanger's eyes, only engenders political
lethargy and private intrigue. And so one repeatedly comes across such disparag-
ing remarks as "ein erbärmlicher Flohzirkus" (334), "ein Häuflein Dreck" (484),
"lauter Spreu," "der Dreck der Uebergangszeit" (471), "Hornochsen," "blöde
Lackel" (322). Such belittling statements are usually uttered by those exiles who,
like Feuchtwanger, stand apart from the majority of emigrants by virtue of their
ideology (Hanns) or their artistic outlook (Sepp Trautwein, Harry Meisel, Oscar
Tschernigg). The others are wretched, quarrelsome, divisive, oppressed by the
petty problems of the day. By employing certain prominent characters as trans-
mitters of his own detachment, and by creating in Tüverlin a self-contained revolutionary spokesman who functions only marginally, Feuchtwanger assumes an
elitist narrative posture that runs contrary to the collectivistic political position
he was asserting at the time.

Dieter Faulseit elucidates Feuchtwanger's artistic position when he speaks
of the latter's "offenen Unwillen gegenüber diesem Gesellschaftssystem [capitalism]
der viele bürgerliche Schriftsteller veranlasst, sich vom Leben abzukapseln und es
gleichsam von aussen zu betrachten. Damit wird aber die Grundbeziehung zwischen
Erzähler und Erzähltem, zwischen dem epischen Subjekt und dem epischen Objekt
abgebrochen." (14) Feuchtwanger becomes guilty of that very A b k a p s e l u n g he
ascribes to bourgeois society in M o s k a u 1937 when he assumes a detached narrative point of view in the novel. The connection with Tüberlin leads one to suspect that he presumes he is serving the cause of socialism by exposing the ills of
communism's arch-rival -- capitalist society, to which the emigrant population
is inextricably bound. In effect, Tüverlin-Feuchtwanger's superiority over the
figures created suggests a politically sectarian attitude running counter to Moscow'
People's Front strategy in the mid-thirties. Prior to Stalin's pact with Hitler the
Soviet Union took a more conciliatory stand toward liberal democracy than its
newly won supporter. Feuchtwanger's pseudosocialist position in E x i l stems from
his inability to integrate figures who actively embody an ideology dialectically
opposed to fascism. (Father Merkle and Hanns are primarily i n t e l l e c t u a l
advocates of Marxism; they portray no realistic function in society from this
standpoint.) Faulseit is quite correct then in concluding from the ideological gap
existing between author and work: "So schlägt die objektive Distanzierung, das
Zurücktreten des Autors als Erzähler dialektisch in eine Subjektivierung um." (15)

Feuchtwanger bases his subject matter on two isolated events to illustrate
(much like Hans Habe) the fractionalized nature and resultant political indetermina
tion of the emigration. The majority of exiles are viewed in relation to the emigrant newspaper P a r i s e r  N a c h r i c h t e n , which has taken up the struggle to

free its eminent journalist Friedrich Benjamin from his Nazi captors. It goes without saying that the artistic manipulation of documentary reality can lead to certain problems when the author is striving for historical typicality. A news-paper like the Pariser Nachrichten was anything but a representative organ of the emigrant population. (16) But Feuchtwanger depicts, in this isolated episode, a syndrome of the ills that presumably lie latent in capitalist society. Certainly such ills as avarice, opportunism, hypocrisy, perfidy, and deceit can be linked to this society when one of its members, the treacherous publisher Gingold, caters to Nazi demands to silence the opposition of an outspoken member of his staff. In his treatment of the newspaper episode, Feuchtwanger blows a documentary source quite out of proportion. In 1935, there was no exiled publisher in Paris as insidious and corrupt as the figure of Gingold presumes to suggest. Yet the author creates the impression that such elements typified the Parisian scene. In his preface he speaks of the "bildnishafte Wahrheit des Typus" (3). In the Nachwort he goes on to say that he sought to depict not "Menschen" or "Geschehnisse," but "Kräfte" (984), an endeavor really more applicable to the socio-realistic literature of bona fide Marxists than to the work in question. If, by "Kräfte," Feuchtwanger means the conglomerate of insipid characters nursing their private whims and lamenting the misfortunes that have befallen them, or the bohemian existence led by Oscar Tschernigg and Harry Meisel, or even the political activity and debates connected with the Pariser Nachrichten and the Nazi journalist Erich Wiesener, then it becomes apparent that this is a misnomer and that Feuchtwanger is really dealing with the individual psychology of "Menschen" and the suspenseful dramati-zation of "Geschehnisse." From a leftist standpoint, which appears to have been Feuchtwanger's ideological position at the time, such a manner of portrayal makes any claim to social typicality unconvincing.

The autobiographical link with the Marxist writer Jacques Tüberlin suggests that Feuchtwanger was more than casually concerned with the precepts of Marxist thought in 1937 and the period following, when most of Exil was written. (17) Moskau 1937 shows that his commitment to the collective solidarity of the Soviet Union, however uncritically expressed, (18) was anything but dilletantish. He seems to have been convinced at the time that the political power molding this collective unity demanded of the writer that he no longer venerate such ideals as humanity and freedom as long as a reality that would reflect them is lacking. The problem that ultimately presents itself in assessing Feuchtwanger's artistic position is a ticklish one. I disagree with other critics' evaluation of Feucht-wanger's dichotomy in point of view only. Where they suggest that Feuchtwanger was directly voicing his own dilemma in Trautwein's vacillation between individual freedom and collective ideology, I would argue that he operated under the delusion that he had overcome it. Actually, the problem still exists in Exil, much to the author's unawareness of it in view of his temporal detachment from the events described. The connection with Trautwein signified an earlier conflict; the more immediate affinity with Tüverlin represents Feuchtwanger's position after 1937, intimating a resolution of the problem of artistic autonomy which, as the novel's structure reveals, still persists.

What we are in fact presented with in Exil is Feuchtwanger's praise, conveyed by other artist figures, of his own product. The author has so far removed himself from the material of his creation that total mastery and objectivity have done an aboutface. In Harry Meisel's novel "Sonnet LXVI" we perceive in miniature form a reproduction of the larger work itself. Little doubt exists that we are dealing with a novel within a novel when we read Trautwein's reaction to Meisel's work:

> Was in den Erzählungen blieb, waren nur Menschen und ihre Schicksale. Dabei hatte sich der Autor nicht etwa entpersönlicht. Aber erfüllt hatte er die ideale Forderung grosser Schriftstellerei: er war aufgegangen in seinem Werk. Er war, gleich dem Gott Spinozas, immer und in allem da, doch niemals sichtbar. Trautwein hatte geglaubt, das Exil zu kennen. Das war ein Irrtum. Jetzt erst, während er die erdichteten Geschichten des 'Sonetts 66' las, erkannte er es. Er begriff, dass er bisher immer nur Einzelheiten gesehen hatte, ein Nacheinander, ein Nebeneinander. Jetzt sah er in Einem die Grösse und Erbärmlichkeit des Exils, seine Weite und Enge. Keine Schilderung, keine Erfahrung, kein Erlebnis vermochte diese Ganzheit des Exils, seine innere Wahrheit, zu offenbaren: nur die Kunst. (170)

The tenor of this description bears a certain resemblance to Feuchtwanger's conception of the exile in "Trübe Gäste." In particular, Trautwein's reference to "Grösse" and "Erbärmlichkeit" calls to mind the "Recken" who have succeeded in transcending the limitations of their existence and the "Elende" who continue to wallow in their own wretchedness (154). The parallel becomes more cogent when one recalls that "Trübe Gäste" appeared in D a s  W o r t under the title "Grösse und Erbärmlichkeit des Exils." (19) Moreover, that Trautwein sends Meisel's novel to none other than Feuchtwanger's persona Jacques Tüverlin -- who receives it most enthusiastically -- is a further indication of the author's predilection for artistic self-portraiture.

Feuchtwanger's portrayal of Raoul, the fascist son of Erich Wiesener, is another case in point. Having experienced the profundity of Meisel's work, Raoul is downright awestruck by the author's air of superiority, his complete mastery over the material at hand ("so erhaben über Gut und Böse und Hass und Liebe," 617). The impression of total objectivity and removal from immediate reality induces in the boy a similar desire for detachment. "Sonnet LXVI" does not inspire him to face the problems of the time, but to escape them. And so he becomes a writer who adopts the impersonality of his model ("Gerade weil er erkannte, wie nichtig die Dinge waren, wurde er leicht mit ihnen fertig," 618). Meisel's novel, depicting the "Grösse und Erbärmlichkeit" of exile -- indeed of Feuchtwanger's E x i l -- succeeds in moving the reader not to a socialistic confrontation with the political demands of exile, but to esthetic sublimation.

Raoul's assessment of the role "Sonnet LXVI" plays in his life prompts an inquiry into the kind of effect Feuchtwanger ultimately had in mind with E x i l. Raoul states: "Da gibt es Leute, die erklären, Literatur sei nur um ihrer selbst willen da und habe keine Wirkung. Was für Narren. Kann einer das Buch dieses Harry Meisel lesen und unbewegt bleiben und sein Leben fortführen wie bisher?" (618). If the "Wirkung" of which Raoul speaks exists on an esthetic plane only, then literature is indeed "nur um ihrer selbst willen da," a point which Feuchtwanger makes no attempt to elucidate. Instead, he issues the comment: "Ihn hat

es [Meisel's book] gelehrt, dass alles, was er bis jetzt gelebt hat, Zeitverschwen-
dung war, barer Unsinn" (618), which by its noncommittal, "objective" character
really comes off as a subtle confirmation of his own detachment. Hans Mayer is
correct in ascribing to Feuchtwanger the "Attitüde eines pseudowissenschaftli-
chen Historikers ..., die gleichzeitig wissenschaftliche Pragmatik anstrebt und
doch auch, nicht ohne künstlerischen Reiz, mit ihr spielt." (20) Thus the interplay
of narrative detachment and self-portraiture in E x i l .

The theme of exile, its "Grösse und Erbärmlichkeit," compounds itself in
the novel. Not only is "Sonnet LXVI" a reflection of the parent work, but Trautwein's "Wartesaal" symphony as well. Trautwein's exuberant endorsement of
Meisel's novel has already been noted. Throughout E x i l , we see him time and
again turning to Meisel for artistic solace as a relief from the monotonous burden
of political writing. This results in Trautwein's renunciation of politics in favor
of art, much in the same way that Raoul's distaste for politics finds an outlet in
Meisel's work. Trautwein's visualization of the "waiting room" reads like a
grandiose fulfillment of the "Ganzheit des Exils" (170) he had perceived in "Sonnet
LXVI." Like Meisel, he too is "aufgegangen in seinem Werk" (170) so as to create
the illusion that the emigrant scene, to quote Feuchtwanger, is "in sich abgeschlossen, übersehbar" (986). The element of time, therefore, loses its historical
reference, and Trautwein, the creative overseer of the exile, transcends the
year 1935, becoming Feuchtwanger's fictitious spokesman for his own work:

> Der Raum war unendlich armselig, er glich den Baracken der Emigranten,
> und, wiewohl durchgrellt von dem scheusslichen, kalkigen, erbarmungslosen
> Licht jener Baracken, blieb er schattenhaft in seinen Winkeln und von un-
> deutlichen Grenzen. Es war aber dieser Saal erfüllt von einem Gewimmel
> von Menschen; nicht nur die Menschen unserer kümmerlichen deutschen
> Emigration waren darin, sondern alle Zeitgenossen Sepp Trautweins. Sie
> hockten da, auf verlumpten Bündeln und Koffern, mit sinnlos zusammenge-
> rafftem Hausrat, sie hockten und bewegten sich gleichzeitig, sie waren auf-
> geregt und resigniert in einem, es war Nacht, denn es brannte ja das kalkige
> Licht, es war aber auch Tag, es war Sommer und es war Winter; man war-
> tete schon so lange, dass es keine Jahreszeiten mehr gab und keinen Unter-
> schied mehr zwischen Tag und Nacht. Die Menschen sassen da und gingen
> gleichzeitig stumpf resigniert, wimmelten durcheinander und rührten sich
> doch nicht von der Stelle. Es ging keiner fort und es kamen immer mehr,
> der Saal war überfüllt und noch immer kamen neue, und es war ein Wunder,
> wie sie Platz fanden. (734-35)

In Trautwein's symphony and Meisel's novel, the motif of waiting evokes
the impression of a group that is hardly ready to implement social change once
the transitional period, seen by Feuchtwanger as historically inevitable, has
passed. Trautwein and Meisel embody distinct aspects of Feuchtwanger's own
elitist stance, for they too view the exiles as a motley group languishing in its
own misery. Feuchtwanger's pseudosocialist detachment, his penchant for manipulating ( s p i e l e n ) the exile theme, the impression that he, through the super-
imposition of one time frame on another (i. e., Tüverlin), has transcended the
static waiting period of the novel all reveal a writer who is still rooted in an in-
dividually oriented literary tradition.

For this reason a discrepancy does emerge between the author's ideological and theoretical premises and artistic function. In the N a c h w o r t Feuchtwanger reflects: "Ich war mir bewusst ..., dass ich mich nicht drücken durfte vor den Widersprüchen, vor dem dialektischen unserer Epoche" (985). Again, as with the earlier question of "Kräfte," Feuchtwanger proceeds from a leftist standpoint, but in the novel intellectualizes the "Widersprüche," that is, he approaches the conflict from a liberal world view (U e b e r b a u) so that the epochmaking dialectical counterpart (B a s i s) is lost sight of. The issue of G e i s t and M a c h t, or art and politics, is "typified" in an individual case and thus lacks a representative function in reality. And when Trautwein finally envisions the appropriate theme for his "Wartesaal" symphony, which enables him to assume an attitude of esthetic distance, the "epochal" significance of his debates with Hanns is greatly depreciated, to say the least. Feuchtwanger errs in thinking that the problem of individualism contra collectivism exemplifies the dialectic "unserer Epoche" inasmuch as the "Elende" appearing in E x i l far outnumber such "Recken" as Harry Meisel, Raoul Wiesener, and Sepp Trautwein, who stand apart from the other emigrants, entertaining not infrequently a certain contempt for their anguish and hardships.

This raises the question as to the motivations underlying Trautwein's activities as a political journalist. A socialistic commitment to anti-fascism would not only make Feuchtwanger's ideological position more artistically tenable, but would also give the G e i s t - M a c h t dialectic a material basis. Needless to say, other reasons seem to account for Trautwein's political awakening. Even in his role as a polemicist he holds rigidly to the idea of freedom from social and political constraint that had always governed his esthetic views. The novel shows him to be totally unresponsive to the social inequities pervading the lives of fellow-emigrants. The scene involving the eminent biographer Sigmund Marnasse is a case in point. This emigrant has become so destitute that he must compete with the dogs for whatever garbage has been deposited in refuse containers. After witnessing this scene, Trautwein reproves himself for having felt concern for Marnasse's plight: "Dass er sich von dem Mitleid mit Sigmund Marnasse hat überrumpeln lassen, daran ist nur seine Müdigkeit schuld gewesen. ... Er ist dazu geboren, Musik zu machen, und nicht die Welt zu ändern. Sollen das gefälligst diejenigen besorgen, die dazu das Talent haben" (741). Marnasse's impoverished state is not an isolated case, but represents one of the conditions perpetrated by the ills of that very capitalism Feuchtwanger lays bare in the Gingold affair. Strangely enough, Trautwein turns out to be the most outspoken opponent of the corrupt practices of his publisher. But when faced with the situation where he might have to transfer his commitment to humanity from the pen to the socio-political realities of exile, he falls back on his primary calling as an artist to avoid any compromise of individual freedom.

Trautwein displays a similar desire for noninvolvement even in his family affairs. It is Anna who takes the economic burden of exile on her shoulders. Her main preoccupation is with the relentless battle for survival. But Trautwein has little use for such banalities; he even rebukes Anna when she brings these urgent matters to his attention. Either he is inspired by the creative implications of G e i s t or by the individual, humanistic ideals it projects. When he gives up music for political writing, nothing essential to his world view has changed. Rather, it is more like a shift of emphasis within the confines of a philosophy of individual freedom.

Friedrich Benjamin's abduction on neutral soil is the catalyst that induces Trautwein to put aside momentarily his work on the "Wartesaal" symphony. His sole intention in joining the P a r i s e r  N a c h r i c h t e n is to effect Benjamin's release through the force of his pen. Once he has achieved this goal, he can return to his music with the satisfaction of knowing that he has not betrayed his obligation to mankind. With the air cleared, an atmosphere once again conducive to artistic freedom can be created. A need no longer exists for him to continue his exposure of fascist tactics. If he can produce results by unmasking the inhumanity of Nazism, then to him that is a victory in the name of humanity (although the Nazis did not release Benjamin for humane reasons, but only because it was politically expedient to do so). The G e i s t - M a c h t dualism crystallizing in Trautwein's repeated confrontations with his son remains largely theoretical; he does not e x p e r i e n c e this conflict as an artist-journalist. Feuchtwanger's penchant for manipulating the exile theme, as evidenced in Meisel's novel and Trautwein's completed symphony at the end, serves to conceal, and by the same token to betray, the actuality of the problem surrounding art and political engagement. In this respect the G e i s t - M a c h t debates do have a bearing on Feuchtwanger's artistic position after 1937, however much this problem appears to be a thing of the past through the author's more immediate affinity with the Marxist writer Tüverlin.

Klaus Jarmatz sees in Feuchtwanger's treatment of the exile the situation of the leftist-liberal writer whose artistic postulates lack the realism necessary for an ideologically progressive integration: "Die Fabel und die gesamte Anlage des Romans E x i l bleiben ... noch im bürgerlichen Lebensbereich, der Schritt zum Gesellschaftsroman, der die moderne Gesellschaft in einer Vielzahl von Charakteren zeigt, wird von Feuchtwanger noch nicht vollzogen. Dadurch vermag er aber auch nicht die geschichtsbildende Kraft der Arbeiterklasse und anderer Volksschichten in der Gestaltung sichtbar werden zu lassen." (21) Jarmatz departs somewhat from this view, however, when he interprets Trautwein as a "Synthese von Kunst und gesellschaftlichem Handeln," (22) or when he sees Trautwein as a bourgeois artist "der durch die Volksfrontpolitik an die Seite der kämpfenden Antifaschisten geführt wird." (23) Had this really been the case, then E x i l would have reflected an ideological basis that lent credence to the idea of historical progress born of socio-political consciousness. As it stands, Trautwein neither achieved a synthesis between art and social reality; nor did his attitude convey the revolutionary spirit of the People's Front. In fact this movement, which by 1935 had become the order of the day among political exiles in France and which also saw Feuchtwanger as one of its most ardent supporters, receives only casual reference in the novel. Feuchtwanger's artistic alignment with the Marxist writer Tüverlin dialectically implies a disalignment from the problem of Trautwein. But the break was not a conclusive one, as this study has attempted to show.

# CHAPTER VI

## BRUNO FRANK: DER REISEPASS

### The Exile as an aristocrat of Humanity

The tradition of liberal humanism, to which the bourgeois writer was heir, underwent a revaluation in some cases after 1933. In their journalistic contributions and artistic works, the liberal authors in exile addressed themselves to issues involving social forces and ideologies that would lend realistic substance to a literary heritage that had fostered individual freedom of expression. Lion Feuchtwanger, Klaus Mann, and Hans Habe saw, if only for reasons of expediency, in the collective struggle of communism the one viable ideological force that could pose a threat to militant imperialism. Habe and Feuchtwanger include in their exile novels separate historical sections showing their discontent with the political apathy of an emigration that had continued to persist in its old ways, unable to suppress private differences and join together in opposition to a common enemy. In Flucht in den Norden, Mann is equally critical of certain reactionary tendencies displayed by various social elements in the countries of asylum. All three writers attempt to resolve the problem of individualism and noncommitted humanism by introducing antipodal figures as bearers of a progressive, collective ideology.

In Der Reisepass, Bruno Frank describes a rather unique exponent of the Hitler opposition. His narrative, centering on the actions of Prince Ludwig of Camburg-Saxony, (1) a descendant of a deposed ruling hierarchy, sheds unusual light on how an exiled liberal writer might confront the politically inept tradition that had facilitated Hitler's rise to power. The scenes characterizing various functionaries of the Weimar government as republicans in form but monarchists in principle reveal an acute perception of the situation as it existed in the 1920's. In the person of Steiger, Ludwig's private tutor and dedicated servant throughout the Republic and in exile, we see exemplified that unpolitical, regressive state of mind typifying a large segment of the officialdom at that time. As a contrast figure, Frank creates an enlightened prince who rejects the former privileges of rank and nobility to which some government officials and intellectuals still aspire.

In the figure of Ludwig, the author erects a model of moral decency. He is the dethroned aristocrat who possesses noble, humane sensibilities, a princely figure in whom bourgeois democratic values of equality and liberty are fostered. Whereas other exiled writers sought to reconcile the concept of humanity to existing reality, Frank goes to the other extreme, embodying this idea in a single figure standing apart from the rest of society. Ludwig becomes Frank's representative of liberal humanism. The "real" spokesmen for the bourgeois class, on the other hand, are portrayed as disillusioned monarchists or fatalistic, resigned exiles.

Klaus Mann and Ludwig Marcuse have both intimated a certain dismay over their colleague's selection of a prince as protagonist in their reviews of Der Reisepass after its appearance in 1937. Since their intention is to bestow more praise than criticism, however, they pay mere lip service to what really constitutes the central issue of the work. Marcuse describes Der Reisepass as "einen etwas problematischen Roman," "ein tolles Wagnis," and considers "manche Partie des Frankschen Experiments" to be "recht fragwürdig." (2) Klaus Mann dispenses momentarily with the usual benevolent tone pervading his reviews when he in turn states: "Es muss Franks Absicht gewesen sein, -- und wir möchten sie fast als eine dichterische Laune bezeichnen, -- uns als antifascistischen Kämpfer diesen Prinzen-Jüngling vorzuführen: diesen Ausnahmefall, dieses nicht-typische Exemplar." (3)

Needless to say, Frank's creation of a verbürgerlichter Prinz is more than simple "Laune." His concern for the defense of human values was just as strongly felt as that of his literary peers. But the author goes about this task in a most perplexing way. Der Reisepass follows Frank's earlier novel in exile Cervantes (1934). In the figures of Ludwig and Steiger, he constructs a relationship that is just the reversal of the lord-servant model in the Spanish writer's famous work. The ideas embodied in the Don Quixote-Sancho Pansa dualism do a complete about-face in Der Reisepass. Here it is the servant Steiger who entertains illusions of grandeur about a ruling aristocracy, and it is the nobleman who holds such fantasies to be obsolete. Appearance and reality, idealism and practicality, have reversed hands in a contemporary reworking of a historical model.

An inquiry into the rationale for such a portrayal of contemporary society is certainly called for. It was noted that Frank creates an aristocrat as a model of humanity. Ludwig's exceptional qualities are hardly representative of the members of his dethroned class. His father Duke Phillip had occupied himself solely with a collection of rare coins following his deposition; the brother Prince August had aligned himself with the Nazi Party; the European nobility attending the mother's funeral in the early 1920's did so for reasons of ceremony, not out of empathy; Ludwig's fellow conspirators in the planned coup d'état, all of whom were deposed nobles and bourgeois sympathizers of the monarchy, were eventually released from prison through personal connections with the upper ranks of the Nazi Regime. Only Steiger, the most zealous spokesman for the coup, which was to have been spearheaded by Ludwig (the "Volksfürst aus altem Blut" (4), remains imprisoned only to be freed by the prince himself.

The rationale for the reversal of the Don Quixote-Sancho Pansa Weltan-schauung ties in with Frank's criticism of Germany's political complacency in the years leading up to the maelstrom of 1933. The satirical emphasis in Cervantes' work rests with unmasking the fruitlessness of an aristocrat's desire to uphold an ideal of chivalry that had since faded into oblivion. His servant, however, is a figure out of the sixteenth century who has surpassed the age of compliant bondage. In Der Reisepass, Frank does not resort to satire as an artistic device for exposing the incongruities of his period. Rather, he allows the ana-chronism of a bourgeoisie espousing an attitude of servility to speak for itself. Observed in a broader historical perspective, this anachronism had its inception with the establishment of the Weimar Republic in which the Wilhelminian monarchy was overthrown in form but not in spirit.

In the figure of Ludwig, Frank depicts a person whose actions are predicated on the principle of democracy and justice. Ludwig is not a typical member of the bourgeoisie, however, but a nobleman reduced to these ranks. Frank refrains from drawing his main character from established middle class ranks, for it was they who had, in part, enabled Hitler to rise to power in the first place. He therefore creates in Ludwig an ideal of the bourgeois class as it s h o u l d be in contrast to Steiger, who represents this class as it is. In showing this servant figure as a venerator of rank and authority, powerless to stand on his own feet, seeking security in the comforting arms of a benevolent protector, Frank exposes a social frame of mind extending beyond Steiger and having its roots in a class that had failed to put into practice the democratic principles upon which the Republic was founded.

The three delegates of the Republic who shamefully present Ludwig's father with his deposition papers in 1918 are a case in point:

> Nach kaum zehn Minuten war der Staatsakt vorbei. Die drei Herren wandelten genierten Schrittes über den menschenleeren Schlossplatz. Dann blieben sie stehen. Der in der Mitte tastete in seiner Mappe umher, als fürchte er etwas verloren zu haben, nahm dann ein Papier hervor, entfaltete es, und alle drei steckten die Köpfe zusammen und blickten hinein. Es war dem zehnjährigen Prinzen auf seinem Balkon klar, dass dies der unterzeichnete Thronverzicht war. (19-20)

Here Frank is not unmasking the delusions of an outmoded aristocracy, but those of a democracy which falters in its self-assurance. With the Republic's downfall in 1933, Frank apparently could salvage little that was honorable from the bourgeoisie itself. The Republic had failed to thwart Hitler's climb to power, and it is its representative members that he intends to expose. In drawing on an outsider so to speak, a prince who willingly strips himself of title and rank, who commits himself to the principle of justice and humanity at personal risk, who makes countless sacrifices to help others, Frank sets up an image of a democratic people as he conceives it ought to be.

This characterization becomes problematic when Ludwig and Steiger are joined together in exile. Even as a youth in Germany, Ludwig had made it clear to his tutor that privileges of rank no longer played a role in his life. In exile he looks upon Steiger as simply a friend and companion whose daring escape from a concentration camp he had planned out of humane motives when he stole back to Germany from Prague under an assumed name. But Steiger fails to get the picture. Experiences in a concentration camp and then in exile in no way induce a changed outlook. He continues to regard his rescuer as the great protector, the concerned noble who never abandons his subjects. Ludwig recognizes the absurdity of such behavior, but lacks an understanding of the serious political consequences that could result from this benign attitude. Unable to enlighten his old teacher, he simply humors him. The conflicting outlooks present in the lord-servant dualism never really interact. Lacking the critical consciousness of the b o r n democratic humanist, Ludwig cannot rationalize his principle of humanity.

Consequently, Steiger demonstrates no awareness of the reality of his changed existence. Expatriation, lack of passport, material hardship -- these circumstances have no effect on him as long as his prince is at his side. While Ludwig provides for the daily necessities by engaging his services as a language instructor, Steiger remains the dutiful servant who takes it for granted that his needs will be met by his lord. He still addresses Ludwig in the third person; he is ashamed of dining with his prince at the same table; and he becomes jealous when Ludwig spends an undue amount of time with Ruth, because he fears in this union a severance of the close relationship between lord and servant. Steiger's home becomes a dream world in which he envisions his prince as the infallible overseer:

> Eine kindliche Dienstbereitschaft war in seinem Wesen, zugleich etwas Zeremonielles. Und Ludwig fühlte, dass er ihn da nicht beirren dürfe. Steiger setzte sich sogar widerstrebend an den Tisch, den er gedeckt hatte. Er wäre lieber hinter Ludwigs Stuhl stehen geblieben, als herzoglicher Ober- mundschenk und Truchsess. Es war eine letzte Zuflucht für seine Träume. Wie er einst den Umgang mit dem jungen Prinzchen nie hatte zur Selbst- verständlichkeit werden lassen, so brachte er es jetzt fertig, im Zusammen- leben auf ein paar Quadratfuss Raum die Distanz zu wahren. In seinem mit- genommenen Geist hatte sich ein Programm und eine Legende gebildet: die Legende vom vertriebenen Fürsten, dem nur ein einziger treuer Diener noch folgt, um ihm Ehren und Hof zu ersetzen. (288)

Frank gives as a possible reason for Steiger's retreat from reality the horrors of the concentration camp and the misery of exile itself. At the British Ministry of Interior, where Ludwig intercedes on his friend's behalf, the impres- sion is conveyed that Steiger's sense of servitude might illustrate a psychological condition stemming from his traumatic experiences: "Steiger sass daneben, mit jenem Ausdruck ergebener Gläubigkeit, der Ludwig teils rührte teils mit einer un- bestimmten Reue erfüllte. Ihm war klar geworden, dass der Freund unter den Schlägen seiner Erlebnisse Schaden genommen hatte" (277). Further on, reference is made to "die Vereinfachung bis zum Kindlichen, die unterm Druck der Erleb- nisse mit ihm vorgegangen war" (297).

Admittedly, such harrowing experiences could have produced these regres- sive symptoms. The state of dejection, for example, to which Rotteck, Ludwig's former university professor, has resigned himself in Prague does intimate a psychological reaction to an abrupt change of existence. Viewing Steiger's situation on a broader scale, however, one spanning the political and social turmoil of the Weimar Republic, we find that he had repeatedly sought solace in the old system when present conditions became too uncomfortable. An authority on the genealogy of the Saxon Dynasty, he had always entertained notions about the Camburg House one day achieving a place in history equal to that of the Habsburgs and Hohen- zollerns. In his opinion, the establishment of the Republic merely presented an undesirable obstacle to a form of rule he thought to be inevitable. To the young prince he exclaims: "Meinen Sie, diese deutsche Republik werde ewig stehen -- eine Republik, die selber nicht wagt, sich bei Namen zu nennen, eine Republik ohne Mut, ohne Glanz, ohne wirklichen Drang zur Gerechtigkeit. Die Leute pfei- fen ja in den Versammlungen, wenn man ihre Staatsform erwähnt" (28). Steiger's reverence for the old order reaches its climax in a conspiracy entered into with other loyal monarchists to overthrow Hitler's regime. More out of sympathy for the desire of the conspirators to rid Germany of the present threat than for the monarchy they wished to see reinstated afterwards, Ludwig agrees to act as a symbolic inspiration to those who would bring about the coup d'état. On this and other occasions throughout the novel he asserts his aristocratic rank for reasons of expediency only. He does not adhere in principle to the reestablishment of a political structure he knows to be passé.

The question to be raised is: What kind of future does Frank perceive in this manner of portrayal? At the end of the novel we are left with an unresolved antithesis between two varying mentalities -- a democratic and a monarchistic. Does the future lie with the Ludwigs or the Steigers? Obviously Frank places his faith in the former. This bourgeois prince represents for him the democratic ideals of a people, a nation that has rid itself of stagnant philistinism, of smug conventionality and political lassitude. Yet, where Frank is adept at pointing out the sociopolitical fallacies of his society, he fails to confront this picture with a realistic counterproposal. Ludwig remains the extreme individualist throughout the work. Despite his self-sacrifice and acts of humanity, he stands out as a figure who, representing neither the aristocracy nor the bourgeoisie, admits of no social classification. By depicting him as an exemplary figure in way of criticism against the reaction of certain members of the intelligentsia, Frank in effect creates his own escape mechanism and accordingly betrays an attitude which, in itself, stands apart from reality. His sympathies very likely do not lie with the dispirited Rotteck, whom he casts as a contrast figure to Ludwig. In spite of the prince's concern for the injustice suffered by others, Frank still places him on a pedestal, showing him as a paragon of virtue who appears self-secure in the knowledge of his own humanity.

Indeed, the abstract cliché -- "preservation of German spirit and culture" -- that is frequently heard in conjunction with exile literature seems most appropriate in Frank's case. For it takes on such humanistic connotations in Der Reisepass that one is inclined to view the author's hero in the framework of Germany's idealistic heritage. Ludwig's initial entrance into exile amounts to nothing but an incredible contrivance on Frank's part to involve his hero in a classical conflict between necessity and freedom, duty and inclination. Ludwig is escorted by the Gestapo to the Czech border, where he is set free with the understanding that his return will mean execution for his fellow conspirators. The following state of exile in Prague thus becomes an individual moral issue. A conflict arises in Ludwig whereby he must choose between action and passivity. Frank does not perceive Ludwig's exile as a political arena from which he could use the freedom alloted him in purposeful anti-Nazi activity. This is clearly evidenced by his unwillingness to align himself with the emigrant newspaper Das Freie Wort. He approaches Breisach, the editor, not to provide him with needed information about the truth of fascist brutality, but to enlist his aid in securing a falsified passport for his return to Germany. The freedom Ludwig senses in exile, tantamount to nonactivity, conflicts with his sense of betrayal of those who still remain imprisoned:

Andere hatten für ihn geplant und gehandelt. Andere waren für ihn ereilt worden. Ihm schnürten Fesseln die Hände zusammen. Aber er würde diese Fesseln zerreissen. Er hatte denen, die für ihn litten, Hilfe zu bringen oder

für sie unterzugehen. ... Jetzt war er zu nichts Anderem mehr auf der
Welt. Wohin er um sich blickte, er ersah für sich keine mögliche Existenz-
form. Aber am unmöglichsten erschien dies: irgendwo unterzukommen und
im Warmen zu vegetieren, während jene Männer Qualen ausstanden und
vielleicht starben. (183)

To intensify the antagonism between freedom and necessity, Frank introduces the
element of guilt incurred by Ludwig through his passionate relationship with
Rotteck's wife Susanna. Now he has no other alternative but to return to Germany
in order to atone for his weakness, his flaw: "Er konnte mit einer Tat bezahlen.
Eine Tat wurde von ihm gefordert, Einsatz seines Lebens zum klaren, fest um-
rissenen Zweck" (203). By arranging for Steiger's escape (the other conspirators
had already been released through the intervention of "private" contacts in the
Regime), Ludwig has executed his obligation to humanity, a daring act requiring
personal courage and self-sacrifice, but completely removed from the political
scene. Ludwig's return to Germany was not undertaken as an anti-fascist venture.
No ideological significance was attached to it. Frank's reason for devising this
plan arises in the final analysis from a desire to heighten the image of his hero
as a humanitarian, one who, needless to say, is wanting in the social conscience
required to reify this abstraction.

We gain a deeper understanding into Frank's penchant for drawing model
characters when we consider his view of history, as reflected through Ludwig's
research on the life and work of the Spanish painter Goya. Nothing against the
portrayal of great historical personalities. But when their sufferings, sorrows,
and conflicts are viewed as singular and outstanding, as something to be appreciated
and relived, then it becomes apparent how rooted Frank is in the historicity of the
nineteenth century. Ludwig's art history professor Johannes Rotteck, an expert on
portraiture, stands in decided contrast to Steiger, the idealistic historian on dynastic genealogy, by virtue of his predominantly empirical approach to his subject
matter. Ludwig's admiration for Rotteck's monumental "Geschichte des Portraits
in Europa" sets the positivistic tone he will initially employ in his study of Goya:

Ein ungeheures Tatsachenwissen war hier mit römischer Klarheit geordnet.
Die Meister lebten, und die sie dargestellt hatten, lebten auch. Ein leerer
Name stand nirgends. Nirgends war deklamiert, nirgends fand sich ein be-
quemer Gemeinplatz, nirgends wurde, nach der Art so vieler neudeutscher
Gelehrter, feierlich die Wolke umarmt. Alles war Substanz, Wirklichkeit,
Fleisch und Leben. Ein illusionsloser Menschenbetrachter redete hier. Ihm
war Kunst nicht eine losgelöste, zu Häupten schwebende Erscheinung, zu
der man emporgedrehten Auges aufschaut. Sie war Daseinsextrakt, Aufschrei,
Trost und Nahrung. Jedes seiner Kapitel malte solid eine neue Phase der
europäischen Gesellschaft. Man wusste, wie in jedem Jahrhundert in Paris,
Siena oder Ulm die Menschen sich fortgebracht, wie sie geliebt, wie sie
einander geehrt oder verfolgt hatten. Alles erschien so simpel, so selbstverständlich, man glaubte, schloss man das Buch, es nacherzählen zu
können. (47-48)

The drawback to Rotteck's seemingly sound scrutiny of historical events and
personages does not become evident until he reaches exile. Here the problems

implicit in a view of history that is inclined to cyclical analysis come to light. The positivist, who rejects speculative, abstract suppositions, perceives history in terms of linear development as opposed to dynamic process. In Rotteck's case this nonidealistic, factual outlook has blinded him towards the existence of change arising from conflicting forces in history. Because he envisages the reigning barbarism in Germany as a modern rendition of the fall of Rome, a new Dark Ages will perforce emerge, echoing in a period of renewed primitivism:

Werden sie kommen, die anderen Zeiten? Nicht für uns, Ludwig. Machen wir uns doch nichts vor. Dieser Einbruch der Werwölfe und Stinktiere ist keine Episode. Ganz so wie wir haben Andere gesessen, als Rom sank, vor einem Jahrtausend und einem halben. In ihren schönen Säulenhöfen haben sie gesessen ... und haben darauf gewartet, dass die Herren Germanen kämen und ihre Bibliotheken und Bäder zerschlügen. Und sie wussten, ... dass nun die Finsternis kam, dunkle Jahrhunderte, dass noch die Kindeskinder ihrer Kindeskinder das Licht nicht mehr sehen würden. (143-44)

Rotteck's resigned outlook no doubt can be attributed, in part, to the uprootedness of exile but, more important, it is symptomatic of a static assessment of man which sees historical epochs in recurring terms of light and darkness, humanity and barbarism.

The author's solution to the problem of Rotteck is to take the quixotic approach to history, as is shown through the exemplary figure of Ludwig. This young art historian, whose empirical method of research is modelled after that of his mentor, takes a similar view of history as his starting point. He draws a parallel between the gruesome images of war in Goya's "Desastres de la Guerra" and the present terror in Germany. The unrelenting cyclical nature of history is uttered time and again in such expressions as: "Ist dies Napoleons Zeit, Spanien, das Gemäuer vor dem schwarzen Himmel Madrid? Nichts braucht man zu wissen. Denn es ist ewig das Selbe" (305); "Vor Verwüstung und schnöder Untat, die der Bestialismus wallte und organisierte und anpries -- damals und heute und immer" (306); "Es war eine ewige Gegenwart" (307); "Geschichte wiederholt sich nicht so genau. Wohl aber wiederholt sich Tyrannei und ihr Schicksal" (308); "Ewig zahlt das Volk. Ewig baumeln Verstümmelte an den Bäumen, ewig schwingt ein rasender Bauer das Beil, ewig ziehen am Strick die zum Tod Bestimmten über die Heide" (308). Ludwig's way of viewing Goya provides us with a clue into Frank's own quixotic tendency in his general portrayal of the exile. It was stated earlier that the author would not appear to share the pessimism and fatalism of the historian Rotteck, who is inclined to interpret the fascist reign of terror as just another inevitable unleashing of man's bestial instincts. Just as Ludwig enhances the image of Goya as a justification for transcending the turmoil of the period, so does Frank transcend a direct confrontation with the political realities of exile by creating h i s model hero.

Unlike his teacher, Ludwig overcomes the ugly reality of the moment by mythicizing the object of his study. He does not grow despondent over Goya's morbid depiction of historical events, as is the case with Rotteck upon describing the current reign of barbarism as typical of a perpetual recurrence of the past. Rather, he finds consolation in heightening the image of the man himself, in elevating Goya above the cruelties and horrors he saw about him and reproduced on canvas. Frank compensates for the present barbarization of the individual by constructing in Ludwig a supraindividual, who in turn exalts the exemplary personage in his study of Goya. Consequently, we see the Spanish painter described as a "Weltherr" and "Jahrtausendgehirn" (308), a "Riesenfigur" (309), who acts as both tragic bearer and vanquisher of the misery of his age: "Da stand der Mann ... an der Scheidung zweier Zeitalter, doppelgesichtig. Ein Gesicht nach der alten, heiteren Welt zugekehrt, sie schwelgerisch auskostend, in Bildern von klarem Glanz ihr zärtlichster Sohn. Das andere einer neuen Zeit zugewendet, der der Massen, Maschinen, keuchenden Kämpfe. Ganz für sich stand er da, inmitten einer Generation, die in seiner Kunst nur das Flache und Schwache hervorbrachte. Er spannte seine Arme aus über zwei Jahrhunderte Malerei" (309).

The image of the preeminent personality who, by his greatness and distinction, symbolizes a source of consolation to a suffering world is also evoked in the immediate setting of the novel. Ludwig's admiration for the unique historical person reverts back to his own situation in exile, where he seeks out actual individuals who reflect the detached nobility of an impeccable humanity. Frank's avoidance of a representative portrayal of exile, which, if undertaken realistically, could only deal with the individual as a product of an impersonal group experience, becomes clear when we observe that his ideal of humanity is magnified almost ad infinitum. The author is so intent on noncommitment to any kind of political opposition in exile, whether it be programmatic or liberal, that he overlooks greatly divergent ideologies for the sake of a common abstract principle of humanity. That Masaryk was a Social Democrat and George V a monarch seems to be of little significance to the author. It is their irreproachable humanity that counts, not the political structure they represent. Frank's historicity takes on such ahistorical connotations that these two exemplary figureheads appear in the guise of timeless overlords, whom history always manages to produce during periods of strife and turmoil.

Frank's artistic design in exile is to superimpose upon the political and social disruption of the time an atmosphere of order and harmony, to preserve those ideals of humanity and decency that are yet unspoiled by the prevailing wave of injustice. He is not content with asserting his unpolitical position in the ideal figure of his hero alone. He even transcends this ideal, picturing in the two detached statesmen model individuals to whom even the idealized Ludwig aspires.

The prince's reverence for Masaryk reflects the same tendency to escapism as was noted in his description of Goya earlier: "Ein alter Professor und Philosoph, klar, wahrhaftig und weise, aller Phrase und Pose mit Heiterkeit fern, Gründer, Schutzpatron, beinahe Gott dieses Staats, zu höchster Geltung aufgestiegen ohne die Menschlichkeit je zu verletzen, ein Blickpunkt und Trost für alle, die in einer Epoche der maulvollen Roheit und des Völkerbetrugs vor Ekel verzweifelten" (148). The consoling figure of the recently deceased George V is treated in no less reverent terms: "Ein Pfeiler, an dem sich der grobe Eigennutz bricht. ... Ein Richtpunkt. Ein Blickpunkt. Einfach ein Mensch, auf den man Vertrauen setzt. ... Ein vornehmer Herr, der sich genau an der Stelle hält, wo die Geschichte ihn haben will. ... Ein britischer Edelmann. Was eigentlich konnte er einer Epoche bedeuten, die in Wehen und Krankheiten kreiste und zuckte!" (273-74

Ludwig sums up his laudation by acclaiming both as a "Sinnbild der Menschen-würde" (275).

In the last analysis, the contradistinctive relationship that Frank purports to show in Ludwig and Steiger is really not so contrastive after all. Frank does succeed in presenting a cogent picture of the H o h e i t s m e n t a l i t ä t of the bourgeois officialdom during the 1920's and in exile. Yet, in trying to offset this submissive mentality by one that demonstrates the true values of humanity, he creates in effect a hero who is just as divorced from reality as his servant-tutor. Frank takes such an extremely individualistic position in the novel that he loses sight of the basic social functionality of the individual. The very fact that he chooses an aristocrat as his model of humanity -- however v e r b ü r g e r l i c h t he may appear -- suggests a tendency to picture the exceptional, the extra-ordinary, the "noble" in man. In actuality, the criticism Frank levels against the regressive attitudes of the Steigers falls back upon himself when he elevates his model figure above the turmoil of the period. One could even go so far as to say that Frank, however unintentionally, entertains a certain admiration for the noblesse oblige, that very frame of mind criticized in Steiger. Throughout the novel Ludwig carries the smaragd his mother had given him as a child. This precious stone, engraved with the coat of arms of Ludwig's dynastic heritage, is a symbol of a noble blood line which serves to enhance the image Frank creates in his hero. That Ludwig sells the stone at the end to obtain money for his beloved's operation does not signify a renunciation of his cherished memories. It is an act of sheer necessity and points once again to the heightened image of the exemplary humanitarian.

The one episode illustrating most vividly Frank's desire to create a world of peace and harmony takes place in the reading room of the British Museum, where Ludwig is diligently pursuing his studies. Both Klaus Mann (5) and Ludwig Marcuse (6) have acknowledged the significance of this scene, although their sympathetic appraisal of its idyllic, Biedermeier setting is wanting somewhat in objectivity. In this "totenstille Halle" (302) Frank has established a place of refuge for the many emigrants who find in the written word a source of solace and inner strength, a haven that shelters them from the discomforting realities out-side: "Dreihundert Leser mochten anwesend sein, einer nahe dem andern an den langen Tischen, aber durch Mauern des Schweigens voneinander abgeschieden, jeder in seiner gesonderten Welt" (302). This picture of philological tranquility, where no sound is heard "vom rasselnden Atem der Millionen draussen" (300), where Ludwig immerses himself "in den hundertsprachigen Schächten des Geistes" (301), reveals an artistic stance that treats the emigrant scene as a sanctuary in which the cultural treasures of the past and individual humanity can be nurtured unhampered by the current perverters of this tradition. (7)

## CHAPTER VII

## ERICH MARIA REMARQUE: LIEBE DEINEN NAECHSTEN

Asylum on the Border

      Erich Maria Remarque has surpassed his literary contemporaries in the production of novels dealing with the German exile. During the reign of the Third Reich he addressed himself on two occasions to the emigrant question in L i e b e n d e i n e n N ä c h s t e n (1941) and A r c d e T r i o m p h e (1946). After 1945 he took up the same theme in D i e N a c h t v o n L i s s a b o n (1963) and S c h a t t e n i m P a r a d i e s (1971). Our interest, of course, lies only in those novels written during Remarque's years as an exile, although in a sense this status prevailed even after 1945 when the compulsory nature of exile underwent a qualitative change to a voluntary one. After the war Remarque did not return to Germany but settled in Switzerland, his initial place of residence when Hitler rose to power in 1933.

      That a writer should confront the exile situation in approximately half of his literary production could lead to false conclusions. One might surmise from this statistic that the frequent appearance of the exile theme pointed to an ideological or artistic dilemma that the author was never able to resolve. This was far from the case. Remarque's experiences in exile had no noticeable affect on his political or creative role as a writer. Where the majority of liberal writers of international repute were pressed to deal seriously with the political function of literature in exile, Remarque remained content to cater to the popular tastes of a vast reading public. He never took a political stand against Nazi Germany in any of the emigrant journals and newspapers, (1) which is somewhat surprising in view of the fact that the book which made him famous, I m W e s t e n n i c h t s N e u e s (1929), was among the first to go up in flames in 1933 as one example of protest literature. Thus his name rarely emerges in conjunction with the liberal humanists, leftist intellectuals, Social Democrats, and Marxists who attempted to form a political front against Nazism after 1935. This is readily understandable when one considers that Remarque never sought political alignment. (2) In his exile novels he assumes an air of detachment towards the lives of emigrants, deriving from the variety of their experiences a wealth of entertaining material with which to captivate the interest of his readers. By adding to these experiences a flavoring of affectation, Remarque assured himself of the widest possible audience. A r c d e T r i o m p h e will certainly testify to this, having reached sales figures extending into the millions. Moreover, that Remarque was settled comfortably in the United States (he emigrated there in 1939) when he wrote his first two exile novels eliminates temporally and spatially any direct affinity with his subject matter.

      In view of these considerations, it is not surprising that contemporary critics on both sides of the fence have taken a rather sceptical view of Remarque's literary merits. He is usually portrayed as the author whose prestige rests on the laurels of his once famous book, and not on anything he has written since. Criticism in the West is often marked by a tongue-in-cheek approach to Remarque, that of the East abounds in downright castigation. Whether scholars speak of Remarque in general terms or with an eye to specific works, they still conclude their remarks with prescribed labels. Marcel Reich-Ranicki lumps all of Remarque's exile novels together with the assertion: "So gewaltig und bitter nämlich die Themen sind, die er behandelt, so sehr macht doch jeder dieser Romane den Eindruck einer protzigen Sammlung von Trophäen, die auf einer skrupellosen Jagd nach Effekten erbeutet wurden." (3) Reich-Ranicki attempts, in the same breath, to qualify this negation by contradicting it, and ends up in an ambiguous evaluation that admits of no clearly defined stand: "Seine Prosa befindet sich im epischen Niemandsland: Sie ist weder ernsthafte Zeitkritik noch arglose Unterhaltung, weder echte Literatur noch gänzlicher Schund." (4)

The Hungarian Marxist Helmut Rudolf attempts to establish his position by concrete reference to three of Remarque's novels. His dogmatic black-and-white method of criticism admittedly precludes the possibility of ambiguity. Yet he too renders an appraisal that fails to do justice to the author. In his examination of Liebe deinen Nächsten, Arc de Triomphe, and Die Nacht von Lissabon, Rudolf restricts his criticism to only certain figures in whom he sees the key to an understanding of the works:

> Die Helden der Emigrationsromane Remarques erfüllen die Hoffnungen
> Deutschlands, ihrer Heimat, nicht; sie stehen nicht inmitten des Stroms
> der antifaschistischen Volksfrontbewegung und der nationalen Bestrebungen,
> die auf den Sturz der Hitlerdiktatur hinwirken. Ihre 'schicksalhafte Bestim-
> mung' scheint es zu sein, sich in der Emigration immer weiter von Deutsch-
> land zu entfernen. Remarque hat seinen Helden weder das Bewusstsein und
> die Kraft noch das moralische Antlitz gegeben, so weit über sich hinauszu-
> blicken, damit sie die Horizonte eines durch ihren Heroismus vom Faschis-
> mus befreiten Deutschland sehen." (5)

Where Reich-Ranicki's comments evince a rather nebulous picture of the author, Rudolf, although he sets out to illustrate his observations, is overly simplistic when he reduces his conclusions to a common denominator. It goes without saying that Remarque's novels bear out certain of their assumptions. Ostentatious display and political indifference do play a role in Liebe deinen Nächsten and Arc de Triomphe. But we must consider these works in their specific historical setting in order to evaluate them properly.

Turning to the novel under consideration, we owe a debt of gratitude to Rudolf for at least initiating criticism on this obscure work and for making scholarship in exile literature aware of its existence. For Liebe deinen Nächsten ranks with Anna Seghers' Transit in realistically depicting the exile condition during the Third Reich. In fact, the two works exhibit pronounced parallels. In both novels a nonpartisan political opponent of the Nazi regime escapes from a concentration camp and flees across the German border. Neither subscribes actively to a political ideology in exile. Such an effort would have been thwarted even if they had attempted to do so. In the one novel the hero must constantly elude the clutches of the Gestapo; in the other he must evade apprehension by an inhuman officialdom. Both figures demonstrate great self-sacrifice at the end. Seghers' hero relinquishes his boat ticket and remains behind; Remarque's character finances Kern's and Ruth's passage to Mexico while he himself returns to Germany. It is also at the close of the novels that the divergent ideologies of the two authors become apparent: where the humanity of Seghers' hero stems from a collective commitment, that of Remarque's is of an individual nature. Viewing the two novels in their entirety, however, we see that both writers set out to portray realistically the conflicts experienced by emigrants confined to a hostile environment. Character motivation is thus determined by the impact this world has upon them.

To approach Liebe deinen Nächsten objectively, without preformed opinion, one must accept Remarque's position as a politically noncommitted writer bent on criticizing society, not inciting it to action through the employment of an anti-fascist ideology. Klaus Mann, Lion Feuchtwanger, and Hans Habe grapple with the problem of opposing Nazism with a left-wing ideology. The difficulties they encounter in effectively portraying this become evident when the bearers of this ideology emerge as isolated figures without a real social following. This often results in an ideological dilemma showing only the author's divided self, with the result that an accurate cross-section of the emigrant population actively functioning in its immediate surroundings is slighted. Habe, for example, does present a diversified picture of the exile, but this is the extent of his portrayal. We rarely see his figures conflicting with the social and economic factors of their foreign environment which lend substance to their actions. Feuchtwanger proceeds in much the same way. We read about the miseries and hardships of the emigrants but seldom are the empirical factors underlying these difficulties brought to light. Mann goes to the opposite extreme in his first novel. He takes to task the reactionary mentality of certain middle class representatives of Western society but incorporates into this milieu only one emigrant, thereby rendering a narrow, one-sided account of life in exile.

Remarque ostensibly never had any second thoughts about his political noncommitment. In Liebe deinen Nächsten he draws people true to life, letting his criticism of society speak for itself as these characters function within it. Helmut Rudolf refers to a "krisenhafte Existenzsituation" (6) in the novels he evaluates, and applies this crisis to Remarque's own situation. He bases his judgment on Josef Steiner's suicide at the end of Liebe deinen Nächsten when he falls into the hands of the Nazis. Yet Ludwig Kern, another figure in the novel who is just as prominent as Steiner, in no way bears out the pessimism and defeatism which Rudolf sees as stemming from the author's presumed predicament. Admittedly, such an "Existenzsituation" could be attributed to the author of Arc de Triomphe, a novel emerging from an international state of war which threatened, however indirectly, Remarque's own existence in the United States. Yet the general impersonalization and resultant objectivity of Remarque's treatment of exile in Liebe deinen Nächsten arises from the fact that a so-called "existential crisis" had not yet become apparent. The defeatism which one might be tempted to read into Steiner's act at the end is offset by the optimistic note underscoring Kern's preparation for travel away from Europe. (7) Like the other emigrants in the novel, Kern also senses the air of disquiet looming over Europe and sees in the voyage to Mexico the only hope for a stable existence. (If Rudolf were to interpret this action as additional proof of Remarque's tendency to avoid a political confrontation, would he also include in this category Anna Seghers, Lion Feuchtwanger, and Heinrich Mann, who also sought asylum overseas?) The point is that Remarque sets out to dramatize the multifarious experiences of refugees in order to make vivid the contradictions and often insoluble problems existing among nations faced with an unprecedented emigration. Herein lies the merit of his book, not in any ideological dilemma.

Remarque takes as his background material the economic, legal, and political difficulties imposed upon exiles in the countries of refuge during 1937 and early 1938. In this relatively late period an important factor must be kept in mind: many German passports had already expired or were about to. An emigrant's presence in a foreign country became most precarious when his status turned illegal. No German consulate would renew or reissue a passport to Jews or political undesirables who had demonstrated their opposition to Nazi Germany by leaving it. The emigrants were no longer recognized as Germans by their own government only the guest countries considered them as such. Remarque elaborates on the problems germane to the passport issue throughout the novel. He shows the necessity for an emigrant to go under cover who lacks permission to reside due to failure in producing legal identification. In a state of incognito the emigrant hopes to survive. Despite their opposition to the Nazi regime the illegal emigrants -- in particular, Steiner, who is a non-Jewish political escapee -- could not align themselves with a political anti-Nazi group or appear openly in such a capacity as long as they were constantly evading local authorities. The internal political situation in Austria at the time, and Switzerland's position of political neutrality would have hindered the practice of these activities to begin with. The liberal exile novel dealing with active political engagement often portray characters who are not legal ly suspect in the eyes of local police. In the figures of Steiner and, above all, Kern, Remarque shows that side of emigrant life complicated by a refugee's inability to claim legal asylum.

Kern is a vagabond from the very beginning. An expatriated half-Jew whose passport was confiscated by the Nazis, he never enjoys a single day of legal status in the many European nations whose boundaries he perpetually crosses as a result of deportation. Steiner, the political escapee from a Nazi concentration camp, improves his situation somewhat when he secures the passport of a deceased Austrian citizen. But even this does not alleviate the economic predicament of exile: "Du hast damit nur das Recht, in Ruhe zu verhungern. Nicht auf der Flucht. Das ist schon viel." (8)

The central theme of the novel is embodied in the less fortunate Kern. It raises the ridiculous assumption that the border itself provides the only domicile for a pursued emigrant ("Die Grenzen sind ja unsere Heimat," 191). This theme illuminates the contradictions inherent in bureaucracies which profess to carry out justice by clinging to the strict letter of the law. The situation is basically the same in the four countries involved, although Czechoslovakia did grant emigrants without visas brief permissions to reside.

Remarque's realistic analysis is shown in the way he portrays the reactions of various legal functionaries to the emigrant problem. He does not indiscriminate place them in an unfavorable light just because the bureaucracies made existence almost impossible for illegal exiles. He draws a distinction between the bureaucratic callousness emanating from genuine social and economic problems in the guest countries and that emanating from the kind of political regime operating the bureaucracy. In other words, Remarque recognizes the dilemma the governments were caught in while trying to control the emigrant population in their respective territories. He therefore sees the greatest contradiction between the principle of humanity and its practical application in those countries whose governments were democratically structured, namely, Czechoslovakia, Switzerland, and France (during Léon Blum's ministry). Austria's regime did not as strongly betray a discrepancy between the spirit and the letter of the law in the late 1930's because of its unscrupulous fascist contingent.

Remarque makes this phenomenon plain at the very beginning. When Kern and Steiner are arrested by the Viennese police as illegal emigrants, they are showered with such outbursts as "Schlagt das Emigrantenpack tot" (12), "Heil Hitler!" (12), "Halten Sie's Maul, Sie Bolschewist!" (16), "Sieht nicht nach kommunistischem Komplott aus, was?" (18). The oppressing political climate in Austria was rapidly approximating that of its Nazi neighbors in the intellectual spheres as well. At the university, Kern witnesses the maltreatment of a Jewish student by young fascist ruffians while professors stand idly by as captivated onlookers. Upon intervening, Kern is promptly arrested for disorderly conduct. The ultimate decision of Kern, Steiner, and other emigrants to move on to France is understandable in view of the ominous political atmosphere prevailing in Austria. There they were hounded not only by a bureaucratic officialdom but were baited by a decidedly hostile government as well. Helmut Rudolf's objection that Remarque led Steiner "in die Ausweglosigkeit" rather than "an die Seite Kämpfender" (9) lacks historical foundation when one considers that Steiner spent most of his time in the one country that revealed no noticeable traces of a collective anti-fascist front among the German emigrants. The political climate in Austria at the time would have promptly stifled the activities of the People's Front. Rudolf's argument would carry more weight if the exile scene in the novel had emerged in its earlier stages. Then the most probable land of asylum for Steiner as a political fugitive would have been Czechoslovakia. That Remarque does not depict his hero in the one country more politically receptive to his background is really immaterial in consideration of the historical period treated. By 1937, Czechoslovakia had begun to restrict the journalistic activities of political exiles so as to avert an intensification of strained relations with Nazi Germany. (10) Hence the "Kämpfende" to whom Rudolf refers were hard pressed after 1937 to find a receptive peaceful democracy that would allow, unconditionally, the continuation of anti-Nazi expression. Since the measures taken in Czechoslovakia were designed mainly to restrict the activities of outspoken German socialists, it goes without saying that the communist exiles fared even worse.

For the most part, the democratic governments were unsympathetic to the plight of "lawless" emigrants, an attitude that often led to a mockery of justice when an outcast's desperate attempt to establish roots became a legal issue. In a Swiss courtroom a scene transpires that typifies the paradoxical behavior of a democracy professing justice and humanity while at the same time pushing off unwanted exiles onto their neighbors. After skirting the police for days, Kern is finally apprehended and brought before the judge for sentencing. To the judge's inquiry as to why he failed to promptly register with the Swiss police after crossing the border, Kern replies:

> Weil ich dann sofort wieder ausgewiesen worden wäre ... Und drüben auf
> der anderen Seite hätte ich mich wieder sofort beim nächsten Polizeiposten
> melden müssen, wenn ich nicht das Gesetz hätte verletzen wollen. Von dort
> wäre ich dann in der nächsten Nacht zurück in die Schweiz gebracht worden.
> Und von drüben wieder zurück. So wäre ich langsam zwischen den Grenz-
> posten verhungert. Zumindest wäre ich ewig von einer Polizeiwache zur
> andern gewandert. Was sollen wir denn andres machen, als gegen das Ge-
> setz verstossen? (266)

This scene points not so much to the dilemma of the emigrant, but to that of the "humanitarian" guest country. It is symbolic of how problematic the asylum question was when even a judge, the interpreter of justice and the spokesman for human rights, can only lament: "Ich habe einen Sohn, ... der ist ungefähr so alt wie Sie. Wenn ich mir vorstellen sollte, dass er herumgejagt würde, ohne irgend-einen Grund, als dass er geboren worden ist --" (267). But the judge is of no help. He gives Kern twenty francs out of sympathy and then sentences him to two weeks in jail, after which he is to be deported to France.

The futility of this situation is brought to light on still other occasions. The elusive Steiner ("Urkundenfälscher," "Falschspieler," "Vagabund," 342), although possessing a (falsified) Austrian passport, deliberately passes as an emigrant at the Austro-Swiss border to avoid the repercussions that would result if the officials were to detect his fraudulent identity. Instead, he confesses to the Austrian border guards that the Swiss police had just escorted him over the line. Since various countries allowed an emigrant to enter illegally for twenty-four hours without taking action, the Austrian guards, welcoming company in their boredom, decide to retain Steiner for the night by striking up a card game. Formalities are quickly dispensed with and they become the best of friends: "Um ein Uhr nachts nannten sie sich bei ihren Vornamen. Um drei Uhr duzten sie sich. Und um vier Uhr wa-ren sie völlig familiär" (292). In the morning they dutifully send Steiner back to Switzerland, with the friendly agreement to play again in the evening when the refugee makes his return trip.

Remarque does not paint this humorous scene just for comic relief. The element of the grotesque is basic to a way of life that turns to deception, cheating, and cunning out of necessity rather than desire. When Steiner pins on a swastika insignia and poses as an important Nazi official in order to avenge the wrong done to Kern by the German agent Ammers, Remarque shows that in a climate of inse-curity, fear, and concealment any anti-Nazi polemic can often only be episodic and spontaneous. Given Steiner's particular situation, his individual but most effective dupery could not have arisen from a joint political effort or an open at-tempt at public exposure, since he himself was existing on the other side of the law at the time. This scene in Murten is one of the most politically revealing of the novel and must be elaborated on. Its polemic is localized, but its effect is widespread for it unmasks the overall treachery and ruthlessness of Nazi agents abroad. Furthermore, it reveals the true attitude of the Swiss government to-wards the presence of fascist elements in its country.

Prior to Steiner's encounter with Ammers, Kern had inadvertently fallen into the clutches of this Nazi agent. Believing Ammers and his wife to be well-to-do emigrants, Kern, desperately needing money to defray the costs of Ruth's hospital bill, thinks this time his peddling (his "profession" in the novel) will bring in a decent return. While Kern is being served coffee, Ammers fetches a Swiss policeman and denounces him as a "vaterlandloses Individuum ohne Pass, ausgestossen aus dem Deutschen Reich" (247). The policeman goes through only the mechanical motions of exercising his duty. As a human being he is completely on Kern's side. In replying to Ammer's demand for protection after Kern has assailed him with curses, the policeman offers what on the surface appears to be a clarification of the verbal assault. Implicitly, it is a sharp attack and its effectiveness is only heightened by its indirectness: "Er hat Sie bis jetzt nur verflucht. Wenn er Ihnen zum Beispiel: dreckiger Denunziant gesagt hätte, so wäre das eine Beleidigung gewesen, und zwar wegen des Wortes dreckig" (248). The policeman's true humanity is revealed afterwards when, upon escorting his prisoner to jail, he voluntarily turns away to allow Kern an opportunity to escape.

In the figure of the Swiss policeman, Remarque shows his admiration for individual acts of humanity, but at the same time he is implicitly voicing criticism against the combined political weaknesses of the democracies. Because this official's remarks w e r e ambiguous and indirect, it shows how dubiously not only Switzerland, but other countries as well, reacted to the spread of Nazi terror. That these nations actually tolerated the presence of German spies in their midst proves their willingness to appease and compromise. Ultimately, it is the emigrants who must pay in this situation: "Immer, wenn in Deutschland etwas geschieht, was die umliegenden Länder nervös macht, müssen die Emigranten es als erste ausbaden. Sie sind die Sündenböcke für die einen und für die andern" (316).

The action of Remarque's novel takes place in 1937 and early 1938. Accordingly, most of the emigrants he characterizes have already spent considerable time in exile. There is nothing affectatious about his descriptions of the anguish and duress felt by these outcasts. He also alludes at one point to "Völkergemisch" and "Wartesaal" (314), concepts reminiscent of leitmotifs in Feuchtwanger's and Habe's novels. Yet the tone of detached superiority emerging in Feuchtwanger's work is absent in Remarque's realistic account of how these exiles thought and felt. His objectivity has enabled him to present a credible cross section of the emigrant population without interjecting personal bias or partiality. At the Parisian police station he renders a gripping description -- one among many -- of an anxiety-ridden refugee awaiting a decision on his application for a residence permit:

Kern sah am Schalter einen Mann mit einem schmalen, geistvollen Gesicht. Seine Papiere schienen in Ordnung zu sein; das junge Mädchen hinter dem Schalter nahm sie nach einigen Fragen, nickte und begann zu schreiben. Aber Kern sah, wie der Mann, während er nur dastand und wartete, zu schwitzen begann. Der grosse Raum war kalt, und der Mann trug nur einen dünnen Sommeranzug; aber der Schweiss drang ihm aus allen Poren, sein Gesicht wurde glänzend nass, und helle Tropfen flossen ihm über Stirn und

Wangen. Er stand unbeweglich, die Arme auf das Schalterbrett gestützt, in einer verbindlichen, nicht einmal unterwürfigen Haltung da, bereit, Antwort zu geben -- und sein Wunsch ging in Erfüllung -- und trotzdem war er nichts als Todesschweiss, als würde er auf dem unsichtbaren Rost der Herzlosigkeit gebraten. Hätte er geschrien, lamentiert oder gebettelt, es wäre Kern nicht so schrecklich erschienen. Aber dass er höflich, in guter Haltung, gefasst dastand, und dass nur seine Poren seinen Willen überfluteten, das war, als ob der Mann in sich selbst ertrank. Es war die Not der Kreatur selbst, die alle Dämme des Menschseins zu durchsickern schien (316).

One must look at L i e b e  d e i n e n  N ä c h s t e n historically with respect to Remarque's second exile novel A r c  d e  T r i o m p h e. In L i e b e  d e i n e n N ä c h s t e n war is not yet imminent, although the international political scene shows definite signs of tension. Austria is about to be annexed and other countries, namely, Czechoslovakia and Switzerland, are finding it increasingly more difficult to accommodate new refugees. This explains why Kern had left Prague earlier in the novel. As a result of these circumstances, more and more emigrants are finding their way to France, a sporadic movement which in the following months is to become greatly accelerated. In the novel we already see the anticipation of what is to come once Austria and Czechoslovakia have fallen to Nazi Germany: "Oesterreich, die Tschechoslowakei, die Schweiz -- das war der Bewegungskrieg der Emigranten -- aber Paris ist der Stellungskrieg. Die vorderste Linie der Schützengraben" (309). In L i e b e  d e i n e n  N ä c h s t e n there is not yet the premonition of the wholesale destruction of mankind that we see in A r c  d e T r i o m p h e. There the relationship between the two lovers Ravic and Johanna is superficial and neurotic, stemming from the climate of impending doom. In contrast to this pair, the love between Kern and Ruth in L i e b e  d e i n e n  N ä c h - s t e n is not self-indulgent. We see in their relationship a genuine mutual respect and sense of sacrifice born from the knowledge that hope still exists in struggle and perseverance.

In his diversified portrayal of the exiles, (11) Remarque depicts attitudes of optimism, despair, decency, and treachery. There is the adventuresome, picaro-like Steiner whose hardened, aggressive appearance shrouds the profound longing for a dying wife, a man who willingly faces peril by returning to Germany as a wanted political refugee so that he can be with her in her last days. Then there are the figures of Binder in Zurich and Krassmann in Paris, veteran "outlaws" who know their way around and are ever ready to assist emigrants passing through. We encounter Kern's former university professor in Prague, a specialist in cancer research who knows nothing about the practicalities of life. Now Kern must give his mentor advice on how to make ends meet. The selling of vacuum cleaners and phonographs is not the answer. One must peddle small items which are in demand from day to day -- soap, perfume, bath lotion, combs, safety pins. In Lucerne the nationalist Jew Oppenheim, a wealthy financier who sets himself apart from other emigrants because of their hostility to Nazi Germany, firmly believes he will return as soon as the situation there stabilizes. After all, he maintains it is the Zionist Jews from the East that Hitler really is down on, not the truly German ones. The former university lecturer Vogt has faced expulsion from one land to the other so often that he finds it a luxury to be able to sit in jail. He hopes that he will soon find a not "allzumenschlicher Richter" (219) who will show "mercy" by shipping him off to the border rather than by putting him behind bars for vagrancy. When he is arrested in Switzerland for illegal entry, his hopes are shattered. The judge is too "human" and Vogt faces expulsion once again. To insure his imprisonment, therefore, he commits robbery. Remarque does not omit the criminal element either. These are emigrants who prey on the decency and innocence of others, whose flight into exile was really an escape from the law in Germany. In Switzerland, Kern has the misfortune of being robbed by such a social outcast who had broken out of a German prison as a burglar, not as a political opponent. Steiner himself learns his card tricks from an emigrant in Vienna who makes his profession as a petty thief and card shark.

Writers in exile have correctly pointed out that the German emigration of 1933 was not a united group willing to suppress individual differences and backgrounds in order to rise to the defense of the "other Germany." Lion Feuchtwanger and Hans Habe have included documentary chapters in their novels for the purpose of illustrating this phenomenon. Remarque, however, joins with Anna Seghers in illustrating -- through direct interaction between emigrant and environment -- the reasons for this diversification and political inactivity.

From the standpoint of overall artistic effectiveness, Remarque's novel falls behind Seghers' T r a n s i t . His penchant for ostentatious digression occasionally detracts from the novel's critical continuity. But episodes of this kind are minor in comparison to the wealth of such "thrilling" scenes in A r c de T r i o m p h e . If we can overlook these sporadic sensationalistic episodes (e. g. , Steiner's pugilistic encounter with the fascist policeman; the woman dying of hemorrhaging during childbirth; Kern's lessons in boxing; or Steiner's suicide at the end), we are left with a piece of critical-realistic prose whose convincing account of emigrant life comes about, in part, because the author was not so directly affected by the typical problems of exile as were other writers. We will note a rather dramatic change in Remarque's narrative attitude, however, upon examination of his second exile novel.

## CHAPTER VIII

ERICH MARIA REMARQUE: ARC DE TRIOMPHE

Escape from Exile

Erich Maria Remarque had already emigrated to the United States when he wrote his two exile novels. In our analysis of Liebe deinen Nächsten we gave as one reason for Remarque's insightful portrayal of the exile scene his removal from the historical setting. Although Hitler's militant expansion was leading most of Europe into either total subjugation or a defensive war when he embarked for overseas in March of 1939, the United States, on the other hand, could still demonstrate a relative degree of political and military immunity. Certainly Remarque's own optimism is implicitly reflected in Kern's and Ruth's hope for the future as they embark upon a new life in Mexico at the close of the novel. The geographical isolation of the United States plus its receptivity to an author of international renown meant that Remarque could write about the disrupted lives of emigrants in Europe without experiencing any direct threat to his own existence. The objectivity and detachment of his first novel went hand in hand with a personal sense of security and noninvolvement.

In Remarque's next exile novel, Arc de Triomphe (1946), attitude and tone undergo such a drastic change that one is almost tempted to recheck the title page to insure identical authorship with the earlier novel. In Arc de Triomphe Remarque no longer portrays a realistic cross-section of exiles conflicting with an antagonistic milieu. Critical objectivity has been supplanted by a subjective, morbidly depressing character study of an individual emigrant's escapades in the bistros, morgues, and brothels of Parisian society. In this novel affectation and sensationalism prove to be the rule rather than the exception. Remarque does not turn to flamboyant display and intimate mind-picking just to digress, as is occasionally the case in Liebe deinen Nächsten; it becomes the underlying artistic principle of the work. The resignation, despair, and cynicism that had characterized some of Remarque's figures in the first novel now become personalized and represent the author's own assessment of the emigration and the milieu in which it is placed.

To explain this transition from objectivity to private impression one must consider the global politico-military atmosphere in which Remarque was writing. At the time he was working on Liebe deinen Nächsten, turmoil and havoc was rectricted to the European continent. When he wrote Arc de Triomphe, the United States itself was involved in armed conflict in two separate theaters of operation -- the Pacific and European. Whereas between 1939 and 1941 Remarque was able to write his first novel with a certain critical detachment because the world situation and therefore his own was not directly affected, the historical scene had changed by the time he turned to Arc de Triomphe. The pervading mood of chaos in this later novel, whose setting is the year 1939, is in effect a testimony of Remarque's political isolation throughout exile. His pacifistic philosophy, born of the senseless slaughter of World War I and laid down in Im Westen nichts Neues, continued to influence his thinking after 1933. In Liebe deinen Nächsten he could reconcile his pacifism to American isolation and noninvolvement in European events in 1939. His ability to portray critically and without personal sentiment the problems of exile in this novel stems, in part, from the material and ideological security of his overseas environment. The isolationism of the United States was a confirmation of his own political escapism, of his refusal to take a defiant ideological stand. Although hostilities on the Continent were already smoldering when he began to write Liebe deinen Nächsten in mid-1939, they had not yet implicated his new country of asylum. In keeping with his pacifist ideology, Remarque could psychologically offset this threat by envisioning the United States as a deterrent to wholesale war. (1)

After 1941, the international political scene had changed drastically. The major powers of the world were engaged in battle, thus making any pacifist view to the crisis meaningless. Where Remarque was able to write from a position of authorial neutrality in Liebe deinen Nächsten, he becomes much more subjective in the next novel, conveying a fatalistic outlook on man as a probable result of a pacifist ideology that could no longer be reconciled to reality. In Arc de Triomphe Remarque imparts to a fictitious exile figure of the past (1939) a pessimistic world view that would seem to extend from the current state of upheaval (1944). If there was an optimistic future hinted at in Liebe deinen Nächsten, then it was embodied in a land away from Europe, one which would remain untouched by the disruptive events taking place on the Continent. Once the United States was involved in the war, Remarque could no longer cloak narrative detachment in the security of his new homeland. Arc de Triomphe is more a product of the author's chaotic world outlook during World War II than it is a realistic depiction of the exile situation in Paris between the Munich agreement and the invasion of Poland. By imposing a fatalistic view on the events of the novel, Remarque sacrifices realism for personal philosophy. Where most writers saw hope for mankind evolving from the international armed conflict with Hitler, Remarque creates the impression that war is an inevitable sign of man's basic destructiveness. The emigrant Ravic has no desire to resist or escape. Like Remarque, he too is a veteran of World War I who interprets the present state of unrest as exemplary of man's inability to effect change. Allusions to the United States are not portrayed in way of contrast to the European situation, but serve to illustrate its morbidity, as is seen in one of the characters who obtains passage on a ship to America. Kate Hegstroem's voyage is a journey into oblivion. That her body is wracked with cancer is Remarque's way of imposing on the setting his own bleak philosophy.

From a documentary standpoint, Remarque re-creates the image of the emigrant that recalls, in part, the illegal status of Kern and Steiner in Liebe deinen Nächsten. Ravic, a former surgeon at a prominent hospital in Nazi Germany, had been tortured by the Gestapo for complicity in opposing Hitler. He escapes from a concentration camp and goes to Spain where he administers to the medical needs of the Loyalists. After their defeat he continues on to France without passport or visa. Aside from the fact that his illegal status would have prevented the public practice of his profession to begin with, French authorities, as a rule, did not recognize foreign degrees in this field. Thus we see Ravic as an underpaid ghost surgeon who performs delicate operations for local physicians too incompetent to undertake the task themselves. Ravic willingly submits to this exploitation in order to insure a meager existence as an unwanted alien. Having been jailed and deported on several occasions, he learns to avoid apprehension by changing his name and residing in cheap hotels rarely raided by the police.

That period of exile in which Remarque places his hero is an especially critical one. Great Britain and France have acquiesced to Hitler by agreeing to Germany's accession of the Sudetenland. While Germany is preparing for war, other nations operate under the delusion that security exists in its postponement. Irresolution, appeasement, submission on the part of the European governments create an ominous feeling of doom culminating in an undesired declaration of war and the internment of emigrants around Paris. Into the atmosphere of futility, fear, and apprehension (2) hovering over Paris, Remarque incorporates a personal world outlook that admits of no hope or struggle, only defeat and resignation.

The author's treatment of exile is limited primarily to the private activities of a single emigrant. Ravic is the lone fugitive whose hatred for the Nazis never rises above the state of personal antagonism. His cynical outlook prevents him from distinguishing between the forces of progress and reaction. Upon observing, at one point, a fascist and communist demonstration, his response is one of total indifference. Since any kind of opposition is futile in a predetermined world, it is pointless to take up the struggle for a cause. Ravic can offer only anarchistic denunciation of the age he is living in, no constructive criticism: "Es ist das lausigste, blutigste, korrupteste, farbloseste, feigste und dreckigste soweit -- aber trotzdem" (3) (meaning one must go on vegetating).

Ravic functions in an atmosphere of moral degeneracy above which he has no desire to rise. A fin de siècle cultural climate of self-indulgence and super-ficiality, of lethargy and purposelessness, pervades the entire work. Images of blood, death, sickness, decay are uttered in the same breath with noble, decent ones. Depravity and humanity are cynically lumped together to show Remarque's disdain for the ideal. He does not paint this depressing picture of society with the intention of showing his hero as a contrast figure. Ravic interacts mechanically with an automatized, dehumanized world stripped of all human values. The criticism leveled against the political impotence and cultural decay of France is subjective and one-sided. Remarque suggests no alternative paths of action -- either among the emigrants or the natives -- which would react against this state of affairs. Society does not follow the dictates of conscience, but impulses of hate, deceit, bestiality and opportunism. Greed, political expediency, fear, delusion -- all point to what seems to be the basic condition of man. Nazism is conceptualized as an ugly growth which even appears to be unmatched by France's malady. Ravic remarks: "Aber ich wollte, Deutschland wäre so korrupt wie Frankreich" (325). The allusion here is to a political hierarchy in France which is so abominable that it surpasses even that of Nazi Germany! Again a manifestation of blind criticism that merely weighs one form of depravity against another. Since human decency has never been powerful enough to subdue the forces of destruction, Remarque sees no purpose in fostering it as a weapon:

Ravic ging in sein Zimmer, um zu lesen. Er hatte irgendwann einige Bände Weltgeschichte gekauft und suchte sie hervor. Es war nicht besonders erheiternd, sie zu lesen. Das einzige, was herauskam, war eine sonderbar deprimierende Genugtuung, dass nichts neu war, was heute passierte. Alles war dutzendmal dagewesen. Die Lügen, die Treubrüche, die Morde, die Bartholomäusnächte, die Korruption durch den Willen zur Macht, die unablässige Kette der Kriege -- die Geschichte der Menschheit war mit Blut und Tränen geschrieben, und unter tausend blutbefleckten Statuen der Vergangenheit glänzte nur selten eine, über der das Silber der Güte lag. Die Demagogen, die Betrüger, die Vater- und Freundesmörder, die nachttrunkenen Egoisten, die fanatischen Propheten, die die Liebe mit dem Schwerte predigten; es war immer dasselbe, und immer wieder waren geduldige Völker da, gegeneinander getrieben in sinnlosem Töten für Kaiser, Religionen und Wahnsinnige -- es hatte kein Ende. (202)

This statement betrays Remarque's inability to view Hitler's rise to power and the emigration it produced as a historical phenomenon created by definite social, intellectual, and political events in Weimar Germany. This ahistoric conception of man and society provides the philosophical basis for the cynical, morbid tone running throughout the novel. In the eyes of the author, history is not based on an interrelationship of conflicting social forces, but is governed by the illogicality of passion and greed. It is thus not surprising that Remarque should regard the emigration in Arc de Triomphe as just another inevitable outgrowth of man's basic inhumanity. Consequently, resistance does not derive from reason and a sense of justice; when it does manage to assert itself, it is merely spontaneous and impulsive.

This explains Ravic's aversion to Haake, the Nazi spy sneaking around Paris. Ravic's reaction towards the wrong done him in Germany is restricted to the sphere of personal dispute. Helmut Rudolf is correct, to a degree, in describing Ravic's "removal" of Haake from the scene as an anti-fascist act. Yet this act is so deeply rooted in personal motives of revenge that it is unlikely Ravic would have performed it in alignment with a political opposition even if the opportunity had presented itself. Rudolf maintains:

Obwohl Ravics Entschluss zur Tat allein durch Haake motiviert ist und sich eigentlich planlos ins Widerstandsgeschehen einfügt, ist sie als antifaschistische Tat zu werten, wenn auch von ihr aus keine Brücke zur Entscheidung für die Teilnahme am Widerstandskampf geschlagen wird. Es hätte im Bereich des Möglichen gelegen, dass Ravic nicht mehr als Aussenseiter handelt, sondern sich einer Widerstandsgruppe der Resistance anschliesst. Er fällt aber nach der Tat in einen Fatalismus zurück. (4)

Rudolf suggests here that Ravic's fatalism was momentarily suspended when he decides to act, that his encounter with Haake signifies, in principle, the initial step towards an alignment with the resistance, which he ultimately had failed to fully achieve. Ravic's political unawareness throughout the novel, however, shows that a commitment to a resistance group fails to approach even the "Bereich des Möglichen." His fatalistic world view explains his irreversible nonreceptivity to any political ideology. We had already noted his indifference to the fascist march and the communist counterdemonstration earlier.

Ravic's disinterested attitude towards any political ideology, whether it be fascist, monarchistic, republican, or communist, is evidenced in the episode concerning the kind of political portrait to be hung in the corridor of the International Hotel. The proprietress has collected a variety of paintings portraying prominent political figures of quite divergent ideologies. The choice of portrait to be mounted depends upon the political background of the refugees residing in the hotel at the moment. At times, politically antagonistic exiles reside together under the same roof, necessitating the stringing of one side of the corridor with pictures of Marx and Lenin, and the other side with those of Franco and Alfonso. Ravic's reaction to this display of conflicting ideologies is marked once again by a listless detachment. The remark by the proprietress -- "Regierungen dauern heutzutage nicht lange" (78) -- merely reiterates Remarque's view of history as cyclical and repetitious. His hero's unconcern for the social realities represented by the various portraits is a testimony to his own political disinterest.

Remarque's predilection for sensationalism and affectation in A r c  d e T r i o m p h e stems from a W e l t a n s c h a u u n g that negates all possibility of human contact. To an extent, he carries on the literary tradition of the late 1920's, which placed emphasis on tangibles, "things," divorced of moral or spiritual attributes. Ravic can murder someone with the same scientific efficiency displayed at the operating table because the human element ceases to play a function. Remarque is not so much concerned with treating the exile situation in its social and political context as he is with picturing the morbid and bizarre as typical manifestations of a dehumanized world. The gruesomely revolting medical scenes in the operating room symbolize man's despiritualization. Here Ravic is in his element. He can exercise a skill dealing with human anatomy, not the heart and soul. In the latter area he has failed with Johanna, and it is in his role as surgeon that he feels most secure. The author does not envision the emigrant as a social being, but as alienated, neurotic, despondent, without hope or ability to act. The exile in French society emerges as an embodiment of irrational forces which defy both freedom of individual assertion and the ability of man to unite in a common goal.

It cannot be disputed that the historical setting of the novel was decidedly unstable. Remarque does succeed in rendering an accurate impression of the political uncertainty plaguing the Continent in the year leading up to the declaration of war. But he uses this documentary data largely as background material upon which to indulge preoccupations which repeatedly detract from the exile scene.

The writer and former exile Robert Neumann has rightly pointed out the "pseudoreality" that describes Remarque's treatment of the exile in not only A r c d e  T r i o m p h e but other novels as well: "Alle Rand-Details, zwar nicht selbst erlebt, aber ausgezeichnet recherchiert, sind 'lebensecht', wenn auch aus zweiter Hand, und garnieren, dekorieren, manipulieren den wohlkonstruierten Leerlauf des Zentralen, Menschlichen derart um, dass für den, der dem Handwerker nicht allzu genau auf die Finger schaut, das Gesamtprodukt zu einer Pseudo-Lebensechtheit aufgemotzt wird, die ... für lebensechter, 'wahrer' gehalten wird als jeder Dokumentarbericht." (5) This attraction would account for the immense success of Arc de Triomphe among American readers. Those who actually experienced emigrant life in France, the exiles themselves, no doubt took a less credulous view of Remarque's works in exile. Neumann states: "Und als er 'Arc de Triomphe' schrieb, und später 'Nacht von Lissabon', lachten viele, die die wirklichen Hintergründe kannten. Woher wollte er das wissen, er war doch nicht dabei!" (6) Actually, Remarque was familiar with the "Hintergründe" that set the scene for Arc de Triomphe. Just prior to the outbreak of war he left the United States in the company of Marlene Dietrich for an eight-week trip to Paris and the Riviera. (7) Thus many of the episodes described in the novel were probably based on direct observation. Remarque's presence in France hardly refutes Neumann's basic argument, however. The author does not treat his situation in exile, but that of the less fortunate who never escaped the problems of the emigration as he had.

From a realistic standpoint, Arc de Triomphe fails to meet certain of the criteria establishing the exile novel as a select category of prose. If one were to attempt to examine this novel in terms of the author's confrontation with his exile environment, one would have to discard it as primarily "fictional" material, for Remarque merely creates an interesting story out of incidents that, for the most part, had no effect on him personally.

Viewing Arc de Triomphe philosophically and in its relationship to Liebe deinen Nächsten, however, one senses that the earlier contrast between assimilation overseas and uprootedness in Europe has been overshadowed by a darkening international political climate. In this context the novel can be defended as a product of exile. The material uprootedness that Remarque never directly experienced is taken over by a psychological and philosophical sense of alienation born of the world crisis after 1941.

# CHAPTER IX

## IRMGARD KEUN: KIND ALLER LAENDER

The Writer in Exile

As a non-Jewish author of popular stories, Irmgard Keun had little to fear in the way of reprisal action when Hitler consigned to flames countless volumes of "non-German" literature on May 10, 1933. Keun's two novels, Gilgi, eine von uns (1931) and Das kunstseidene Mädchen (1932), (1) were hardly considered provocative literature on the day of the infamous book-burning. On the contrary, such "unproblematic" books could only have promoted the ultraconservative cultural politics of the Reich Chamber of Literature (Reichsschrifttums-kammer). Keun soon realized this state of affairs herself. After refusing to join this agency (2) and enduring the suppression of free thought for three years, she saw no other recourse but to leave Germany. With the aid of the Allert de Lange publishing house, (3) she was able to escape via Brussels to Holland in 1935. Keun's flight from Germany signified an act of political denunciation. Like her bourgeois contemporaries in exile, she too saw that a conservative attitude in literature only supported, however indirectly, a regime whose policy it was to eradicate all liberal, democratic expression. That Keun persevered in Germany until 1935 had its merits, at least from a literary-critical standpoint. In Nach Mitternacht (1937), she could write from direct experience about conditions in the Nazi Reich, something which those authors who had emigrated in 1933 could only do from written sources or hearsay. In this anti-fascist novel, Keun lays bare the psychological complexes of that segment of German society -- the lower middle class -- which saw in Hitler's assumption of power a bolstering of its own inferior egos. (4) In the novel following, Kind aller Länder (1938), she turns to the exile scene for her material and is no less critical of the follies of society than she was in the preceding novel.

If a writer other than Lion Feuchtwanger had authored the essay "Die Arbeits-probleme eines Schriftstellers im Exil," (5) one would be inclined to select Irmgard Keun as the most probable originator. Feuchtwanger himself had presumably experienced a number of the frustrating conditions outlined in his essay, but that he was seriously affected by them materially is unlikely. The relatively comfortable existence he led in his villa at Sanary on the Riviera created an atmosphere hardly adverse to writing. The material difficulties of exile as they relate to the writer which Feuchtwanger discusses in his article refer less to internationally renowned authors than to those whose material existence could not be sustained by a continuing income from book royalties. We single out Irmgard Keun in this respect because her novel Kind aller Länder deals specifically with the situation of the writer in exile. The issues Feuchtwanger raises -- the gap between writer and audience, the constant struggle to cope with the exigencies of a foreign environment, the endless maze of bureaucratic red tape, perpetual interruptions of the writing process -- are central to Keun's work as one of her characters tries desperately to eke out an existence for himself and family through his writing.

First of all, we must visualize the exile period in which the novel is placed. All indications would seem to point to a time in late 1938. Austria had capitulated to Germany and Hitler was entertaining thoughts about advancing on Czechoslovakia, thus implying that the Sudetenland had already been Nazified. The arrival of new refugees in Belgium from Czechoslovakia suggests, furthermore, that Keun is dealing with a period subsequent to the Munich agreement of September. The atmosphere of unrest produced by the fear of imminent war means that not only had a sizeable reading audience been eliminated for the exiled writer, but that the remaining German-speaking territories -- Switzerland and the Alsace -- were proving to be a less reliable market for exile literature as attention turned to the threat of invasion.

This problem emerges in Keun's treatment of the precarious situation of the exiled publisher, a probable allusion to her own association with Walter Landauer at the Allert de Lange publishing house. The publisher depended on the writer's literary contributions to keep his firm operating; yet the writer's progress was constantly being impeded by material obstacles. Both, in turn, relied on a reading audience that was rapidly diminishing in size. Hans-Albert Walter appropriately concludes: "Hitler's 'friedliche Expansion' in Europa verkleinerte das Absatzgebiet erheblich. 1935 ging das Saargebiet verloren, im März 1938 Oesterreich, im Herbst des gleichen Jahres die deutschsprachigen Gebiete der Tschechoslowakei, kaum sechs Monate später, was von dem Lande noch geblieben war. Es kam ein immer wachsender Druck auf die Buchhändler hinzu. In der Schweiz beispielsweise wurden die Bücher der Exilierten zwar noch verkauft, sehr häufig aber nicht mehr in die Auslagen gestellt. Es versteht sich, dass das zu Umsatzeinbussen führte." (6) In addition, the Western countries began tightening their entrance requirements. Visas became a scarcity. If one expired, the emigrant often had no place to go. He either languished in a hotel room or led a Bohemian existence, adopting an unconventional life style as an answer to the limitations imposed on his physical activity.

Irmgard Keun copes rather unusually with these distressing realities in her novel. One is taken aback, at first, by the narrative perspective she employs. Even in the most disruptive of environments this author of youth literature and love stories retains her innocent, unimposing style. The events of the novel are related in the first person by the ten-year old daughter Kully, a technique which seems to produce a discrepancy between form and content. In that Keun confines the unnerving experiences of exile to the restricted vision of a child, allowing her to tell the story from her point of view, one is impressed with what seems to be a simplistic portrayal of emigrant life. By retreating into a child's imagination, the author inhibits the uncertainties and complexities of her own existence. The young girl's impressionable mind registers the events of the novel as they happen, without imposing upon them a moral judgment or a sense of indignation. She describes each direct experience with the same childlike simplicity seen in her reflections on nature or past occurrences linked by association. At times, her observations are quite penetrating, but they are made with a naiveté uninfluenced by the seriousness underlying them. The gravity of a subject matter dealing with the destitution of a family seems less cogent when depicted through a child's eyes. The most important figure of the novel is the father. He is the one upon whom Kully and her mother depend for their existence and about whom the events revolve. Furthermore, he stands closest to Keun by virtue of his profession, a status central to the novel's theme. Yet Peter, the father and writer, does not tell his story, nor does an objective third-person narrator. Keun appears to subdue the hectic nature of his experiences by transferring their account to the mind of a child still incapable of fathoming the reality of frustration, despair, and hopelessness plaguing this exiled family. The grim realities of exile seem to be misrepresented by a narrative attitude that is too credulous, too oversimplified.

Escapism, however, is not one of Irmgard Keun's artistic attributes. Her intention is to draw a sharp contrast between right and wrong. Accordingly, she employs a narrative perspective that is yet unspoiled by the callousness of man. The innocent, naive observations of Kully reveal with frightening accuracy those contradictions of society perpetrated by elders. The Marxist writer Fritz Erpenbeck refers to Kully's "naiven aber gesunden Menschenverstand" in a review of the novel in 1939. (7) The liberal author Hermann Kesten advances similar views. He associates truth with Kully's naiveté, and blindness with the frantic search of grown-ups, most notably of Peter, to acquire success where such is impossible. (8)

Erpenbeck's appraisal of Keun's work is most interesting from the standpoint of the People's Front effort for which this writer was naturally an ardent spokesman. Hist article appeared in Das Wort early in 1939, at a time when the communists were still attempting to lend impetus to the movement through a rapprochement with the bourgeois liberals. Erpenbeck's sympathetic and uncritical analysis of Kind aller Länder must be understood in this context. By interpreting the struggle of the exiled family in an optimistic, future-oriented context, he betrays an ideological bias which does not coincide with Keun's intention. Towards the end of the essay, he concludes: "Es ist ein Optimismus, der sich im menschlichen Kampf der Figuren zeigt, -- selbst wenn diese oder das Beste in ihnen bei diesem Kampf untergehen." (9) Erpenbeck sees the daily struggles of exile as an act of protest against fascism. Emphasis is thereby shifted from the immediate effects of these experiences to the collective idea behind them. Kully's closing statement -- "Manchmal habe ich Heimweh aber immer nach einem anderen Land, das mir gerade einfällt" (10) -- reflects, in his opinion, "eine furchtbare Anklage gegen die Schänder Deutschlands. Er weckt den Hass gegen den Fascismus, von dem Irmgard Keun mit uns weiss, dass sein Ende kommen muss ..., denn Kullys Vater ist trotz aller menschlichen Schwäche ein Antifascist, der in unseren Reihen mit uns streitet, mit uns den Sieg erleben und mit seiner Familie heimkehren wird." (11) Here Erpenbeck shifts the interpretive point of view from the empirical realities of exile to an ideological conflict with Nazi Germany. He does allude to Keun's criticism of capitalist society, but fails to delve into the issues relating to this phenomenon, a perplexing omission indeed for a dogmatic Marxist. More startling, yet, is Keun's own critical point of view. It is just such a capitalist society that she is primarily taking to task in Kind aller Länder. Through the eyes of her heroine she repeatedly lays bare the ill effects that money can exert on society. Inhumanity, greed, deception -- all these factors emerge in the novel as we relive the experiences of a father trying to uphold his decency in a frantic rush to success. Kind aller Länder is not so much a defiant protest against fascist tyranny as it is a criticism of the evils of capitalism among the liberal democracies.

Needless to say, Erpenbeck pays only lip service to this overriding idea in the work. Why? As a Marxist he ought to have capitalized on the opportunity of distinguishing Keun's novel as a prime example of the contradictions inherent in the capitalist system. His interest in the author would then have been a logical outgrowth of historical analysis, for she would have exemplified, according to Marxist thinking, the type of bourgeois humanist whose critical realism was still bound up in a process that would ultimately culminate in socialist realism. The explanation for Erpenbeck's apparent disregard for the obvious issues in Keun's novel is no doubt a strategic one. In line with the policy of nonsectarianism set forth in the Communist proclamation of the People's Front in 1935, priority was placed on gaining the anti-fascist support of the bourgeois writers, not on revealing the contradictions of the society to which they belonged. That Erpenbeck should read into Kind aller Länder a meaning contrary to Keun's intention is a direct reflection of this policy. Keun's exposure of the evils of capitalism, however, does not necessarily make her a staunch follower of the anti-fascist People's Front. Certainly the novel gives no evidence of this intent.

The figures in the book comprise anything but a politically defiant collective. The humanity they portray is individualized, springing from mutual love and consideration. Kully, Peter, and Anni are victims of immediate circumstances with which they must contend each day in order to survive. The optimism to which Erpenbeck refers is not ideologically motivated, but reflects rather a determination to persevere, to not succumb to resignation and despair. What Erpenbeck merely refers to as "eine endlose Kette trauriger, manchmal tragikomischer Alltagssituationen ohne 'dramatische' Höhepunkte" (12) really strikes at the center of the novel's form, which is inextricably tied to the leitmotif of money. The material privation of the family, brought on by their constant lack of finances, frequently creates situations that appear ridiculous and incongruous, to the point where the comical and tragic become fused.

Time and again we see Kully confined to cafés as collateral for unpaid bills. When her father returns to settle accounts, it is usually with borrowed money. Peter, the breadwinner of the family, is caught up in a vicious cycle from which there is no escape. Burdened with debts, he rarely reaps the rewards of his literary efforts: "Mein Vater bekommt hauptsächlich Geld für seine Bücher aus Holland, aber das hat wenig Sinn, weil das Geld von ihm schon ausgegeben ist, bevor es ankommt. Darum sagt mein Vater, es müssen andere Verbindungen und Quellen gesucht werden" (8). Thus, while he is away trying to arrange for advances on royalties through various literary connections, Kully and Anni register at hotels with no intention of signing out by virtue of their inability to pay. Their quarters become a virtual prison. The longer the stay, the higher the bill. Yet, if they were to attempt to leave, they would face arrest as frauds.

Kully's simple, but revealing reaction to this situation is representative of the novel's tone. It betrays Keun's own sense of outrage over the selfish refusal of the wealthy -- including other emigrants as well as foreign acquaintances -- to help the less fortunate in a time of need:

Ich verstehe ja, dass man anderen Menschen nichts fortnehmen darf, aber
ich verstehe garnicht, warum man andere Leute nicht um Geld bitten soll,
wenn sie was haben. Es ärgert mich nur, wenn Leute kein Geld hergeben,
obwohl sie was haben und obwohl man das Geld doch braucht. Sonst würde
man sie ja garnicht drum bitten. Wenn mein Vater Geld hat, gibt er immer
anderen Leuten was davon, wenn sie was haben wollen. Tiere und Kinder
darf man nicht einfach verschenken oder liegen lassen, aber Geld ist doch
nichts, was unglücklich ist oder weint, wenn man es verlässt. (47)

Only the greedy lament such a loss. There is Max Popp, an exiled calendar manufacturer who has business connections in Brussels and Paris. Peter intends to
supply him with ideas for advertisements, but must survive in the meantime. To
request payment in advance, however, from a man who tries to conceal his wealth
is unthinkable: "Er wohnt in einem ganz kleinen schäbigen Hotel, natürlich hat er
Geld. Nur reiche Leute leben so sparsam" (21). Or there is Peter's Swiss friend,
a watch dealer, whom he had asked to finance a literary journal, but who is apprehensive about the risk involved and hence rejects the proposal. "Wir haben aber
immer wieder die Erfahrung gemacht," Kully explains, "dass reiche Leute eklig
sind und nie Geld geben, daher sind sie ja reich" (154).

Peter has one outstanding "weakness" in a world hostile to poor emigrants --
his charitable humanity. This noble quality merely aggravates the material predicament of his family. At the same time it allows him an element of freedom that
others lack who are enslaved by money. Hermann Kesten has drawn a credible
likeness to Joseph Roth, whom Keun knew personally in exile. (13) Like Roth,
Peter too empathizes with the poor and oppressed, writes while drinking in sidewalk cafés, is very gregarious. In the United States Peter, although on the verge
of starvation, lends his last dollar to a negro to help pay for the burial expenses
of his deceased wife. Upon returning later to the negro's house for repayment,
Peter discovers that the body was exhumed because the husband had used the money
to drown his sorrows in drink.

Keun portrays in Peter a clown-like figure who can adapt to any situation.
Money is never an object when he has it. When he is destitute, he resorts to all
sorts of harmless deceptions to sustain himself and family. While in the United
States, he sends a telegram to distant relatives in Holland announcing his own death
under an assumed name. He appeals to the generosity of his miserly kin by re-
questing that they send money for Kully's return passage to Europe so that she may
rejoin her mother. When money does arrive, a meager sum, they are assured of
a meal -- for the time being at least.

Such a state of affairs raises the question as to Keun's intent. Do her sympathies lie with the eccentric, Bohemian writer or with her young narrator, whose
revealing observations serve to unmask the folly of this mode of existence? Very
likely with both, which points out Keun's own dilemma in exile. It is highly improbable that she herself led the kind of existence characteristic of her literary
model and acquaintance Joseph Roth. But she undoubtedly saw in this Bohemian
way of life certain qualities that allowed the materially deprived writer of 1938 to
transcend the confinement of his situation. The unconventional artist manifested
a degree of flexibility that permitted him to cope with the hostile milieu about him.
In a world pervaded by contradictions, eccentricity assumed an appearance of

normality. Prevented from leading a secure existence, writers like Peter had to deviate from conventionality so as to survive. Sidewalk cafés and restaurants became common rendevous points for vagabond writers who saw in their peers the only source of literary recognition. It became increasingly difficult for them to sell their products on the market, so they "sold" them to each other in these literary salons.

It goes without saying that countless novels never reached completion in view of the obstacles posed under material deprivation. At one point in the novel, we see Peter's publisher Krabbe anxiously awaiting the conclusion of his writer's manuscript, which had been long overdue. Peter realizes he cannot continually tap his publisher for advances on royalties. In sheer desperation he sends his wife to Amsterdam to inform Krabbe that the novel is finished, but that she does not yet have it in her possession. While she is holding him off, Peter plans, in the meantime, to rush back to Belgium from Poland and complete the remaining two hundred pages in eight days. But he cannot return unless Krabbe forwards him the money for travel expenses. This the good-hearted, but impatient publisher agrees to do. The equally good-hearted Peter gives the money, in turn, to someone who needs it more. Thus he is still stranded in the East and the novel remains a fragment. When Peter does manage to finish it much later, Krabbe informs him that it is his best work to date, but that he is unable to sell it due to the poor market.

In view of these circumstances it is no wonder that prolific letter writing became such a popular pastime with many exiled writers. In this genre they were at least assured of terminating that which they had started. Peter deplores in a letter to Anni such an inadequate substitute for the novel: "Siehst Du, jetzt fange ich schon an, einen Brief-Roman zu schreiben. Das ist wohl ein Zeichen, dass ich vollkommen liederlich geworden bin. Ein Romanschriftsteller soll sich in seinen Briefen nicht literarisch gehen lassen" (60).

In Kind aller Länder, Keun produces an image of the pursued writer. In contrast to his nonliterary acquaintances, the well-to-do businessmen, Peter is the perpetual victim of poverty by virtue of a profession whose demand has steadily diminished. In a period of political and social turbulence, where the threat of war is imminent, people still heed the call of money, not the word of truth and humanity. Keun shows that the situation of the writer in a capitalist society can be especially problematic, for his profession is dependent upon the salability of his product. Yet the intrinsic nature of his product is noncommercial; it transcends any utilitarian value. The problem is only compounded when the writer attempts to continue his profession in exile. If he had acquired international fame -- a status which only a few exiled authors enjoyed -- he could turn to the proceeds from his translated works at a time when the German-speaking audiences were coming increasingly under Nazi rule. Keun makes it quite clear that she is dealing with a writer of at least some repute. The anti-fascist articles and book Peter had written while in Germany account for his very presence in exile. We can infer from Keun's novel that Peter had enjoyed a degree of popularity in the early years of emigration, but only when the German-speaking countries still enjoyed a degree of political independence. As these countries began to fall in 1938, Peter's profession suffered correspondingly. Indeed, such was the fate of numerous exiled authors, not to mention Irmgard Keun herself. Even limited translations often did little to relieve the material burden of exile. While one of Peter's books is being displayed in the window of a Polish bookstore, its author is seen travelling through Warsaw, Prague, and Budapest in a frantic effort to secure a means of income.

It would seem, after all, that the employment of a child-narrator does indicate a retreat on the part of the author. But it is not an escape from reality; rather, it provides Keun with an artistic medium for exposing it. This narrative perspective enables her to contend artistically with the incongruities and hardships of exile to which she was undoubtedly subjected herself. The truthful simplicity of a child allows Keun the distance needed to render an accurate account of an unstable existence, one with which adults are too directly involved to be able to assess clearly.

In concluding, we must address ourselves to the issue of the United States as an exile country and Keun's probable reaction to it. In late 1938, many writers were entertaining thoughts about leaving Europe. A few had already made the move by that time, sensing that catastrophe was in the making and that Western Europe was doing nothing to thwart it. Keun travelled widely in exile, visiting, in addition to several European nations, the United States itself. The dubious note on which her novel ends produces definite problems regarding her choice between the two continents. We know, of course, that she returned to Europe after her sojourn in the United States. Like Walter Landauer, she too was stranded in Holland in 1939 and was unable to obtain a visa for France. (14) In 1940, she escaped the clutches of the invaders by returning to Cologne with a false passport. There she lived in concealment until Germany's surrender.

The question we must ask is why she came back to Europe. The United States was apparently one of the last countries she visited, implying that her novel was written soon after her return. The closing scenes of Kind aller Länder remain suspended between Europe and the United States. Peter had only gone abroad to arrange for the filming of a book. He had not intended to remain there, but does so nevertheless. His daughter, who accompanied him, returns to Europe for the purpose of fetching her mother for the eventual trip back. At this point, all logicality is dispensed with. Kully and her father both possess roundtrip boat tickets. If their final decision had been to remain in the United States, then one or both of these tickets could have been sent to Anni for her passage over. Yet Kully makes the trip back just so they can return together. Here the novel closes.

Keun probably had second thoughts about remaining in the United States herself, an assumption born out by her decision to return to Europe. The frustrating, morbid picture she creates of life in the United States would dissuade even a native from remaining there. While Peter and Kully await the results of their business agreement with a New York publisher -- which never materializes -- they virtually live from hand to mouth. As a last resort, Peter presumes on the hospitality of a former school friend, who eventually tires of him, and Peter and Kully must again take to the streets. Living in utter destitution with still several days remaining before their boat is to embark for Europe, they suddenly stumble upon a miracle. Peter is contracted to write stories for a New York newspaper. He stays and Kully goes.

The author's ambivalence at the end of the novel is exemplary for an untold number of writers. The last thing many wanted to do was to abandon their home continent. As the threat of war drew nearer, however, they realized they had no alternative. Keun certainly sheds dubious light on the cliché that describes the United States as a land of "unlimited opportunity." Just the opposite is the case in the novel. Yet her optimistic surprise-ending suggests, perhaps, that she too would soon have to face an existence in the United States of a much longer duration. This conceivably was her intention during the months leading up to the invasion of Holland. By depicting a hopeful picture of Peter's situation, she was easing the displeasure of the return voyage she sensed to be unavoidable. But her true affinity seems to have been with Europe, where we view Kully together with her mother at the end.

# CHAPTER X


## RENEE BRAND: NIEMANDSLAND


### Political Captivity and Esthetic Freedom

Lesser known authors in exile have revealed some strikingly original reactions to the state of exile in their works. This was noted in E in Mensch fällt aus Deutschland, where Konrad Merz's penetrating treatment of youth as both a traditional and contemporary concept is so problematical that the one analysis offered in this study hardly exhausts the possibilities of interpretation. Irmgard Keun, although she had enjoyed a degree of popularity in Germany, is still counted in the class of minor writers in exile. But it was perhaps due to such a lesser status that she was able to provide us with the only exile novel depicting the many obstacles interfering with the writing process. Robert Groetzsch, the only Social Democrat confronting the emigration in the exile novel and whom we will treat in a later chapter, has left behind another significant work in W i r suchen ein Land. Here we gain an understanding into how a former member of the Workers' Youth Movement (A r b e i t e r j u g e n d b e w e g u n g), who had eventually joined the ranks of the middle class as an intellectual and journalist, reflects the dichotomy in a writer's attempt to do justice to the two conflicting classes -- the proletariat and the bourgeoisie.

In the case of Renée Brand, we run into definite problems of literary classification. A cursory glance at N i e m a n d s l a n d (1940) raises the question as to any individual artistic merit whatsoever. To the best of our knowledge her name, like Merz's, never received even so much as a footnote reference in the wealth of literature emerging from the emigration. In view of the genuine artistic worth (which some critics might dispute) of Merz's novel, this omission was unjustified from a critical standpoint, although one can understand how its objectionable passages might have offended the more refined tastes of some of the exiled literati. One wonders, however, whether in Brand's case disinterest and nonrecognition was not in fact justified. I myself was tempted, at first, to write her novel off as mere popular literature, as a slavish imitation of the Romantic past. Had the novel rested solely upon such a re-creation, I would have discarded it without further ado, for it then would have transcended the exile situation and reflected a different category of prose altogether.

It is somewhat ironic that the conservative (i. e. , Neo-Romantic) writer who turns to the exile scene for his subject matter cannot be all conservative. A confrontation with the experience of exile -- as shown through the dilemma of a group of exiles confined to that strip of terrain (no man's land) separating one legal border from another -- implies, on the author's part, an involvement with the political scene giving rise to this condition. We see, then, in Brand's alternation between realistic portrayal and Romantic nostalgia an illustration of how a conservative writer might deal with the exile problem. We had observed in Bruno

Frank's case a similar incongruity between critical exposure and escapism. The exile scene in Der Reisepass was portrayed as a sanctuary for shielding the noble virtues of humanity from the wave of terror across the English Channel. Renée Brand also exhibits a tendency to escapism in Niemandsland, but in a much more problematic way. Aside from the fact that she depicts a diverse group of people in exile -- which Frank, for the most part, fails to do, addressing himself primarily to the solitary individual -- Brand also creates a situation which, by its peculiar nature, lends credibility to the invocation of an idealistic past. Where the early setting in Frank's novel shows a guest country to be generally solicitous to the problems of the refugees, such a setting is absent in Niemands- land, which describes the precarious situation of exiles just prior to and at the onset of Hitler's invasions.

Unlike Frank, who separates political protest (Ludwig in Germany) from individual freedom (Ludwig in exile), Brand continuously addresses herself to the two. She divides the setting of her novel into two distinct spheres. There is Western society, the "Europäer aus Frankreich, England, Holland, Schweiz," (1) and there is the contrasting barren field to which the unwanted fugitives are restricted, a piece of soil that is real and idyllic, that is a product of political turmoil as well as a realm intact, an actual and a symbolic no man's land "Ausserhalb von Mond und Erde: In der Sphäre der absoluten Indifferenz" (7). The strip of land separa- ting the German border from other boundaries is not geographically defined. It is immaterial to the author whether the "friendly" border on the other side is French, Swiss, or Dutch. The field is to display universal significance. For that reason it is bordered on the one side by Germany, on the other by the rest of Europe. The narrative point of view Brand employs is a decidedly tendentious one. The audience to whom her story is directed is Europe itself; the frequently recurring "Du" re- fers to the Western nations who are reproved for the suffering experienced by those populating the "Feld ... AUSSERHALB" (7), which the "free" nations have created in conjunction with Nazi Germany. This narrative perspective serves, then, as a connecting link between the two estranged worlds. Brand's no man's land is not shown as an existential antipode to a rational, humane Europe. Rather, this barren patch of land enclosed by barbed wire fencing constitutes a world that is socially and culturally sound as opposed to the one outside which is not. She creates in her no man's land a scene that contrasts sharply with the spiritual and cultural bankruptcy of a Europe whose vacillating and indecisive reaction to Nazi treachery is an extension of the ineptitude it displays in trying to deal with the question of asylum: "Mitten im Krieg verhandeln sie Frieden und Landesverteidi- gung. Aufrüstung und Nichtintervention. Nichtintervention, das ist Frieden um den Preis, den die anderen zahlen" (14).

Brand purports to preserve culture and civilization and, at the same time, to warn against its impending massacre. This explains the twofold significance of her no man's land. To preserve her ideal of art and humanity, she must trans- cend the chaotic reality threatening this tradition. To admonish the other nations for their lack of humanity, she must address herself directly to this harsh reality. Brand presents us, therefore, with a dualistic concept of art. Side by side, with no common basis, stand two estranged artistic perspectives. The one rejects the timelessness of pure estheticism when it confronts the empirical situation, the other overcomes the limitations of this situation by transcending it. The ahistorical art form of the conservative is juxtaposed with the realistic polemic of the defiant liberal humanist. What we have here is the situation of the conservative writer whose exile experience compels her to political protest. Yet her actual concept of art is so strongly rooted in an idealistic tradition that she is unable to renounce it altogether. Attack and retreat, confrontation and escapism, constitute the almost schizophrenic structural basis of the work.

A dual interpretation is imparted to the concept of captivity in the two worlds Brand sets up. The emigrants who populate the neutral strip of soil separating the political boundaries delineated by barbed wire and border patrols are depicted as both free and imprisoned, depending upon the point of view. A group of emigrants flee Germany with the intention of finding refuge in another country, but never reach their destination. It is not freedom they find, but a continuance of its abuse. The emigrants can neither go on nor can they return. Yet the very neutrality of this no man's land implies in itself freedom from oppression by acting as an area that is off limits to "friend" and foe: "Haben sie über dies Feld zu verfügen? Sollen sie bestimmen, wer hier bleiben darf, wer nicht?" (125). The freedom-captivity dialectic is applied, in turn, to Europe itself. Where the enclosed emigrants are physically incarcerated but intellectually and spiritually free (because no political power will attempt to encroach upon the rights and privileges of this neutral soil), the equally enclosed European nations enjoy physical freedom, but are captives of their own inhumanity and injustice. The "Stacheldraht" imagery (7-8) must be viewed in this dualistic context. The Western nations have, in effect, fenced themselves in by refusing to open their borders to humanity. Conversely, the exiles in no man's land are not fenced in but out. They are not affected morally, esthetically, and spiritually by the cultural deficiency of their insensitive neighbors, only legally and bureaucratically. From a political standpoint they are captives, from a human one they are free. This disparity between ruthless politics, on the one hand, and unspoiled culture, on the other, is brought into focus by the contradistinction portrayed in the two kinds of existence. Brand's no man's land signifies banishment to an area where exiles must endure extreme hardship, but one which also is untouched by Europe's cultural depravity: "Der europäische Geist ist Lüge. Die europäische Kultur ist Lüge. Europa gibt es nicht mehr. Europa ist das Chaos" (162).

Brand's artistic design is to reestablish culture and civilization before the eyes of a European public that has lost sight of man as a social, spiritual, and esthetic being. And so her barren field is inhabited by figures from every stratum of society: a physician, a laborer, an artist, a teacher, school children, a government official, a lawyer, a pregnant mother, and lovers. Out of nothing ("sie richten sich ein im Nichts," 24), these deprived refugees are able to form a kind of community in which the members, despite personal differences, strive to work for the good of the whole. The polarity between uprootedness and community is explained by the peculiarity of the historical situation. No man's land indicates the last station in exile prior to its dissolution through wholesale war. Brand is intent upon upholding her ideal of culture and humanity and, in doing so, creates a plot of European land that would still allow for comradeship, love, esthetic-spiritual exchange. Her no man's land represents a twilight zone between peace and war, an "unfreiwilligen Kriegsschauplatz" (8) upon which the inhabitants, in contrast to outsiders, have proved themselves to be noncompromising by virtue of their exile. Their patent rejection of conditions in the Third Reich acts as an admonishment to Europe for its fear and irresolution: "Sie kämpfen nicht um des frisch-fröhlichen Kampfes willen. Sie wären gerne gerade so 'neutral' wie du. Aber sie haben nicht die Wahl. Morgen hast auch du nicht die Wahl" (8).

With this argument Brand, in effect, betrays the apolitical attitude of certain conservative intellectuals in Germany who had preferred to be noninvolved until they were forced to declare themselves. Despite the variety of emigrants occupying her no man's land, none of them, according to his background, can really be described as openly anti-fascist. That they emigrated at such a late period implies that they had elected to persevere throughout the thirties as silent dissenters. Brand's exiled group displays diversity only in numbers. Politically, its membership is quite unidimensional, manifesting nuances of the author's basic, conservative Weltanschauung: "Hinter den Stacheldraht gelangten diese hier aus vielfachen Gründen: sie sind Juden oder Christen, Demokraten oder Pazifisten, Sozialisten oder einfach verantwortungsbewusste Menschen gemäss der Vorstellung, die wir bisher vom Menschen hatten, und die gewissermassen verknüpft ist mit dem Urbilde, nach dem er geschaffen wurde, und an das er sich halten sollte" (17). Here a tendency to idealize emerges which overlooks the greatly divergent political differences inherent in the classifications. Brand's primary concern is with the common denominator that unites this group generically (as belonging to the family of man), but fails to differentiate it socially and politically. As Brand recalls the experiences of these figures in Germany, we see that their reactions to Nazism all point to one universal symptom: moral indignation over the insult done to humanity. The worker who comes closest to the class of "Sozialisten" referred to above, but whom Brand describes as "ein ganz privater Mensch" (16), had resisted the cruelties committed by the Third Reich on impulse only: "Der Ingenieur hatte ein weiches Herz und konnte Misshandlungen von Wehrlosen nicht ansehen. Er wurde plötzlich verrückt und stellte sich auf die Seite der Wehrlosen" (17). In the description of the circumstances surrounding the worker's act of protest, we gain an insight into the author's inability to penetrate beyond the mere humanistic aspect of resistance: "Das geschah eines Morgens auf der Baustelle, als ein halbes Dutzend SA-Stiefel auf einem am Boden liegenden Arbeiter herumtrampelten, der sich gegen irgendetwas, gleichviel was, aber dagegen ausgesprochen hatte. Der Ingenieur liess das Halbdutzend wegtreten und zog den Mann in die Höhe. Er schleppte ihn zum Brunnen und wusch ihm das gemarterte Gesicht. Nun ist der Ingenieur ... hier gelandet. Er hatte persönlichen Mut bewiesen, der Ingenieur" (17). The specific nature of the victim's protest is immaterial to the author ("gleichviel was"). She is more concerned with the act of protest (dagegen) than with its political ramifications. We observe this in the figure of the "Ingenieur" who does not relate to his co-worker in a social context, but as an individual empathizing with the sufferings (but not their causes) of another human being. Had this incident not disrupted the worker's routine existence, chances are he would have remained in Germany doing the same thing he had always done.

Such is the case with most of the refugees populating Brand's no man's land. They would have continued on as they normally had throughout the thirties if some occurrence or sequence of occurrences had not forced an abrupt halt to their routine existence. The Jewish members of the group -- Niemand, the former lawyer whose horrible experiences in a concentration camp had led to mental derangement; Rose, the pregnant woman thrown through the window of her textile shop; and the physician who was beaten and sheared while performing an operation -- must of course be regarded as special cases, for their very presence in Germany, irrespective of their politically philosophy, meant sure oppression and persecution.

Brand asserts her conservative-humanistic position most vividly in the non-Jewish figures of the government official, the painter, the teacher, and the clergyman. These emigrants had come to the conclusion that further existence in the Third Reich signified a total compromise of the traditional artistic, ethical, and religious views they had been able to espouse unimpeded thus far. Since their personal political philosophies amounted to nothing but an extention of the conservative-idealistic outlook they had held prior to the establishment of the Third Reich, they were powerless to oppose the reactionary fascist philosophy with an ideology that functioned constructively in social reality. Hence, as long as they could rest on the ideals of their humanistic conservatism, they experienced no need for protest. The moment the Nazis clamped down on their political neutrality, however, they were faced with only two choices: either they programmed their philosophies to conform to the barbaric principles of fascism, or they retreated altogether in an effort to uphold what they traditionally had believed in. This explains, in part, the neutrality of Brand's no man's land, an area which, because it is temporarily free of political intrusion, allows for the furtherance of an apolitical W e l t a n - s c h a u u n g .

It is in this light that we see the artist, whose too idyllic paintings of Romantic scenes evidently were not heroic enough for the esthetic tastes of the Nazis, continuing in exile his idealization of love which recognizes fulfillment only in death. In the style of the Romantic poet Novalis, he senses artistic perfection only upon capturing the essence of his object: "Wenn ich dir sagte: die Liebe. Wüsstest du mehr? Du wüsstest weniger. Es gibt nur noch eine Kraft, deren Unerforschlichkeit dieser gleichkommt. Der Tod" (103). If one can speak at all of a leading character among this group of exiles, then it is the artist-painter, the one figure with whom Brand would most likely sympathize the most. And it is indeed to this figure that she devotes the largest part of her characterization, for it is the painter himself who poetizes the no man's land the author has created: "Dies trostlose Feld, jener Baum, der Himmel, ist mehr, anders, als nur Baum, Himmel, Feld. Hinter allem wird plötzlich ein geheimnisvoller Zauber offenbar. Die Welt schwingt in den Wundern der Sphären, und in Baum, Himmel, Feld schwingst auch du mit. Du bist in der Schöpfung, die Schöpfung ist in dir, du bist daheim. So vermag hie und da ein Begnadeter in einem Lächeln die Schöpfung wieder zusammenzufügen, rund, ohne Riss" (75).

Brand depicts the clergyman in no less mystifying terms. Up to the point where he chances upon ("ein Gotteswunder," 66) Rose lying on a patch of ice in a pool of blood after having delivered her own child, we see him as the despairing apostate who associates exile with the loss of congregation. He bickers with the Almighty because it was He who sanctioned the Nazi intrusion upon his church community. The clergyman's flight into exile was not perpetrated foremost by political conditions in Germany; it was decreed by Providence. He finally realizes the divine purpose of his exile when Providence guides him to the spot where the bleeding mother and infant are stranded: "Jetzt hat er wieder eine Gemeinde. Er ist abberufen und auf einen neuen Posten gestellt worden. Das Kind, das er wie durch ein Wunder gerettet hat, lebt" (86).

Brand's attempt to restore order out of impending chaos is evidenced repeatedly by her employment of t o p o i suggesting cosmic harmony. Her novel is even structured along the lines of a Romantic fragment. The depiction of the harsh realities of exile is constantly interrupted by idyllic digressions which seem infinitesimal. Long discourses on the overpowering passion of love; Romantic folksongs echoing the wonders of God's creation ("Deines Schöpfers weiser Wille," 127-28) or the redeeming quality of suffering and virtue ("Ueb' immer Treu und Redlichkeit/Bis an dein kühles Grab," 178; "Ach ich bin des Treibens müde," 166); the transformation of no man's land into an object of esthetic beauty; the invocation of the spirits ("Geister ziehen Geister an," 164) of great musical, literary, and artistic geniuses of the past; religious-philosophical discussions about death and rebirth -- all point to the creation of a world without limitation, a kind of U n i v e r s a l p o e s i e, which time and again transcends the ominous reality of the moment.

In this vein the teacher sets out to resume his profession in exile, unhindered by the lies infecting the life of every schoolchild at home. The children in no man's land must, in his opinion, be reintroduced to the mysteries of the universe. Romantic idealism had been perverted and brutalized in Germany; here its wondrous features can be explored free from the influence of dirty politics: "Er lehrt sie Ehrfurcht vor der unendlichen Vielfalt der Schöpfung in dem einen grossen Raum, dem Weltenraum, vor der unendlichen Vielfalt der Völker: Menschenvölker, Tiervölker, Pflanzenvölker, Steinvölker. So lernen sie die Religion der Religionen" (131). Here one detects a certain appeal exerted by the word "Volk" on some of the conservative members of the German intelligentsia. Although this teacher had the presence of mind to reject Hitler's blood and soil ideology, his preoccupation with the concept suggests that its daily propagation by Nazi racial experts might have left an imprint, however innocently the teacher chooses to use it.

It was stressed earlier that the political world "outside" clashed with the idealistic one "within," and that Brand is addressing herself partly to the former as a way of protest against Europe's inhumanity and cultural deficiency. Since her individual views on art and philosophy constitute an apolitical retreat into intangible spheres, however, she really presents the European public with a further inducement to regress to the past. Throughout the novel her narrative viewpoint vacillates between confrontation and escapism, denunciation and preservation, thus only intensifying the polarity already existing between her world and the one outside. The humanistic principles she envisions in her idyllic interludes become so estheticized and abstract that they actually exert a retarding effect on the more concrete pleas for humanity emanating from her criticism of European society. Indeed, her recurrent lapses into an idyllic realm of U n i v e r s a l p o e s i e convey to her European audience the deceiving impression that the situation in no man's land is really not so precarious after all. Brand's portrayal of harsh reality, followed intermittently by its Romantic poetization, reveals a characteristic attitude of the conservative writer intent upon keeping life and art in their respective domains. Those scenes which do point out the actual plight of the refugees as an outcome of Europe's inhuman bureaucracy are admittedly quite provocative. It is when we consider the novel in its total perspective, however, that we perceive a reduction of critical effectiveness brought on by Brand's predilection for alienating art from reality.

The episodes depicting the border officials on both sides of the fence are an illustration of the critical side of the novel. Brand describes the inhuman actions of the German and European police patrols in identical terms, to the point where they interact as "colleagues." In drawing a mutually reflective picture of the two, she levels a stinging attack against Europe by intimating that its bureaucratic inhumanity towards the stranded exiles is just as reprehensible and shameful as the treachery of the Nazis. The fugitives encounter identical responses when, in the case of the European guards, they request passage to obtain refuge and, in the other case, they set out to gather branches from the German forest for bedding on the frozen ground:

> Die Beamten schoben die Mützen von den gutmütigen, wohlgenährten Ge-
> sichtern zurück und kratzten sich verlegen den Kopf. ... 'Ohne Pässe?',
> Achselzucken. 'Ohne ordentliche Papiere?!', Kopfschütteln. (29)
> . . . . . . . . . . . . . . . . . . . . . . . . . . . . . . . . . . . . . . . . . . . . . . .
> Die Soldaten schoben die Mützen zurück und kratzten sich den Kopf, mit
> der gleichen Bewegung und dem gleichen Gesichtsausdruck, wie ihre Kol-
> legen von der gegenüberliegenden Grenze. Nein, es ist unmöglich, Sie
> dürfen nicht passieren. (115)

The satiric implication in this likeness is most incisive. The European and German guards resemble marionettes who mechanically follow ("Grenzmaschinen in Menschengestalt," 32) the directives of their governments, with the distinction being that the European governments' flagrant disregard for human dignity is shrouded in a fetishized veneration of a stamped piece of paper, while the Nazi regime openly professes its animosity towards undesirables.

Equally incisive are those scenes portraying delegates from the League of Nations who provide the suffering refugees with charitable handouts (sleeping bags) but not their safety and security. While a commission is deliberating over the disposition of the exiles, the latter continue to endure untold hardships. Brand lashes out bitterly against the European nations for allowing this state of affairs to persist:

> Was meinst du? Ist die Welt gross genug? Unter uns brauchen wir uns ja
> nichts vorzumachen. Sage mir, glaubst du wirklich, es lässt sich auf der
> Welt ein Platz finden für diese Menschen? Oder handelt es sich nur um eine
> trostreiche Handbewegung? Handelt es sich um eine edle europäische Geste
> der Menschlichkeit, handelt es sich um Worte?
> Nun wir werden ja sehen. Wenn die Menschen nicht inzwischen erfrieren,
> verhungern oder wahnsinnig werden, werden sie schon noch erfahren, wie
> das alles gemeint ist. (138)

Whenever Brand turns her attention away from subjective digression and confronts the problems at hand, she creates a cogent picture of the emigrant scene. In this respect her narrative point of view is most effective. By addressing her account of the exiles' plight to a specific audience within the story, she succeeds in actualizing the tension between the two realms of existence, demonstrating thereby the gross disparity between superficial gestures of kindness and true humanity. The European democracies act most charitably in supplying the refugees with a circus van containing staples for everyday use. Nevertheless, this gesture of decency is accompanied by a certain suspicion about fugitives whose misery and confinement is legally sanctioned. The European people do not relate this banishment to their own internal fear and anxiety, but to some kind of transgression that the refugees themselves must have committed: "Etwas muss ja doch mit diesen da los sein, das man sie so behandelt, eine Bewandtnis wird es schon haben, ganz aus der Luft gegriffen kann es doch wohl nicht sein?" (111). Brand unmasks this fallacy by pointing out to her audience that it was their own complacency and political insecurity which had created this situation:

> Erkennst du dein Gesicht nicht, dein Europäer Gesicht, das gut hinter Gardinen geborgen, durch das noch unzerschlagene Fenster späht? Du protestierst. Nein, dies sei dein Gesicht nicht. Du habest eingegriffen, wo es möglich war. Wie hast du eingegriffen? Mit beiden Händen hast du die Grenzwälle verstärkt, an die die Wogen der Verzweiflung branden. Kommissionen hast du ins Leben gerufen, damit sie beraten, wie geholfen werden könne. Ehrenwerte Männer und Frauen bemühen sich. Konferenzen tagen. Das Elend aber nachtet. (136)

If we take a closer look at the international political situation prevailing at the time, we can see why Brand's denunciation of European injustice, however warranted it may be, must ultimately fail to produce results. In late 1939, as Hitler was preparing to engulf the whole of Europe in war, the panic-stricken nations of the West were taking special precautionary measures with respect to the admittance of German refugees who had elected to remain in the Third Reich up to that time. The problem was only compounded when such late arrivals were unable to produce identification papers at the border. To aggravate the situation even more, the government of France by this time had been corrupted by a contingent of fascist disciples bent on keeping additional emigrants out and imprisoning the ones that were in. The smaller governments, in turn, had reached their capacity and were opening their borders mainly to those emigrants who could produce visas showing they were in transit. Brand's characters had gone into exile at a time when the letter of the law had to be strictly observed. The daily handouts provided the refugees by the neighboring countries were a sorry excuse for humanity, but under the prevailing circumstances it was perhaps all that could be expected when Hitler's armies were about to advance on the West.

If we compare Brand's Niemandsland to Walter Hasenclever's Die Rechtlosen, which portrays the exile predicament in a French internment camp in late 1939, we realize how hopeless the dilemma was for escapees who were first seeking asylum when it was seldom granted. In effect, the neutral plot of soil between political borders gives a paradoxical impression of the emigrant scene. The fugitives find themselves in exile and then again they do not. The idyllic past that Brand was able to construct out of her no man's land could only have been undertaken in a realm free of outside laws and restriction. Such a state of neutrality would have been unthinkable under "actual" exile conditions within the countries themselves. The dualism between physical captivity and artistic freedom gives concrete form to the peculiar exile state created in the novel. These polar extremes -- the one outlining the exile condition, the other transcending it -- explain the structural uniqueness of the work. Reality and unreality exist side by side, reflecting the paradoxical character of the exile setting. The people inhabiting the area called no man's land, who are uninfluenced by activities in the outside world and hence are not subject to established laws and customs, form their own culture and society whereby they are at liberty to enact their own system of justice and social intercourse. This is clearly evidenced in the strange relationship that develops between the former Nazi government official and the mentally withdrawn Jewish lawyer. The minister, who had never openly supported fascist racial brutality but then never denounced it either, joins the group as a repentant sinner. He takes the reticent lawyer completely under his wing, catering to his every wish and need in an effort to make up for the injustice done to him by the Third Reich. But Niemand shows no signs of responding to the minister's act of kindness. In a mock trial scene around a bonfire, the lawyer suddenly snaps out of his stupor and condemns his enemy to death. Humanity and mercy play no role in this macabre scene which exercises justice on the basis of an eye for an eye: "Wir hier sind auch hinter Stacheldraht. Und hier, in meinem Bereich, werde ich für Ordnung sorgen. Ich werde geordnete Zustände herstellen. Der Angeklagte ist schuldig. Leugnen ist sinnlos. Bekenne deine Schuld, Angeklagter, und nimm deine Strafe auf dich" (190). The minister submits to his guilt and is found dead the following morning. Kneeling beside him is his judge holding a pistol. Nobody knows whether it was suicide or execution. The lawyer is unable to answer for he has once again become the silent Niemand.

Although Renée Brand avoids exact reference to time in N i e m a n d s l a n d, she mentions, at one point, two events that would place the novel in late 1939: "Ein Deutscher baut sein Fundament auf einem verschneiten Feld zwischen Stacheldrähten im Niemandsland, während sein Land soeben die Grenzen erweitert: Gau Oesterreich, Gau Tschechoslowakei ... Gau ... wer weiss ... Welt, wer weiss ..." (93). The allusion to winter is dubious. It could have only symbolic meaning with respect to the deplorable physical conditions to which the refugees are exposed. In fact, this seasonal reference remains constant throughout the novel. If the reference to winter is to be interpreted historically, on the other hand, then one could assume that Nazi Germany has already embarked on its invasion of Poland, an event that triggered an ambivalent and often hostile reaction towards emigrants in the countries of exile and hence the emergence of the internment camp. And when no man's land is overrun by invaders at the end of the novel, we receive the impression that Hitler has commenced his military campaign in the West. Here the reference to winter is totally inaccurate if it is to be interpreted realistically. For emigrants were not freezing ("das Blut fror ihnen in den Adern," 193) when the Nazis turned to the West in May of 1940. It could mean, however, that Brand is merely anticipating events to come. If the invasion of the West had not yet taken place when she wrote the novel, then the question of historical inaccuracy with regard to the season of winter would be irrelevant. Symbolically, this reference also serves to heighten the atmosphere of doom that had befallen the exiles when no man's land ceased to exist.

Brand's identification with many of the characters in the novel, revealed by the commonplace references to "Ach" (35, 41, 102, 106) and "die Unseren" (109, 111), suggests that she may have experienced a similar exile. She certainly did not share their fate at the end, however, when the stranded refugees fall into the clutches of the advancing troops. In Schriftsteller im Exil: Zwei Jahre deutsche literarische Sendung am Rundfunk in New York, (2) Peter M. Lindt states that Brand had escaped to Basel where she pursued academic studies until she was granted an American visa. Her novel was written during her exile in Switzerland and appeared in translation (Short Days Ago, 1941) prior to her arrival in the United States.

## CHAPTER XI

WALTER HASENCLEVER: DIE RECHTLOSEN

The Internment Camp and the Freedom of Captivity

In Kurt Pinthus' preface to his anthology of Walter Hasenclever's works, he quotes the dramatist's reaction to his urgent request to make immediate preparations for resettling in the United States. Hasenclever's reply, dated June 14, 1939, reads: "Sollte Stück (S c a n d a l  i n  A s s y r i a) oder Roman Geld bringen, so würde ich gerne für diesen Betrag als Visitor herüberkommen, um Euch alle wiederzusehen und die Möglichkeit des dortigen Lebens und Arbeitens zu studieren. Tatsache ist, dass ich hier mit Haus, Garten, Gemüse, Tieren, Garage, Auto in der herrlichen Landschaft nebst Weib mit 75 Dollar im Monat als 'besserer Herr' existieren kann -- für welchen Betrag mir in Amerika die Badeschnur des armen Toller winken würde. So was gibt man nicht ohne zwingenden Grund auf." (1) Hasenclever's description of his cozy domicile in Cagnes-sur-Mer hardly creates the impression of an exile living under the material and psychological strain of hoemlessness. It evokes rather the image of a writer who is quite content with the new home he has made for himself in the German emigration. This is not surprising when one considers that Hasenclever had been residing outside Germany since 1925. In France, where he spent most of his time, he was more artistically at home than in his native country. "Merkwürdig ist," states Pinthus, "dass im Ausland Stücke Hasenclevers aufgeführt wurden, die in Deutschland weder im Druck noch auf der Bühne erschienen. Das Merkwürdigste aber: etwa die Hälfte von Hasenclevers Gesamtwerk ist in Deutschland überhaupt niemals veröffentlicht worden, darunter sicherlich einige seiner besten Arbeiten." (2) From the standpoint of artistic repute, therefore, Hasenclever did not sense the loss of a German reading public that was to become the fate of many writers upon moving to foreign surroundings in 1933.

When Hasenclever was compelled to remain in France after his books were consigned to flames in May, 1933, his newly acquired status as a political emigrant effected no change in his private life, his pacifist philosophy, or his idea of artistic autonomy. The renowned expressionist's traditional distaste for the restraints imposed upon individual freedom by any organization -- whether it be religious, political, or literary -- continued to determine his thinking after 1933. (3) Like Erich Maria Remarque, he led the life of a lone wolf in exile, remaining aloof from the group activities of other writers who attempted to come to terms with the artistic and political demands of the crisis at hand. In his autobiographical novel D i e  R e c h t l o s e n Hasenclever includes a brief episode which clearly establishes the individualistic position of his first-person narrator. When asked whether he was ever a member of the S c h u t z v e r b a n d  d e u t s c h e r  S c h r i f t - s t e l l e r  i m  A u s l a n d, the narrator responds disparagingly with the reply: "Dieser Redeklub eines bedeutungslosen Grüppchens war mir immer ein Greuel.

Ich kenne den Vorsitzenden aus langjähriger Erfahrung. Was ihm in Berlin nicht gelang, hat er endlich in Paris erreicht. Drüben hat man ihn ausgelacht und hier darf er quatschen. Umhüllt von einer politischen Toga, spielt er sich auf seinem Pöstchen als Gesinnungsrichter der emigrierten Literatur auf. Dass er kein Talent hat, mag noch hingehen. Leider ist er auch ein Dummkopf. " (4) That Hasenclever should single out Rudolf Leonhard as the object of his invective is not surprising. Their views on art had always been sharply opposed. In a debate over the creative function of the writer, held on radio in 1929, Leonhard argued for a form of art that reflected social change, while Hasenclever insisted on treating it as an autonomous product of the intellect. (5)

In his preface Pinthus makes frequent reference to Hasenclever's propensity for idyllic quietude, an atmosphere that enabled him to write his personal confession Irrtum und Leidenschaft intermittently over a five-year period. He completed it just prior to his first internment in Fort Carré near Antibes in September, 1939. Pinthus speaks of Hasenclever as living "in ziemlicher Ruhe" in Nice in 1934. His following trip to the "fast völlig von der Aussenwelt abgeschlossenen jugoslavischen Insel Sipanska" finds him with his sister and her husband for a brief period. In 1936, after a short stay on the Riviera, he travels to the vicinity of Florence where he buys a farm. This "ländliche Idylle" is interrupted, in 1938, by fascist Italian police, who imprison him for ten days as a favor to Hitler who happened to be visiting the Duce at the time. Following his rapid departure from Italy, Hasenclever settles in his villa in Cagnes, "seine letzte glückliche und friedliche Zeit" before the era of the internment camp. Pinthus' comment on Hasenclever's letter, quoted above, points out the two events playing a key role in the creation of Die Rechtlosen: "Der Beginn des Zweiten Weltkriegs und die französische Mobilmachung rissen Hasenclever aus diesem Idyll." (6) For the purpose of our interpretation, this comment also points to another critical issue, namely, that Hasenclever's exile status after 1933 becomes a reality to him the moment his personal freedom stands to be jeopardized. From January, 1933, to September, 1939, Hasenclever appears to have lived like a permanent vacationer in a foreign country. His residence outside Germany after 1933 was a continuation of the one he had established previously. His expatriation, the most apparent manifestation of his new status, very likely facilitated his psychological integration into a foreign society by engendering a conclusive break with his past.

Considering Hasenclever's mythical view of history, which had envisioned an apocalyptic upheaval of universal society as a predetermined outcome of man's fate, it is not surprising that the year 1933 failed to bring about a change in the apolitical outlook he had fostered since the twenties. His perception of fascism as a cosmic embodiment of human corruption precluded any kind of rational political opposition since such a force was predestined to unleash itself. Thus the transition from residing in France to being exiled there produced no noticeable effect on his Weltanschauung. On paper he was expatriated, but the legal implications of this status did not make a real impression on him until he saw his existence threatened by the international political and military scene in late 1939. This is reflected in the main part of the novel depicting emigrants stripped of their rights in a French internment camp.

Due to the imminence of a German invasion, French authorities felt it necessary to intern German and Austrian emigrants for reasons of national security. Exceptions to this policy were made (in theory, but not in practice) on the basis of age and health. Those emigrants who possessed a German passport, or none at all, were to comply with the internment order even though they were prepared to prove their loyalty to the guest country by joining its armed forces. Because of their nationality, they were indiscriminately interned until their loyalties could be documented through statements made by personal friends or organizations in France. Internment applied initially to those who had been, in fact, officially expatriated, a predicament in which the narrator finds himself in September. Although a legally expatriated status was proof of an exile's disavowal of any political allegiance to his homeland, it still did not give sufficient evidence of his unconditional loyalty to France. This country still regarded expatriated emigrants as Germans and, as a precautionary measure, had them interned along with other exiles whose rejection of Nazi Germany could not be supported by evidence.

Hasenclever opens Die Rechtlosen in medias res. The relatively peaceful exiled existence the narrator had been leading extends into the scenes depicted prior to the actual exile condition in the internment camp. The seclusion of the narrator's home conveys the impression that the occupants have assimilated quite satisfactorily into their environment. All the comforts of life are enjoyed: villa, garden, private library, maid, dog. Although the narrator has been an exiled German all along, he does not seem to have suffered any of the psychological and material effects of this status. It is the ominous presence of a fellow emigrant named Wohlgast which acts as a catalyst awakening the narrator to the grim reality of his situation ("So oft Wohlgast auftauchte, lag Unglück in der Luft," 395). The narrator's life as a recluse is shattered by the emergence of this intruder, whose presence is a reminder of the precarious position of the emigrants in France in the face of imminent disaster. The narrator depicts him as a kind of incarnation of fate and impending doom. Throughout the scene he tries to evade the threatening implications of the approaching crisis by interspersing comments about Wohlgast's unpopularity with women. Yet war looms in the background despite his reluctance to accept this reality. He sees himself, finally, as a victim of irreversible cosmic forces, culminating in the emergence of fascism as the incarnation of evil and destruction.

This opening scene, followed by episodes portraying life on the Riviera as a den of iniquity, sets the stage for the dual form of existence created by the world outside the internment camp and the one within. Kurt Pinthus correctly points out this structural peculiarity in his introduction:

> Bald nach seiner Heimkehr begann er den Roman 'Die Rechtlosen', in dem er in autobiographischer Ich-Darstellung eine Doppel-Existenz schildert: das fast sorglose, bescheiden geniesserische Leben der deutschen Emigranten in Südfrankreich und, im Gegensatz dazu, das erniedrigende Vegetieren der im Lager Inhaftierten, die sich aber bald der neuen primitiven Situation anpassen und eine Art geschlossenes Gemeinwesen mit grotesken und tragischen Episoden und einer intellektuellen, diskutierenden Oberschicht entwickeln. In der letzten dieser Debatten gibt Hasenclever sein geistiges Testament, gipfelnd in einem hymnischen Bekenntnis zum Buddhismus. (7)

Hasenclever frequently contrasts the communal atmosphere of the internment camp to the aimless existence led by those who are free on the outside. He draws on a passage from Tolstoy's W a r  a n d  P e a c e to illustrate the dualism erupting from the current setting: "Das Leben jedes Menschen hat zwei Seiten: das persön-liche Leben, das um so freier ist, je abstrakter seine Interessen sind -- und ein elementares, ein Herdenleben, in dem der Mensch unweigerlich die gegebenen Ge-setze erfüllt" (408). The twofold form of existence appearing in the novel would seem to reflect this polarity. The concept of freedom takes on special meaning in light of the situation presented. Who is actually free? The interned elite who, in the midst of physical captivity, engage in theoretical debates about the future of man, or the people who have escaped incarceration but are captives of their own irra-tional instincts and petty indulgences? One receives the impression that Hasen-clever's narrator actually prefers the intellectual autonomy born of the current crisis to the "normal" reality prevailing outside the camp. Following his release at the end, the narrator states: "Aber ich wurde meiner Freiheit nicht froh" (498). When he returns to his interned colleagues to bid a final farewell, he reflects: "Die Gemeinschaft war versammelt -- ich hatte die Empfindung, als sei ich zu Hause. ... Die Schicksalsverkettung schien unlösbar. Hier sassen die Rechtlosen, zu denen ich gehörte. Bei ihnen war mein Platz und nicht in Cagnes" (499).

Hasenclever portrays a condition of man which, in its present "cosmic" state, is unable to reconcile the polarity expressed in the passage from Tolstoy. He illustrates this antagonism in the case of Dr. Marcus -- one of the more outspoken adherents to the principle of human solidarity in a crucial situation -- who sub-sequently resumes a life of private dilettantism outside the internment camp. And so the narrator points out:

> Männerfreundschaften entstanden, die für die Ewigkeit geschlossen wurden, aber die Dauer der Internierung kaum überlebten. Geriet der Entlassene wieder in sein gewohntes Fahrwasser, dann füllte ihn die Ehe mit ihren An-sprüchen völlig aus. Vergessen waren Schwüre und Beteuerungen. Die Leidensgenossen entfremdeten sich ebenso schnell, wie sie sich gefunden hatten. Kaum dass ein Mittagessen, eine flüchtige Teestunde die einst Un-zertrennlichen verband. Die Alltäglichkeit eigener Interessen überschwemm-te sie, und das Ausserordentliche existierte nur noch im Schauer der Er-innerung. (473-74)

Hasenclever's displeasure over the fractionalized existence he sees in society extends beyond Marcus' case ("Spiessbürger schlimmster Sorte," 476) to include the "Herdenmenschen" in general. The narrator's sardonic description of these figures suggests a certain repulsion towards an anarchistic mode of existence that stands in sharp contrast to the idyllic one he had enjoyed prior to its disruption by the appearance of Wohlgast. The social outcasts of the Bohemian subculture in Cagnes, replete with sexual perverts, alcoholics, and dilettantes, are portrayed with the detached cynicism that explains the author's preference for the abstract realm of G e i s t emerging in the solitude of the internment camp. His deprecating exposure of the den of iniquity ("Sündenbabel," 398) on the Riviera is a further manifestation of his philosophical view towards man as an incarnation of hell, an apocalyptic unleashing of irrational cosmic forces. Even the group of artists with whom he closely associates are regarded in this manner. The panderer Sesam and Didi's lesbian relationship with the bisexual Angelika are also described in a disapproving tone.

Paradoxically, the world of the internment camp provides the author with a setting for a retreat to freedom. The irrational impulses determining the lives of exiles in the "real" world are momentarily suspended in an "ideal" environment removed from the anarchistic one outside. In light of the unique setting created in the camp, the many philosophical and religious speculations dealing with the future of man take on the appearance of an intellectual repartee an sich. The elite circle of intellectuals senses "Zusammengehörigkeit" (466) in the realm of Geist, an ideal state produced by a condition of physical confinement. A friendly battle of abstractions takes place, with the result that theories and hypotheses provide the stimulus for a sense of community: "Trotz grosser Divergenzen hielten nach aussen alle geschlossen zusammen. Kein Unbefugter drang in ihren Kreis. ... Klarheit und gesunder Menschenverstand bewahrten die Teilnehmer vor den zermürbenden Einflüssen der Massenpsychose" (477).

The various arguments and opinions on the nature of humanity and ethical conduct transcend social reality when viewed in the context of the novel as a whole. This comes especially to the fore in the case of those internees (e.g., Dr. Marcus) who fall back to their earlier pattern of life when set free. So much theorizing, probing, and deliberating; yet those individuals espousing proposals for the future fail to abide by their principles when the opportunity really presents itself, namely, in the world outside where they are free to act. No permanent change of outlook is ever realized Discussions on humanity and one's obligations towards a social mission later on become speculative chatter by virtue of the intellectuals' asocial attitude within the camp to begin with. That this group is a closed unit comprising only select members raises some question as to how they plan to realize a changed society when they make a practice of intellectual isolationism. Their intolerant attitude towards other internees merely attenuates their formulations of a solution for the future state of Germany. If the platitudes, unrealistic speculations, and metaphysical visions they espouse are to become guidelines for a new world after the holocaust, then these exiles have not learned a great deal from the social and political realities which produced the era of the internment camp. By describing their prison as a "neue Heimat," a "Vaterland" (484), they fabricate an existence that transcends the inexorable reality of the period (the similarity to Brand's novel becomes apparent here). If solidarity can come about only in a crisis (the captive world within), after which this sense of community disintegrates when a normal life is resumed, then one wonders how these hypothesizers can justify a new humanity of the future once normalcy has been restored upon the termination of an even greater crisis (the war).

In essence, the various participants in the discussions profess elitist beliefs which serve to preserve a degree of individuality without reflecting a basis in reality. The narrator's retreat, for example, to Buddhistic asceticism is one of several personal formulae for human conduct. Hasenclever reconstructs within the confines of the internment camp a pseudoidyllic setting (an extension of the earlier one he had known prior to the novel!) in which the intellectual elite form a kind of stoic immunity to the physical inconveniences imposed upon them. A la

Goethe's Unterhaltungen deutscher Ausgewanderten, they are bent upon upholding the intellectual freedom of Geist amidst an atmosphere of turmoil. Matthias Wegner sums up Hasenclever's artistic position quite fittingly when he states:

> Eine so neuartige Lebensform wie das Exil wird in die alten Begriffs- und Erkenntnis-Schemata eingepasst, die äussere Abkehr von Deutschland löscht nicht die tiefe geistige Beziehung zu seiner Kultur. Die Erfahrungen der Gegenwart werden mit denen der Vergangenheit verschmolzen, — die Vision von einem weltweiten Wandlungsprozess wird wieder aufgenommen und für die Sinngebung des Exil-Schicksals herangezogen. Das Exil verliert damit als besondere Situation an Relevanz. Indem es nur noch als äusseres Symptom für einen die ganze Menschheit umgreifenden Prozess angesehen wird, sind auch die spezifischen Bedingungen des Emigranten-Daseins von untergeordneter Bedeutung. (8)

Wegner refers here to Hasenclever's conception of the approaching war as a revelation of an "ungeheurer Umwandlungsporzess" (493) that already had its inception in 1914. Expressionist writers at that time had viewed the first war as a necessary prelude to the birth of the new man. The conflict between intellect and nature, formulated in the reference to Tolstoy and depicted in the world outside the internment camp and the one within, will remain unresolved until the Menschheits-dämmerung erupting from the upheaval of the next war frees man from the basic contradictions of his existence. The emigration of late 1939 is but another manifestation of the dualism between freedom and captivity, spirit and nature.

The narrator's retreat to the realm of Buddhistic mysticism, in which the extremes of thought and action, reason and irrationality, become fused, (9) recalls in part Klaus Mann's metaphysical solution to the current crisis in Der Vulkan. He too transcends the realities of the period by envisioning in man a coincidentia oppositorum that only obfuscates the historical significance of the German exile.

## CHAPTER XII

ERNST NEUBACH: FLUGSAND

The Orthodox versus the Western Jew: Exile as an Extension of the Diaspora or a Preparation for Assimilation?

Ernst Neubach's obscurity as a writer is not necessarily due to artistic inferiority, but to his apparent nonmembership in the profession of belles-lettres. His only work, F l u g s a n d (1945), presumably is the story of his own life in exile as recounted by a first-person narrator named Josef Berger. The absence of additional information about Neubach, either by outside sources or through personal statements in exile, leads one to believe that the author turned to writing for reasons other than esthetic. He evidently did not consider himself a belletristic writer. Certainly this solitary work would not have sufficed to bring him that kind of recognition. Renée Brand is the only other author who, to the best of our knowledge, turned out just one work in exile. But then, in her case, she is dealing with a situation in which esthetics and politics represent a problem of the liberals as a class of writers. Berger-Neubach's harrowing experiences in exile, beginning with the fall of Austria and terminating with Berger's flight from Southern France to Switzerland in 1942, seem to have produced a set of narrative criteria in which a moral and didactic interpretation of real events takes precedence over the problem of creative freedom contra political polemic.

Neubach calls his work a "Dokumentarischer Roman eines Heimatlosen." This designation, in itself, implies a certain "artistic" intent, one which is normally not attributable to simple autobiography. In the dedication, addressed to a certain Margrit J., Neubach draws the distinction between creative phantasy and the art of reality: "Du weisst, dass ich nichts zu erfinden brauchte. Die Phantasie verblasste vor der Wirklichkeit." (1) Neubach takes the position that the empirical reality of exile does not require alteration in order to meet certain demands of the novel. To dispel the notion that he is not just relating past experiences in the form of an autobiography, he creates a fictitious narrator who becomes a part of the action described. The author incorporates this figure as a vehicle for structural unity amidst a disparate, often traumatic chain of events. In addition, selectivity and typicality meet the requirements of the novel without sacrificing documented reality: "Schreib alles auf! -- sagtest Du einmal. Wie könnte ich das? Zu ungeheuer ist die Materie. So kann es nicht Aufgabe dieses Buches sein, das Flüchtlingsproblem erschöpfend zu behandeln. Trotzdem ist mein J o s e f  B e r g e r keine Einzelperson: Er ist W i r !" (7). Neubach closes the dedication with: "Im Exil, Zollikon-Zürich, 1943/44." In a footnote later on, he states: "Bei Abschluss dieses Buches meldet die Weltpresse, dass die Regierung de Gaulle in Algier die unmenschlichen Wärter des Konzentrationslagers Hadjerat am 3. März 1944 vor das Gericht in Algier gestellt hatte. ... Die im Jahre 1940 gemachten Aufzeichnung des Verfassers wurden somit vier Jahre später gerichtlich bestätigt" (263). By inference, Neubach must have written his novel after obtaining refuge in Switzerland, basing it on diary entries he had made during his actual experiences in Nazi-occupied Vienna, the two French internment camps, the Sahara Desert as a Foreign Legionaire, and the unoccupied French zone from where he (Berger) slipped across the Swiss border in 1942, the point at which the novel closes.

Without the addition of a fictitious first-person narrator, whose participation in the events portrayed evokes an illusion of immediacy and actuality, the work would read very much like an autobiography, a genre not pertinent to the category of prose under study. Countless autobiographies were written in exile and after 1945, with the distinguishing feature being that of distance created either through time or physical removal from the scene. Those autobiographies emerging out of the exile period itself were mainly written away from the European zone; those created in Germany after Hitler's defeat were even more removed from the urgent problems arising from the exile situation. The significance of Neubach's documentary novel is that it was written at a historical turning point (1943-44) in the twelve-year reign of exile. Hitler's armies were suffering untold losses in Russia, the strength of Rommel's tank divisions was wavering, and the allied invasion of Normandy was but months away. Neubach's novel marks a transition from a hopeless, chaotic state of turmoil to an outlook transcending the exile condition and anticipating a rebuilding of a humane Europe. A sufficient number of years had elapsed to allow for the treatment of the exile in the form of autobiography. That the author's exile status had not yet terminated, however, accounts for the intent he lends to the events recalled. F l u g s a n d acts as a final revue of life in exile, extending from Hitler's uncontested dominance over most of Europe to a gradual weakening of this position on various fronts by late 1942. The years in which the novel was written constitute a turning point from the past to the future.

It would be superfluous to treat, in detail, the numerous episodes Berger relates in the novel. These disruptive events have come up time and again for discussion in the works covered thus far. The flight of panic-stricken refugees scrambling to get out of Austria after its capitulation was a natural culmination of occurrences that had occupied a major portion of Remarque's L i e b e   d e i n e n N ä c h s t e n. The situation of the emigrant in France following his escape recalls typical themes of uprootedness, joblessness, and destitution (e. g. , Feuchtwanger's E x i l, Mann's D e r   V u l k a n, Keun's K i n d   a l l e r   L ä n d e r ). In the year leading up to the outbreak of war, Neubach makes several references to the hectic gaiety pervading certain segments of the French population, a situation reminiscent of the narcotized atmosphere distinguishing the morbid tone in Remarque's A r c d e   T r i o m p h e. Neubach's description of life in a French internment camp needs little elaboration. Hasenclever's D i e   R e c h t l o s e n portrays the humiliation and disillusionment felt by those who had considered France to be a nation responsive to the plight of refugees. Berger's cry of protest -- "Wir waren also Z i v i l g e - f a n g e n e. Nicht mehr Flüchtlinge. Einfach Feinde! Hier Feinde und dort Feinde! Sandkörner in den Staatsmaschinen der Völker" (98) -- reiterates the central theme of "Rechtlosigkeit" in Hasenclever's work.

Berger's release from the internment camp on the condition that he serve in the Foreign Legion is merely an extension of his earlier form of existence: "Man war gekommen, um Soldat zu sein, und hatte doch eigentlich nur ein schlechteres

Konzentrationslager mit einem besseren vertauscht" (210). The narrator's unnerving experiences as a Legionaire in the Sahara Desert are unique to the exile novel seen up to this point. Yet they add nothing problematically new to the political turbulence of a wartime environment. His contractual agreement to serve the French nation in this capacity only for the duration of the war becomes a meaningless slip of paper after France's surrender in June, 1941. The Nazified Vichy government regards these soldiers as enemies of Germany and dishonors the agreement by shipping the exiles to a forced labor camp in the desert. When Berger finally returns to the unoccupied French zone to join his wife and child, who in the meantime have been interned by authorities, he becomes a captive of the same kind of bureaucratic machinery that forms the theme of Anna Seghers' T r a n s i t. The harassment by razzias, the constant threat of deportation, the necessity for concealment, application for permits to leave the country, capture by the Gestapo, last-minute release through the intervention of influential contacts, the final closing of the border to Jews and outspoken political enemies, the perilous flight into Switzerland -- the entire scene in Southern France vividly recalls the nightmarish labyrinth in which Seghers' exiles find themselves.

This brief resumé of the external action shows that the novel contributes nothing original to the exile condition from an experiential standpoint. The striking aspect of the work, rather, lies in the character of Berger himself. In contrast to the orthodox Jews whose A h a v e r existence resembles a perpetual Diaspora, Berger is a European Jew, a W e s t j u d e, who renounces all bonds with his past when he is baptized into the Christian faith. This conversion takes place prior to Hitler's march on Austria. Yet he is still compelled to flee as a Jew, a stigma he believed to be removed through his efforts to assimilate into the European community by subscribing to the dominant religion. Thus, in exile, he really finds himself in a kind of Christian Diaspora. The conflict Neubach tries to solve through his narrator is of a religious-cultural nature and can be formulated as follows: the only hope for a peaceful Europe lies in man's respect for humanity based on the Christian principle of love. Despite Berger's conversion to Christianity, he is still branded a Jew, a reality he has to face in Southern France when refused a permit to depart by reason of his heritage. Berger experiences the dilemma of the Western Jew who rejects the traditional beliefs of his descendancy, but whose subsequent Christianization still fails to effect the desired assimilation. Early in the novel he states: "Ich entfernte mich von der jüdischen Religion, obwohl ich einerseits die Tiefe ihrer Weisheit ehrfurchtsvoll begriff, andererseits aber das starre Festhalten an nicht mehr zeitgemässen Gesetzen, den strengen Konservatismus nicht mehr verstand. Ich näherte mich dem Christentum, weil ich die Liebe suchte, obwohl der Rahmen, der das schlichte Bild des Märtyrers umgab, mir zu prunkvoll erschien. Klarheit brachte mir erst eine Nacht in der Sahara. Bis zu dieser Nacht kannte ich wohl Gründe, aber nicht den Grund meines Schrittes, den ich nun unternahm" (18).

The "Grund" underlying Berger's conversion touches on a sensitive religious-cultural issue relating not only to Berger's (and the author's) individual predicament at the moment, but to the situation of assimilated Jews in general once the ludicrous racial myth propagated by fascism has been dispelled in a renewed world of peace. The dramatic scene in the desert, however isolated from the sequence of events presented, is central to an understanding of the novel's didactic quality, suggested in Neubach's hopeful outlook on the future. Berger, the Christianized Western Jew, engages in a debate over the hypocrisy implicit in non-Christianized Western Jewry. In the company of such Jews, fellow Legionaires of Berger, the convert argues for an unconditional commitment to either the West or the East. One is either a European or an orthodox Jew. He criticizes those who ambivalently pay homage to both such greatly divergent traditions. The polarity between the two traditions is clearly established when he states: "Ich betone vorerst, dass ich das Judentum als Nation absolut nicht ablehne. ... Der Charakter einer Nation wird nicht durch die Sprache, noch durch die Rasse, noch durch sonstige Eigenschaften bedingt, sondern durch Erziehung, Lebensgewohnheiten und insbesondere durch den freien Willen derer, die der Nation angehören wollen! Ich will dem Judentum als Nation nicht angehören, weil ich hierzu einfach kein Recht habe. Zur Nation gehören diejenigen, welche Gesetze und Gebräuche der Gemeinschaft zu erfüllen gedenken" (304-05).

Berger denounces the false nationalism of Western Jews who fail to abide by the dictates of a religion to which they profess to belong. He brings to the attention of the group certain European habits they have acquired which contradict the strict laws of Jewish religion and culture:

Du, Philipp, ... schleppst Gebetbuch und Riemen mit dir herum. Das tust du, weil dein Vater es so tat. Aber in Sidi hast du an einem Sabbath ... in einem Restaurant einen ausgezeichneten Schweinebraten gegessen. An anderen Sabbathen sassen wir gemütlich im Bordell, und während eines Gottesdienstes warst du es, der dauernd fortzugehen drängte, weil du ins Kaffeehaus wolltest, um Karten zu spielen. Von dir, lieber Hornstein, nehme ich an, dass du weder Gebetbuch noch Gebetriemen bei dir trägst, wahrscheinlich nicht einmal Hebräisch kannst. Worauf ich hinaus will? Auf das Thema Ost- und Westjuden! Hier liegt der Kern des Judenproblems und auch seine Lösung." (305)

Berger wishes to impress upon his comrades the sharp distinctions dividing the orthodox and European Jews. In his opinion the latter have no right to call themselves Jews because of the non-Jewish culture into which they elect to be assimilate His conversion to Christianity symbolizes a categorical break with the past and, in turn, a "Lösung" of the problem relative to the ambivalent position of the Western Jews. Berger's main point of contention centers on the irreconcilability of co-existing religious cultures. Since Western Europe manifests predominantly a Christian culture, Berger sees the rise of anti-Semitism as an inevitable reaction to beliefs foreign to the overriding religion. Therefore, he recognizes the necessity of providing the orthodox Jewish people with their own homeland. The concept of nation necessarily embodies a way of life organic to the majority of the people comprising it. If two sharply opposed cultures clash, then religious (not racial) discrimination will result for the minority culture:

Die Nation bilden die Ostjuden! Sie fühlen sich in der Diaspora lebend, halten zähe und mit jahrhundertelangen Leidens- und Blutopfern an Glauben und Gesetzen fest. Sie allein sind das Judentum. Ihnen hat die besitzende Welt eine Heimat zu geben. England, Amerika und Russland hätten nicht zusehen dürfen, wie diese Menschen jahrhundertelang gepeinigt wurden. Es gibt einfach keine Ausrede, dass für das jüdische Volk kein Platz auf dieser Welt vorhanden ist. Den gläubigen Juden, die sich zur N a t i o n bekennen, muss ein Land gegeben werden, denn sie verstehen zu verwalten, aufzubauen, zu kolonisieren; sie haben in der Sandwüste von Palästina gezeigt, was sie zu leisten vermögen. Sie haben die Lüge, dass Juden nur Händler sind, ad absurdum geführt, sie haben als Bauern, Pflanzer und Züchter einfach Vorbildliches geleistet. Wenn solche Juden einmal mit einem palästinensischen Pass in der Tasche nach Europa kommen werden, als Gäste, als Reisende, wird kein Antisemitismus sie beleidigen. Antisemitismus wird nur immer dort bestehen, wo Angehörige der anderen Religion als Minderheit unter der Mehrheit leben. Daher wird auch nach diesem Kriege kein Schutz von Bajonetten den Westjuden vor dem unsichtbaren Antisemitismus schützen. Wohl wird man ihn endlich körperlich in Frieden lassen müssen, aber immer wird er nur geduldet sein, wird nie werden können, was er so gerne sein möchte: Franzose, Deutscher, Engländer -- jüdischer Religion. Ihr assimilierten Juden seid eben gar nicht assimiliert. Aus atavistischen Gründen seid ihr zu schwach, um den Glauben abzulegen, den ihr gar nicht mehr befolgt. Ihr schielt mit einem Auge nach dem Volke, unter welchem ihr lebt. Euch schmeckt ein fetter Schweinebraten ausgezeichnet, aber ihr esset ihn am liebsten allein in eurem Kämmerlein, eingedenk des Verbotes, vom unreinen Tier zu essen. Solange ihr aber auch nur innerlich andere Gesetze befolgt oder nach ihnen lebt, wird euch das Volk, unter dem ihr lebt, nicht als zugehörig betrachten. (305-06)

Berger advances the view that discriminatory attitudes will, of necessity, emerge when a nation fears the compromise of its own beliefs through the intrusion of alien ones. The prevention of discrimination can only be effected if this danger does not present itself. And so the convert gives as the solution to the Western Jewish problem: "Nein, schliesslich und endlich ist die Annahme der christlichen Religion die einzige dauernde Rettung!" (306).

The religious debate in the Sahara and the racial discussion transpiring later between a Nazi father and his son in Southern France lend a perspective to the novel that removes it from the factual nature of documentation. In view of the time in which the book was written, Neubach conceivably did not intend for his ideas to have an effect on the immediate exile situation, a period which was gradually drawing to a close by 1943-44. Furthermore, the novel's publishing date (1945) marks the transition from disruption to relative stability in the opening of a new era of peace. It would appear, then, that Neubach was considering the future when he wrote F l u g s a n d. In the dedication he states: "Den Jungen der kommenden Generation aber, berufen, Hüter ihres Jahrhunderts zu werden, möge dieser Bericht einen Begriff geben vom Wahnsinn, der die Welt schändete. Eine Macht, die Nächstenliebe mit Eigenliebe verwechselte, Kadavergehorsam vor den Verstand setzte, die zehn Gebote Moses bespuckte, konnte niemals Grundlage einer neuen menschlichen Ordnung werden" (6). The political discussion between father and son complements the religious one in the desert. In order to prepare European society for the recognition of "former" Jews who desire assimilation, Neubach proceeds to eliminate the racial myth that had given rise to Jewish nonmembership in the Western community thus far. The father, who has come to terms with the fallacy of racial intolerance, proves to his son the irrationality of a belief postulating as "biologische Notwendigkeiten" (352) the liquidation of a social group ruled by "plutokratisch-jüdisch-bolschewistische" elements (352). The elder Nazi points out the illogicality inherent in this juxtaposition: "Und wieso bolschewistisch? Ist diese plutokratische Oberschicht [the capitalist magnates] vielleicht für Gleichmacherei? Oder sind die Juden, denen man nachsagt, geldgierig zu sein, Bolschewisten?" (353). By allowing a N a z i to expose the ruthless myth of his own movement, Neubach lends weight to a recurrent motif in the novel which proclaims man's basic humanity. In the dedication he reveals this didactic purpose in his work: "Denn der Mensch ist gut -- nur schlechte Führung macht schlechte Menschen" (6). The novel's preoccupation with a direct account of the miseries of exile is to be a lesson in man's inhumanity to man. The Nazi father's denunciation of the past anticipates a state of society in which man can live in harmony because he has learned by his mistakes. Once the spirit of humanity has been instilled, discrimination on the basis of race will cease to exist. This sensitive issue seems to be Neubach's main point of concern as a Western Jew. If racial intolerance is allowed to continue, then complete integration into European society can never be achieved, even though a Western Jew may have proven his willingness to assimilate through his conversion to Christianity. Racial discrimination is a negation of the principle of Christian love and charity. Neubach sees, therefore, in the practice of the latter concepts the solution to the assimilation problem of the Western Jew. The religious dispute in the desert and the argument of the Nazi father revealing the inhumanity of fascist racial theory extend beyond the documentary setting of the novel for the purpose of laying down a set of values affecting the future state of man. This transformed Nazi, who by 1942 recognizes the seeds of destruction and downfall inherent in the onetime "invincible" Third Reich, considers the future in terms of a realistic assessment of the past. He warns his son:

> Hoffentlich bist du nicht einer von denen, die nach diesem Kriege am lautesten 'mea culpa' schreien werden. Ich schäme mich schon heute der Deutschen, die bisher aus dem Hitlertum eine Religion machten, die später aber alles Deutsche verdammen und Ravel über Mozart, Dostojewskij über Goethe stellen werden. Die Schuld unserer hysterischen Weiber und brutalen Landsknechte werden wir leider einmal bitter abtragen müssen, das ist gewiss. Hoffentlich tragen wir sie mit Würde! Vernichten wir den Krankheitskeim des Weltbeherrschungstraumes, legen wir in die Herzen unserer geschändeten Jugend den Keim zur Liebe zum Mitmenschen, welche Sprache er auch sprechen möge. Zeigen wir den V e r t r i e b e n e n unser brüderliches Mitleid. Nur so wird Deutschland l e b e n !" (356-57)

In his dedication Neubach fosters a similar view based on learning and moral upbringing: "Lehren wir unseren Kindern sich zu schämen, wenn Unrecht zu Recht wird, der Starke den Schwachen überfällt, der Reiche den Armen demütigt. Und die kommenden Generationen werden sich unserer schämen! Tun sie dies, dann geht die Menschheit endlich einer besseren Zukunft entgegen" (7).

Josef Berger acts as the author's spokesman for the future, conveying Neubach's Christian optimism through his unshakeable faith in the victory of good over evil. The transitional period of exile, as Berger recounts it, is viewed from the standpoint of a misguided humanity. Nazi Germany and the Vichy government stand out as prime examples of "schlechte Führung" (6). Neubach is less concerned about the political factors explaining their emergence. This comes to light in one of the rare cases in which Berger addresses himself to the topic of politics: "Politik war mir jederzeit und in jeder Form ein Greuel. Ich muss sogar eingestehen, dass ich niemals einen Wahlzettel abgegeben hatte, so weit war meine Abneigung gegangen. ... Mein Bewusstsein, immer nur meinem Vaterlande, niemals aber einer seiner Parteien gedient zu haben, hielt mich ab, nun plötzlich Agitator zu werden" (82-83). The Diaspora in which Neubach places his narrator is an indication of the author's apolitical assessment of fascist tyranny as a sort of timeless persecutor. In the Sahara, Berger reflects: "Meines Vaters Erzählung vom Frondienst der Juden in Aegypten klang in meinen Ohren. Vor Tausenden von Jahren schleppten unsere gequälten Vorfahren auf dem gleichen Kontinent die Steine zum Bau der Pyramiden, und heute schleppten wir Nachfahren sie wieder zum Bau einer modernen Pyramide in gestreckter Form [the building of a trans-Sahara highway under forced labor conditions]" (282).

The sequence of episodes appearing in the novel resemble stations of a martyred humanity that has been victimized by an overpowering manifestation of brutality. Cries of protest are usually directed against the flagrant acts of inhumanity, not against their historical causes. Neubach betrays his heritage by really assessing the exile period in terms of the Jewish Diaspora, a condition which subsequently can be overcome only by an unconditional assimilation into a Christianized European society: "Wir Flüchtlinge litten überall, denn der Arme muss überall leiden, und der Mensch ohne Heimat ist der Aermste der Armen. Daher dürfen wir, die wir am meisten gelitten, aufstehen am Tage des Gerichts und den höchsten Richter bitten, ein gerechter Richter zu sein. Das wundert Dich, liebe Freundin, die Du nach allem was ich Dir erzählte, den Schrei nach Rache erwartest? Nein, nicht Rache braucht die Welt, sondern endliche Versöhnung. Nur so wird unser Martyrium den Kindern zugute kommen" (5). Berger's conversion to Christianity and concomitant relinquishment of all traditional bonds are to provide a solution to the Western Jewish problem in a new world receptive to the idea of assimilation on the principle of Christian love and charity.

A discrepancy arises, however, in Neubach's perception of the future when one attempts to reconcile Berger's faith in Christian love and humanity with his insistence on establishing a homeland for orthodox Jews on the premise that European and Jewish cultures can never co-exist. In his assertion, "Antisemitismus wird nur immer dort bestehen, wo Angehörige der anderen Religion als Minderheit unter der Mehrheit leben" (306), Berger is exchanging one form of bigotry (racial) for another (religious). When he finds the "Annahme der christlichen Religion" (306) to be the only solution to the question of Jewish admission into Western society, he concedes a discriminatory attitude, however unintentionally, which contradicts the principles of love and charity professed in Christianity. If, in principle, orthodox Jewry cannot co-exist in harmony with the Christian religions because the latter would not tolerate it, then one must question Neubach's overriding plea for Christian humanity, which is predicated on the assumption that an alien religion will not be present to undermine it. Berger's sincerity about the future of the orthodox Jews as a nation certainly cannot be disputed. That he advocates the removal of the orthodox Jews from the European scene on the necessary grounds of religious intolerance, however, sheds dubious light on his concept of Christianity, a religion to which he subscribes, but only on the condition that it be allowed to reign supreme.

In essence, Neubach's anticipation of a "humane" Europe has not progressed appreciably from traditional discriminatory practices towards the Zionist Jews. He is correct in denouncing fascist persecution of the Jewish people on the basis of race. He is also right in forming the analogy between a people and the nation which it comprises. But until a land can be provided for the establishment and perpetuation of the Jewish nation, the Zionists will continue to sense a state of rejection in the Diaspora, a condition only aggravated by the religious discrimination directed against them. If the author's outlook on the future of Europe had been rooted in genuinely human principles, then it would indeed have reflected a progressive stand. The moral-didactic nature of the novel, predicated throughout on a mere abstract restoration of humanity, would then have taken on almost revolutionary characteristics in the realm of Western Christian culture. A polemicized didacticism, arguing for a true Christianity on a co-existing basis with another religious culture, would have resulted in a view of the future that advocates a less bigoted treatment of the homeless Zionist Jews. As it stands Neubach undertakes, in his enthusiasm for the Christian religion, to erase the stigma attached to Western Jewry by virtue of its Zionist heritage, and in doing so establishes a religious-cultural polarity which carries on a tradition that had originated in the nineteenth century with the so-called Jewish emancipation. The Western discriminatory superiority, in contrast to fascist racial persecution, will simply appear in a more sophisticated and less barbaric guise. In place of the Nazi myth of racial impurity, there will emerge, instead, a kind of chauvinistic European "Volksgemeinschaft" (7) which admits only a member who is a "Produkt ... seiner Umgebung und Erziehung" (7).

## CHAPTER XIII

ROBERT GROETZSCH: WIR SUCHEN EIN LAND

## Inner Emigration in Exile

It is our fortune in being able to locate an exile novel written by a member of the Social Democratic Party. Seeing the problems related to the German exile from the perspective of a non-Marxist Socialist helps to fill the void separating the politically noncommitted liberal camp from the orthodox revolutionary one. The Social Democrat's confrontation with exile produces a special kind of dilemma. In contrast to the nonpartisan bourgeois writer, he in a sense has a responsibility towards liberal intellectualism as well as the revolutionary demands of socialism emerging from the crisis of 1933. We are not speaking here of the left-wing socialists who were discontent with their party leadership in the late 1920's and on into exile. These elements were generally sympathetic to the idea of revolutionary socialism and did not find it too difficult to reformulate their goals along more radical lines. Rather it is the revisionist socialist to whom we are referring, the traditionalist whose bourgeois sensibilities in exile inhibit a reversion to an ideology that regards the masses as the true opponent of Nazism. As we will see in Wir suchen ein Land (1936), the idea of socialism as it pertains to the anti-Hitler working class becomes problematical in light of the author's unwillingness (or inability) to apply it in concrete historical terms.

In 1933, Robert Groetzsch made his exodus into exile along with a number of his compatriots after the S.P.D. was officially outlawed by the Nazis. Prior to the fall of the Republic, he was chief editor of the Dresdner Volkszeitung. Afterwards, he continued his journalistic work and also turned to literary writing. In addition to Wir suchen ein Land, two other works of rather minor significance were written: a kind of documentary, Gerechtigkeit: 14 Bilder aus einem Freiheitskampf (1936), and a second novel, Tormann Bobby (1938). Groetzsch was exiled in Czechoslovakia until 1938 and then moved on to France, where he remained until 1940. The last six years of his life were spent in the United States.

This sketchy data says nothing about Groetzsch personally, but information collected about the life of his journalistic and literary mentor might. Franz Diederich (1) was educated in the natural sciences and ethnography before joining the socialist movement as an exponent of the Darwinian school. He became a member of the S.P.D. in 1885 and began, at that time, his journalistic activities with various workers' newspapers. His subsequent encounter with Friedrich Ebert in Bremen ostensibly played a role in the more liberal course he was to pursue henceforth. In Bremen he was involved in the activities of the Goethegesellschaft until 1903 when he moved to Dresden and took over the editorship of the Sächsische Arbeiterzeitung. It was here that he began promoting journalistic talent from the ranks of the Workers' Youth Movement (Arbeiterjugendb e w e g u n g) of which Robert Groetzsch was a member. Diederich was apparently well versed in the works of German classicists and the V o r m ä r z. His published anthologies on Hölderlin, Goethe  Heine, and the obscure dramatist Adolf Glassbrenner show his concern as a liberal socialist for all stratums of society in literature. In Dresden he seems to have undertaken the task of educating his proletarian followers in a liberal, humanistic spirit. Like most S. P. D. members of the old school, Diederich's affinity with the working class was imbued with a sense of morality and ethics. The political outlook of his new writers was to reflect the principles of liberal socialism fostered by the bourgeois Socialist leaders. Thus the idea of class conflict gave way to the idea of liberal social democracy within a class structure. In W i r  s u c h e n  e i n  L a n d there is ample evidence showing that Groetzsch had assimilated many of the ideas of his old teacher, ranging from an interest in science (geology, ethnography) to purely esthetic endeavors.

The early exile scene in Groetzsch's novel is portrayed in various run-down refugee homes alongside a river on the Bohemian frontier. The group depicted, all political exiles, form what is called "Herkner's Kolonne," (2) a designation characterizing the migrant life these refugees lead. Later joined by the artist-journalist Justus and the university student Eva, the Kolonne refrains from demonstrating the anti-fascist spirit they had once fostered in Germany. Groetzsch "farms them out" to a peaceful rural area divorced from the bustling political activity of other comrades in urban centers.

The backgrounds of most of the Kolonne seem to have one thing in common: a kind of political anarchy. Ernst had fled Germany after assaulting a leader of the Hitler youth; Herkner, an S. P. D. worker, had fled to Czechoslovakia after giving some young SA upstarts a thorough thrashing; Peter and Paul also had to escape because of their assault on an SA leader in a Nazi work camp; Frosch, a former member of the R e i c h s b a n n e r, was forced to flee after being implicated in a local coup; Moses finds himself in exile because of his racial background and also due to his alignment with the R e i c h s b a n n e r.

In most cases Groetzsch stresses the individual act of resistance rather than a collective one. The emigrants are workers, both young and old, whose motives for going into exile spring from an elemental predisposition to fight. The only reference to any organizational means of resistance is the one made to the R e i c h s b a n n e r. Yet this group was not founded upon the principle of worker solidarity, but was largely a paramilitary organization established to defend the liberal ideas of freedom and democracy during the remaining days of the Weimar Republic. The only worker showing direct party affiliation is Herkner. But his reason for fleeing was spontaneous and retaliatory too; it was not based on any organizational or ideological effort, but arose on impulse. Like the others, his revolt was instinctively directed against the abusers of nature.

Throughout the novel Groetzsch avoids treating the proletarian Kolonne as a unified collective body. A descendant of the old order who persists in viewing the masses as a body to be integrated into capitalist society, not as one which opposes it in terms of the class struggle, Groetzsch advocates a kind of precapitalist socialism in which natural simplicity and a primitive naiveté form the basis of collectivism. This Rousseauistic view of the proletariat could be interpreted as a reaction to efforts being made by left-wing socialists and communists to enlighten the workers at home and in exile about the revolutionary role of their mission against Nazism. The Sopade, the exiled executive branch of the S. P. D. , and other older party liberals like Groetzsch could not accept a form of resistance which perceived the struggle in Germany along these lines. This situation was especially tense in Czechoslovakia, the country providing a haven for the majority of political exiles until 1938.

Groetzsch separates his political escapees from the ideological battles being waged elsewhere in order to preserve a condition of the worker as it existed prior to the so-called Entfremdung produced by the division of labor. The term "work" (or "worker") takes on special significance in the novel. It is not displayed in a context related the united anti-fascist front, which is how it is applied in Fritz Erpenbeck's Emigranten. The qualitative social connotation of the term, rather, has been taken over by an inherent quantitative one -- that of productivity, growth, and development. It implies also a direct participation in the workings of nature. The worker interacts with elemental forces, becomes a part of them, molds them into something useful. The scenes along the river do not evince the quasi-existential predicament of exile that appears, at times, in other novels. The common exile themes of uprootedness, longing, homelessness are compensated for by a primitive drive to activity. Groetzsch rechannels the energies of these exiles into unpolitical activity which acts as a temporary substitute for the loss of homeland.

Rather than confront the exile condition as a political phenomenon, Groetzsch treats it in accordance with recurring laws of nature. The Hitler tyranny and its opposition are not so much a reflection of antagonistic political groupings as they are of the perpetual struggle between the productive and destructive forces in man and nature. The vicissitudes of emigrant life relate symbolically to seasonal changes, the transitory flow of water, the growth and dying of nature's products -- all of which create an illusion of both permanence and change. The hardships, uncertainty, and privation under which the Kolonne labors are countered by its determination to make the best of things, by its productivity and simple belief in man's constructiveness. Constancy and turmoil, productivity and dying, guide the destinies of these exiles in a way that the laws of nature are subject to conflicting forces. The treatment of exile in terms of natural philosophy is unique up to this point, for the historical situation as it relates to the future is now seen in a context other than socio-political or ideological.

The cyclical nature of the universe with its alternation between temporality and permanence is symbolized by the threefold appearance of the raft bearing identical passengers over an extended period. The Kolonne changes its habitat three times in the novel, but always along the bank of the same river that flows into Germany. The emigrants' encounter with the raft is connected metaphorically to the cyclical nature of their existence at the riverbank. They meet the raft as they are about to depart from their first home; it appears again when they are settled in the "Spinne"; and it mysteriously emerges at the end when they move on to their third home. The river, linking the present with the past, the emigration with home, implies a transitory condition of exile, one which will not prevail indefinitely. The exiles' perseverance and will to turn a desperate situation into a useful one suggests, in turn, a sustaining quality which will survive the hardships brought on by the corruption of tyranny (or, symbolically, by the more harmful forces of nature). Their capacity for productivity amidst the discomforts of exile enables them to impose stability on the uncertainty created by Nazi barbarism: "Vor einem Jahre wurde euch dies Gestade hier zur zweiten Heimat. Euer Vaterland hat euch misshandelt und verstossen. Mit nackter Brust kamt ihr, abgekämpft und verfolgt: mit ebenso nackter Brust werdet ihr morgen von der Villa Wanja scheiden. " (3) In each habitat the emigrants go about building order out of disruption, after which they are forced to leave and begin anew. The first refuge, the Villa Wanja, was found in a neglected condition ("leer, verfallen," 8). After a year's time it was molded into a livable domicile ("das Haus hatten sie gereinigt, verjüngt, erneuert," 8). Once the house is made habitable again ("das urbargemachte Haus," 9), the owner sells it and the exiles move on. Towards the end of their stay in the Villa, the mother Gusti makes a remark that illuminates the harmony brought about between man and nature through work: "Es ist nicht leicht, dreissig Mann immer bei Laune zu halten, wenn keiner weiss, wie lange er die Frucht der Arbeit ge- niessen darf" (12). In the second home the cycle begins to repeat itself ("eine ver- fallene, alte Spinnerei! Neue Dreckarbeit, neue Ungewissheit," 12). Again construc- tive work restores order out of ruin. The innate drive to productivity sustains the exiles through each phase of migration. At the end of the novel we see the Kolonne about to set out a third time in search of a haven: "Ein neues Heim war in Sicht. Weiter oben am Flusse, einsam und verloren zwischen zwei kleinen Orten. Der Besitzer in Prag. Leer stand das einsame kleine Haus; ein Einbruch war auch schon verübt worden. Reif für eine Besatzung. Der Garten verfallen, na ja, ihr kennt das" (229). Throughout the work Groetzsch directs the energies of his exiles into activities which detract from the idea of the working class as a political unit conscious of its historical role in the current period of oppression.

Accordingly, the position the exiles take towards Hitler's hegemony is pre- dicated on a humanity-nature relationship. Fascist Germany is not perceived as an exploitative or totalitarian power, but (cf. Marion in D e r  V u l k a n) as an eruption of the corrupt, destructive side of nature. In Germany, Herkner had supervised the construction of a playground until it came under the control of the Nazis. The theme of taming the unbridled elements of nature through humane efforts is contrasted with the abuse of these elements through barbaric intrusion. In retrospect, Herkner visualizes the playground as a "geschändeter Sportplatz" (18) after its confiscation by the Nazis. A parallel is drawn to the present situation in exile in which the wilderness surrounding the "Spinne" is to be tamed in a man- ner similar to the episode recounted in Germany: "Der Platz, auf dem Herkner zu- hause gewesen, der hatte einst noch etwas wilder ausgesehen als das Gelände bei der Spinne" (25). The workers who had joined together in Germany to mold a wilderness into a community is related to the image of the Kolonne working the soil and renovating each dilapidated house in the move from one shelter to the next: "Es waren nur zwei Dutzend Männer und junge Burschen, die da tagaus, tag- ein schaufelten, karrten, hämmerten, walzten, aber jeden Tag wurde ein neues Stück geglättet. Menschen, die unter Untätigkeit litten, hatten ein Feld der Gemein- schaftsarbeit gefunden" (25-26). The unity of man with nature through the medium of work is that which creates a collective body. The social note of the novel does not emanate from class struggle, but suggests a preindustrial environment in which man is not estranged from the benefits of his labors by exploitation or inequitable return. The nonpolitical collective Groetzsch describes in Germany reflects a sense of comradeship attained through a cooperative communion with nature: "Hier auf ihrem Sportplatz war Sonne, Luft, Kameradschaft" (26); "hier lebte Gemeinschaft gleichstrebender Menschen" (27). Humanity, mutual respect, love, justice are virtues evolving naturally from work that is beneficial to all. Groetzsch sets out to re-create this idyllic setting in Bohemia. The proletarian members of the Kolonne do not acquire a sense of class identity and solidarity as a result of the current political crisis. The author insures that all indications of defiance and disorder are subdued, funneled into other areas. A picturesque, rustic setting is thus established despite the material hardships plaguing the exiles.

The recurrent motif of an innocent "nakedness" is frequently evoked as a sign of Groetzsch's design to render his workers politically harmless. Time and again we see the younger members frolicking about in the river, carefree and immune to the reality of their situation. Indeed, it would appear that Groetzsch fears any kind of activity which would tend to disrupt the harmony between man and nature. When Eva appears on the scene, Gusti becomes worried over the possible harmful effect her presence could have on the innate drives of the vigorous youngsters. Again the sublimating function of work is the answer to this predicament. When the neighboring villagers enlist the aid of the emigrants in laying a stone terrace for a vineyard, Herkner quickly sees this as an emotional outlet for the impulsive boys: "Die Burschen brauchten Arbeit, sonst meuterten sie" (83). Passion in all its forms is repressed in the novel, kept in check, lest it become too "revolutionary." One wonders if Groetzsch is not using as a literary model the post-Romantic period of the Biedermeier, which saw in homely simplicity and idealized nature an outlet for the sense of uneasiness created by the political injustice reigning at the time.

The figure of Eva would seem to bear this out. Groetzsch makes every attempt to avoid the possibility of a direct political confrontation in exile. All his characters are political opponents of Hitler; this factor plays no role, however, in their actions later on. The young members of the Kolonne happen upon a political newspaper Eva had read that bears the caption: "Das Volksrecht ... Drei Pfeile am Kopfe" (33). They immediately draw the conclusion that she is a "Genossin," implying a collective political opposition to the Hitler regime. But Groetzsch, in his apparent reluctance to develop the implications of this reference, lets his heroine retreat to her world of rare stones so that she may pursue her doctoral research.

The description of the smug, comfortable surroundings housing Eva and her sister Thekla betrays the literary heritage underlying Groetzsch's escape to the picturesque and idyllic: "Im Garten unten lärmten die Vögel, die alten Biedermeiermöbel ringsum schliefen. Von der Wand schauten Eva's verstorbene Eltern. Der Vater bärtig und mit schütterem Haar, die Mutter vollbusig, die beiden Töchter auf ihren Knien -- ein altes Familienbild, beinahe ein anderes Jahrhundert" (65). Eva's romantic search for the essence of stones ("die Seele der Steine," 59) reflects Groetzsch's attempt to shroud reality in idealized sentimentality: "Aber Eva litt eben unter romantischer Ueberspanntheit, ein Prinz sollte es sein, schon als Kind hätte sie Märchen gedichtet, die Prinzen wohnten alle in Zauberschlössern und unterirdischen Palästen, deren Wände aus Krystallen, Edelsteinen, Korallen und märchenhaft flimmernden Steinen bestanden" (69). Groetzsch is so intent upon evoking an illusion of harmony that one cannot help but recall certain scenes in Adalbert Stifter's works which view any sort of passion as disruptive. In a realistic setting the attractive student would not have enjoyed such an innocent comradery with the youthful members of the "Spinne." In this harmless relationship between the sexes Groetzsch merely reiterates his intention in the novel -- to keep unbridled nature in check: "Nett waren die Burschen, bisschen kräftig manchmal im Wort, dafür natürlich, unverbildet, unaufdringlich, Kameraden. Wenn sie sich in den Weiden umkleidete, hielt jeder mindestens fünfzig Meter Abstand" (70).

The unpolitical characterization of "political" exiles shows the ambivalence of the S.P.D. writer who is for the downfall of Hitler but against the political organization of German workers in exile. Admittedly, scenes do appear in which a propaganda link between socialist elements in Germany and Czechoslovakia is discussed, but to the exclusion of any emigrant involvement. Ignaz, a Czech-German from the Sudetenland, undertakes the task of passing onto German contacts at the border political leaflets to be disseminated among the opposition in the Third Reich. The exiles refrain from participating directly in this mission, expressing merely their moral support for its success without helping to insure it themselves. Instead, they give a romantic character to the present situation. Groetzsch instills in his workers a nostalgia for the homeland that springs from his own tendency to sentimentalize. His refinement of the proletariat, in effect, insures their political inactivity and hence his own artistic freedom. And so the workers sing Bohemian folk songs which serve to reenforce the unproblematic, benign role in which the author places them:

> Wo ist mein Heim? Mein Vaterland?
> Wasser rauscht durch grüne Triften.
> Kiefernwald auf Fels und Klüften.
> Frühlingsblumen auf der Flur.
> Paradies ist die Natur:
> Das ist meine schöne Heimat:
> Böhmerland, mein Vaterland! (132-33)

In line with Groetzsch's Social Democratic humanism, there are historical reasons that explain the political noninvolvement of his proletarian exiles. W i r s u c h e n   e i n   L a n d was published in 1936, which means that it was probably being written around the time the People's Front was proclaimed at the Seventh World Congress of the Comintern in August of 1935. This proclamation advocated the unification of all Nazi opponents, regardless of ideology. Many liberal Social Democratic exiles were sceptical about a plan originating in Moscow which sought the international organization of the working class as the revolutionary nucleus of a popular front. Although the events of the novel precede the era of the People's Front, it is conceivable that Groetzsch chose to portray his exiles in a passive role in anticipation of these later developments. On the other hand, his manner of portrayal could have been a reaction to the actual period reflected in the novel.

Prior to the People's Front era, the communists in Prague initiated a campaign to sectarianize all socialist workers from their S. P. D. liberal leadership in an attempt to organize a revolutionary united front from below. This movement alone would have been inducement enough for Groetzsch to create the harmless setting he does in Wir suchen ein Land. When we discuss Erpenbeck's Emigranten in the next chapter -- a novel dealing with the revolutionary consolidation of all workers from below -- it will become plain that the liberal S. P. D. body, indeed, had a problem on its hands in the early exile period.

This background helps to elucidate the historical motive for Groetzsch's unpolitical characterization of his escapees. Such an idyllic, harmless portrayal could then be defined as an expedient retreat applicable to the moment. There are also philosophical reasons explaining this idealized treatment of exile. Here we must again draw on indirect evidence to explain Groetzsch's artistic position. Gerhart Seger, a former Social Democratic delegate to the Reichstag in Leipzig and, like Groetzsch, a political journalist has made some revealing comments about the incapacitation of the exiled political opposition which could represent a trend of thought among certain liberal socialists. In his Reisetagebuch eines deutschen Emigranten (1936), such statements as "zur Untätigkeit verurteilt am Rande des Weltgeschehens" (4) and "Aussenseiter der Geschichte" (5) appear to border on an existential predicament but actually betray a very real problem of the political emigration. The partisan anti-fascist exiles did, in fact, stand "am Rande des Weltgeschehens." By 1936, the Third Reich had erected such an effective police network for dealing with the opposition that any further resistance could only be undertaken piecemeal. This meant, in turn, that propaganda materials smuggled into Germany by exiled political groups were, more often than not, intercepted by Nazi agents. Seger's pessimistic view is understandable when considered in this context. He goes on to say: "Es entsteht das drückende, bedrückende Gefühl, dass man aus dem Strome des Weltgeschehens ausgeschaltet ist; heimatlos zu sein bedeutet in diesem Zusammenhange zugleich -- mindestens für eine lange Zeit -- ziellos zu sein." (6) In contrast to the communists, who along with the left-wing socialists had perceived the confrontation with fascism as an ideological struggle which would one day see the workers as the sole governing body of Germany, the liberal socialists were not about to subscribe to an ideology which openly pitted the proletariat against the bourgeoisie. Seger makes a definite distinction between the real forces of opposition and those who are compelled by their physical isolation to sit out the struggle: "Der Kampf selbst, die Entscheidung darüber, was nach Hitler in Deutschland kommt und getan werden kann, wird nicht in der Emigration gefällt, sondern das kann nur in Deutschland sich abspielen." (7)

These statements lend insight into Groetzsch's philosophical-esthetic position in Wir suchen ein Land. He creates a character in his own image in Justus, a former editor of an S. P. D. newspaper in Germany who has taken up literary writing in exile. In the novel he is working on, he voices Groetzsch's own opinions on society and history. Justus' views on art really set the theoretical tone of Wir suchen ein Land. He is writing a book about "die sozialen Träume und Schäume der Menschen" (42). It is to be a roman à clef dealing with the parvenu Creon, the "Urtyp des skrupellosen Demagogen" (42). The figure of the artist-intellectual provides us with the philosophical key to Groetzsch's idyllic treatment of exiles. In his novel, Justus perceives historical figures in cyclical terms and envisions Hitler's prototype Creon as a recurrent destructive force in nature ("Es war alles schon dagewesen," 42). Justus looks at history as an antithetical play of forces, an eruption, in part, of the catastrophic elements of nature, without examining the specific social factors that give a rational explanation for the unleashing of such forces: "Versunkene Zeiten tauchten aus unergründlichen Schächten, stürmten auf ihn ein, stiessen mit der Gegenwart zusammen" (420). Justus and his creator both assess the present state of turmoil in Germany as a repetition of the past; only names, places, and dates have changed.

Groetzsch's artistic partiality to a kind of G e f ü h l s s o z i a l i s m u s is in perfect keeping with his ethical, liberal tradition which views history as a clash between human values and their barbaric perversions, not between conflicting class elements in society. The leading motif of the novel appears at both the beginning and the end: "die Ahnung vom ewigen Kreislauf der Dinge ... und dass alles einmal wiederkehrt" (33, 229-30). This leitmotif influences the structure of the work and explains the author's approach to art as a revelation of timelessness and universality. Groetzsch's retreat to the idyllic suggests a nurturing of an idealistic tradition until such time as the current barbaric threat has run its cyclical course and has been overtaken, once again, by the humane forces of history.

In the politically unconcerned bourgeois socialists Justus and Eva, certain class issues are called to mind which are reminiscent of the unstable political structure of the Weimar Republic. Younger socialists in exile had shifted to the far left b e c a u s e they remembered how ineffective their party was in regulating the social problems of Germany. Liberal, democratic socialism carried little weight when the masses went hungry. As an exponent of the old school, however, Groetzsch persists in keeping things the way they were, holding them intact, until liberal social democracy can be reinstated. In Justus' ambivalent remark -- "Die Menschen brauchen soziale Träume, lasst sie vernünftig träumen" (75) -- we see the problem of the liberal Social Democrat who views the masses not in terms of a material, but a bourgeois-ethical socialism which obfuscates the class issue. Justus' statement is an interesting example of intellectual acrobatics, but it suggests a social setting that is quite nebulous, to say the least. Eva's reaction to Justus' words of wisdom reflects Groetzsch's own tendency to escapism in the novel: "Ausserdem war es schön, zu hören, wie er Gedanken auf Gedanken türmte. Endlich jemand in diesem Neste, mit dem man reden konnte, ohne dass ein abgegriffenes politisches Flugblatt draus wurde" (75). An earlier comment about Justus himself attests to the attitude Groetzsch holds throughout: "In der Spinne kam Justus erheblich billiger weg als bisher, zahlte einen bescheidenen Satz, brauchte sich nicht an der Kollektivarbeit zu beteiligen, konnte seiner Schreiberei obliegen" (54).

Here the political disharmony between the bourgeois and the proletarian socialist comes to light. The author had already made the transition from a material to a liberal-socialist philosophy when he came under Franz Diederich's tutelage. It would appear, on the one hand, that the strong representation of workers in the novel intimates an affinity that Groetzsch feels out of sympathy as a former member of this class himself. On the other hand, he cannot portray the image of the proletariat in a manner consistent with his earlier tradition due to his political development to the right-center. In his treatment of the exile he takes a downright conservative position, going as far to the right as limits will allow in order to insure the preservation of a socialism that purports to eliminate class antagonisms by an overriding ideal of humanity.

In the portrayal of the two bourgeois socialists, intellectual endeavors are merely academic; in the depiction of the workers, an idyllic nature setting constitutes the unrealistic counterpart of an intellectual elitism. Groetzsch's novel reveals the problem of the older S. P. D. writer unable to reconcile an idealistic tradition to the current struggle of the working class. As a liberal and a socialist the author's tone is understandably sympathetic to both the Kolonne and the two intellectual outsiders. Yet these parties go their own way, never establishing a common ground. The politico-ideological foundation of social reality, as it ought to be represented by the working element, remains obscured and oversimplified. Correspondingly, the bourgeois idealism of Justus is just as unconvincing for lack of a realistic basis. The novel's leitmotif, which postulates a cyclical pattern in history between the conflicting harmonizing and disruptive forces in nature, is illustrated in Groetzsch's attitude towards art and the masses. Elemental nature, as shown in the interaction of man with his environment through the medium of work, must necessarily be kept in check if the more progressive elements of Geist (which could become too revolutionary) fail to interact. By the same token, if the artist confines his idea of humanity to the intellect alone and fails to integrate this idea into the social element present in the novel, then one cannot agree with Justus more when he envisages for the future an eternal Nebeneinander of Natur and Geist: "Neben der ewigen Rohheit, neben der unvergänglichen Dummheit gibt es eine Elite, für die man lebt. Und auf die Dauer bestimmt diese den Gang der Geschichte" (97).

Groetzsch avoids the possible repercussions that could result from the creation of a thinking proletariat in the novel. He reserves intellectual autonomy for the bourgeois factions intent on upholding a tradition that could be jeopardized if the masses were to unite on an international scale. Groetzsch's motives for isolating his workers stem from the urgency of the historical situation as well as a liberal philosophy bent on self-perpetuation. The portrayal of a proletariat which lacks a political awareness of its historical mission in the struggle against fascism must be considered in these contexts. A thinking proletarian class is a disruptive one in Groetzsch's eyes. And so he removes any tendency to socially-directed intellectual activity by involving his Kolonne in the harmless workings of nature. The nature image which Justus sees embodied in Gusti, the mother of the Kolonne, echoes Groetzsch's aim in keeping the activities of the workers in check: "Das ist Gusti. Die ist richtig. Von allen in der Spinne trägt sie mit am Schwersten, aber sie weiss alles das in den grossen Kreislauf einzuordnen, ohne nachzudenken. Sie ist Natur" (129).

## CHAPTER XIV

## FRITZ ERPENBECK: EMIGRANTEN

### Programmed Left-Sectarianism in Early Exile

In Communist emigrant circles, particularly in Czechoslovakia, efforts were already being made in the early part of the German exile to launch a front campaign against fascist tyranny -- to the exclusion of bourgeois humanists and Social Democrats, however. The years preceding the official proclamation of the People's Front at the Seventh World Congress of the Comintern in August, 1935, marked a period of programmed sectarianism which saw the hard-line adherents of Party policy concentrating their aims on mustering a united front from below. The old disagreements that had split the Communists and Social Democrats into hostile camps during the Weimar Republic became even more aggravated in the early exile as a result of renewed claims made by both parties on the rightful leadership of the German working body. Thus official Communist policy in 1933-34 was not to unite all anti-fascist elements, but only the workers in their revolutionary struggle against the Hitler regime along with its "reactionary" complement. This included the various remnants of the old order: the Reichswehr, the monarchists, the petty bourgeoisie, the intelligentsia, and above all the "social fascist" leadership. For it was this party, the S.P.D., that had rivaled the Communists in their efforts to lead the workers, and if there was anything the latter wanted to prevent after 1933, it was certainly the perpetuation of a divided proletariat.

Fritz Erpenbeck's novel Emigranten (Russian, 1937; German, 1939) reflects the left-sectarian position of the German Communist Party executive when it was still pursuing a unity-action program from below. In 1934, Erpenbeck began writing the novel while he was still in Prague. He completed it the following year in the Soviet Union, where he remained for the duration of the exile. The novel probably reached completion prior to the Comintern's official announcement of the People's Front. It exhibits no evidence that would point to the liberal alignment strategy promoted later by Moscow. Erpenbeck holds to the earlier Communist position which still regarded functionaries of the fallen Republic as enemies of the working class. In line with this position, the true leadership of the workers rested with the Communist Party as the only socialist organization that represented their best interests. By winning Social Democratic workers over to its side, both in exile and through the German underground, the German Communist Party hoped to gradually realize a conclusive ideological split between the Social Democratic leaders and their members, and thereby render fruitless any further attempts by this party to establish a potent rival organization.

These party politics create the historical setting for Emigranten, which takes place in Prague and depicts all aspects of the fractionalized political emigration. The one group attesting to any kind of anti-fascist unity at all is the German

Communist Party. In contrast to this following, the city literally swarms with nonpartisan liberals and conservatives, labor union members, pacifists, Trotskyites, National Socialist members of the Black Front, and irresolute Social Democratic functionaries, all of whom emerge as obvious opponents of the concept of a united front from below.

The task Erpenbeck undertakes in Emigranten is of an ideological-formative nature. In attempting to build a unified front of all workers, he must momentarily dispense with a hard-line dogmatism that could have a dissuasive effect on the newcomers. Erpenbeck shows the integration of the Social Democratic labor force into the Communist Party to be a process of learning and development. On the one hand he must "liberalize" the more radical elements of the Party to make them receptive to outsiders; on the other he must turn outside workers into good Communists without sounding too doctrinaire.

The innate human qualities of the proletariat take precedence, for the time being, over party authoritarianism. Erpenbeck's image of the worker as one who is selfless and courageous, who gives of himself for the benefit of others, and who willingly endures hardship is important to the idea of a united proletarian front, in which certain fundamental ideological differences between the two socialist parties must be overcome in the struggle against a common oppressor. Erpenbeck portrays Jakob as a model of proletarian unity. Although a worker with no party affiliation, he is still singled out as the ideal proletarian who places collective goals above individual ones. It is this "Genosse" who, in the opening scene, smuggles the Social Democrat Karl Damrow, the nonpartisan leftist Oskar Gundel, and the Communist Peter Röhl across the Czech border and then returns to Germany to assist others in their escape.

As a Marxist, Erpenbeck works consistently within the framework of a political philosophy that postulates as inevitable the disintegration of the bourgeois class and the resultant rise of the working man. But the condition of exile, which to the worker means an abrupt break with comrades and jobs in the homeland, can produce bickering and dissension even among the most devoted of revolutionaries. Erpenbeck, therefore, sees the emigration as a test of determination and courage for the proletariat. Discord within the party itself and the differences that traditionally had separated the two socialist camps must be reconciled if a viable force is to be mustered against the spreading fascist tyranny.

The Communist Peter Röhl provides the ideological stimulus for proletarian unity. The issue of a united front of the workers produces frequent clashes between him and Max and Inge, two loyal Communists who are suspicious of any acceptance of outsiders into party ranks. Their nonconciliatory views conflict repeatedly with Peter's plan to join forces with the neighboring Social Democratic refugee home. Max still harbors animosity towards members of the opponent party. He indiscriminately blames the workers for the failures of the Social Democratic Party during the reign of the Republic and fears the dissemination of reformist ideas through an alignment with this group. Acting just as intolerantly, Inge is concerned with the formation of a Communist front only, not a general united front from below, which would include Social Democratic laborers as well as certain select intellectuals, members of the Social Workers' Party, and proletarian nonpartisans.

The recurrent motif of "Abgrenzung" emerges from this insistence on isolation and it becomes Peter's task to counteract it. In the Communist refugee home he makes the members aware of the fact that a proletarian united front had failed in Germany and that now the time was ripe for its implementation. If this is to be effected, the Communist Party, which is to spearhead the united front, must first become cognizant of its role in exile. Peter's critical speech promoting revolutionary unity of all proletarian forces in Germany and on the outside sets the tendentious tone the author employs throughout the work:

> Man hat uns aus der Feuerlinie zurückgenommen, hat uns sozusagen in die Etappe geschickt. Aber sind wir deshalb keine Soldaten des Klassenkampfs mehr? Gewiss doch. Und müssen wir nicht eines Tages unsern Kameraden drüben Rechenschaft ablegen können, wenn sie uns fragen: Und ihr, was habt ihr getan, während wir in der Feuerlinie standen? Nein, Kameraden, ... unsere Emigration darf nicht Selbstzweck werden! Wir haben hier die Gelegenheit, besser als unsere heldenhaft kämpfenden Genossen drüben, unsere Waffen zu schärfen, zu lernen und wieder zu lernen! Wir haben die Gelegenheit, ihren Kampf von hier aus durch unsere Arbeit zu unterstützen. Darum nochmals, Kameraden: Arbeitet, lernt, es wird der Tag kommen, wo euch eure Klasse ruft, den einen früher, den andern später; dann muss die Spreu vom Korn geschieden sein, dann sollt ihr nicht nur ebenso gute Kämpfer wie die Genossen drüben -- nein, ihr müsst, sonst war eure Emigration sinnlos, geschulterte Kämpfer sein ..., nur deshalb hat uns unsere Klasse für kurze Zeit aus der Feuerlinie beurlaubt. (1)

In theory, the establishment of a united front from below ought not to have presented a great deal of difficulty in the emigration because all workers were bound together by a common destiny: exile. Erpenbeck recognizes, however, that the transition from homeland to exile does not necessarily indicate a corresponding change from division among workers' ranks to proletarian solidarity. The tendentious design in the novel lies in the reeducation of the workers in the principle of class struggle. This means ridding the two major parties of old prejudices and scepticisms that had been carried over into exile. The theme of "Abgrenzung" within the Marxist ranks stands in contrast to that of "Abwarten" among the body of Social Democratic workers. Whereas some of the Marxist workers persist in clinging to a traditional orthodox policy that had defied conciliation, members of the Social Democratic Party continue to follow the guidelines set down by its liberal leadership.

To remedy this problem, Peter functions in a liaison capacity between the Communist and Social Democratic workers. Through his spokesman, the author attempts to clear the air of dogmatism by stressing the revolutionary role of the worker per se, and not so much the leadership of the Communist Party in matters governing the actions of the proletariat. Once the character of the worker has been demonstrated along the principle of collective participation in a common effort, then one can begin demanding party loyalty (the political atmosphere describing Stalin's regime at the time!). The workers are to sense a purpose in their emigration. They must be provided with a constructive assignment, not only to relieve their boredom and material hardship, but more importantly to prepare them for the future. And so Peter undertakes to bring the parties together and to establish a propaganda link with comrades in the Third Reich by involving the exiles in the preparation of illegal material.

In his dealings with the Social Democrats, Peter tactfully goes about the task of molding the proletariat into a unified body. Erpenbeck shows this educational process to be a painstaking one. The Social Democrat Karl Damrow, who had escaped with Peter across the border, persists in complying with the directives of his party. In their discussion over proletarian unity, Karl refuses, at first, to follow the example set by some of his comrades in the refugee home. Seven workers had been severely reprimanded by their party for speaking out in favor of a unity-action program with the Communist exiles, and Peter tries to persuade Karl to stand up in defense of this proposal. To make matters more difficult, the director of the refugee home, a liberal Social Democrat (cf. Groetzsch), takes a dim view of any kind of collaboration with the Marxist refugee home. Karl is not about to overstep authority. He believes in carrying out the wishes the Party has expressed, and it is to this point that Peter addresses himself in attempting to win Karl over to the cause: "Aber was ist denn eine Partei? In jeder gibt es Dummköpfe, Bonzen, Bürokraten und sogar Gesindel; selbst von Verrätern und Verbrechern kann sich keine Partei reinhalten, auch keine Arbeiterpartei" (346). If read out of context, this polemic could be construed as a criticism of any party leadership, to include even the Communists. It reflects quite accurately, however, Erpenbeck's strategy in the novel. For purposes of expediency, he places emphasis on the people, and the only way Karl can ever join forces is if he is made to believe that his own leadership is usurping the interests of its workers. Even in the speech delivered by Peter earlier, attended only by Communists, Erpenbeck refrains from drawing attention to Party orders. Rather, the stress now lies on the workers as a class, and class solidarity can be achieved only if authoritarian party politics are momentarily suspended. (2) Only in this way can the extremes of "Abgrenzen" and "Abwarten" be synthesized.

In the discussion between Peter and Karl, the groundwork for proletarian unity has at least been laid. Peter impresses upon his socialist comrade the need for solidarity and mutual cooperation, for Party regulations only mislead the workers and engender a division of interests. Peter criticizes Karl for not coming to the aid of the seven workers. He sees this as a breach of trust which stirs up internal disorder among the ranks of the workers. Once again Jakob is cited as a model of the dedicated proletarian. Despite his nonpartisanship, his commendable service to others is still mentioned in reproof of Karl's indetermination.

Throughout the novel Erpenbeck consistently hammers away at those political factions of the emigration which, in principle, tend to alienate the workers from the revolutionary task for which they are destined. The main adversary is, of course, the Social Democratic Party. At the home of the Czech Social Democrat Dr. Albert Šif, Peter and his Communist comrade Hans, the Social Democrat Kurt Hörschel, and the nonpartisan bourgeois Pauline Schöller assemble to debate the united front issue. The three non-Marxists, all liberals who lean to the left, are unsure of where one should place one's loyalties -- with the party or the people. In Peter's analysis of the weaknesses of the Social Democratic Party as an organization imbedded in capitalist tradition, the author's polemic intent once again comes

to the fore. Peter reprimands the Social Democratic traditionalists for entertaining a "Politik des Abwartens, die Hoffnung auf ein Abwirtschaften des Gegners
und vor allem der Wunsch, sich lieber mit der Bourgeoisie, mit den offenen Fein-
den, zu verbünden als mit den Klassengenossen -- mit uns" (364). This criticism
reflects the attitude of the Comintern in the early exile period and explains the
motive behind the German Communist Party's desire to muster a united front
from below. It also explains the author's left-sectarian strategy in the novel: the
split w i t h i n the working class, precipitated in Germany by the bourgeois Social
Democratic leadership, is to be supplanted by a split b e t w e e n the workers as
a reunited whole and the carry-overs of the fallen Republic.

In addition to the remnants of the old order, many anti-Nazi splinter factions
appear which, until they were officially recognized as allies during the People's
Front era, are still considered as indirect advocates of the Third Reich because
their individual interests reflect that class mentality which enabled Hitler to rise
to power with the help of major capitalist enterprises. Here Erpenbeck paints a
totally black and white picture of the early political emigration. Either an escapee
is for the worker and hence the revolutionary struggle against the capitalist forces
of tyranny, or he is abetting the interests of the Nazi regime, however much he
fosters a dissident position.

A third motif, "zersetzen," emerges frequently and points to those political
exiles whose very presence among the workers exerts a disruptive influence.
Erpenbeck carefully chooses the kind of nonpartisan political emigrant to be soli-
cited for the cause of the class struggle, and insures the expulsion of those who
would in any way jeopardize it. Indeed, it is not enough to be merely "links einge-
stellt," which is how Oskar Gundel is described (47-48). A leftist without a
practicable ideology has no place among the revolutionary ranks of the workers.
Gundel had left Germany voluntarily because he was simply fed up with Nazi tactics.
Erpenbeck takes the stand that the political emigration is a forced condition and
refuses to accept the argument that an exile could leave of his own free will. Otherwise he may as well have remained in Germany.

It is in this context that Erpenbeck views a number of political exiles in the
novel. Although they are decidedly anti-Nazi, they are also adverse to the idea of
class struggle, and thus are useless to the cause of the proletariat. The psycho-
analyst Erna Arne expounds sexual theories "auf marxistischer Grundlage" (53),
but does not particularly care to examine their realistic implications in a classless society. The religious pacifist Professor Erwin Horgarth would like to engage
himself politically, but is afraid to. He becomes a lone wolf who eventually commits
suicide out of despair over the fact that no one wants him. It goes without saying
that the Trotskyites command little favor in Erpenbeck's eyes. He rates them on a
par with the Social Democratic leaders because of the position both take toward the
concept of revolution. Whereas the former believe in an anti-Stalin Marxist revolution, the latter aspire to a revolutionary ideal also, but along liberal-humanistic
lines rather than in an anti-capitalist framework.

At the Club House International, a meeting place for Social Democratic
functionaries, journalists, Trotskyites, Nazi spies, and informers, Erpenbeck
illustrates the reasons why the anti-leftist elements of the emigration are destructive ("zersetzend") to the unifying efforts of the working class. While the members

are intellectualizing about the pros and cons of revolution, the private secretary of one of the journalists proceeds to compile an attendance list. This he promptly delivers into the hands of a spy in an adjoining room, who in turn provides same to the editor of a Czech newspaper. The following day the participants of the meeting suddenly read about the agitative revolutionary goals of the local emigration, an undertaking they never would have dreamed of actualizing in the first place. Erpenbeck intends to expose this lot for what it is -- as a group of bickering theorists who exhibit no awareness of the practical side of revolution in terms of class struggle. In 1934-35 public political meetings of this kind were particularly frustrating to the Communist who saw the revolutionary goals of the r e a l opposition placed in jeopardy when they became the object of extreme criticism on the domestic scene. The problem resulting from Communist efforts to organize was that it could attract the attention of the Social Democratic Czech government if carried out indiscreetly. Even this just government was forced to compromise its political hospitality when it suspected agitation among the exiled population. Active leftist opposition to the Hitler regime could smell of internal politics, and this is just what the Czech officialdom wanted to avoid.

In the case of the proletarian Willi Bonsel, a braggart and adventurer who thinks he is serving the cause of the workers by cooperating with members of the National Socialist Black Front, Erpenbeck demonstrates the theme of "zersetzen" within the working class itself. He shows how the front effort can be jeopardized when one of its followers chooses to act on his own initiative. Willi and Dieter von Eckstädt, a Nazi spy posing as a member of the Black Front, conspire to steal anti-fascist letters sent to the Black Front journalist Rudolf Schlözer by his brother in Germany. Schlözer refuses to release the letters for publication for fear of reprisal action against their originator. Willi's intention in confiscating the letters is well-founded, for their public release would expose the truth of Nazi corruption. In his impetuosity, however, he fails to look into the real motives of his accomplice. Eckstädt wants the letters to insure that their contents remain undisclosed and at the same time to use them as a justification for incapacitating Schlözer's brother.

Willi's thirst for action is quenched on another occasion. The Czech newspaper editor who had been printing "dirt" about the political emigrants had issued one falsehood too many. Thinking he is doing his comrades a good turn, Willi takes revenge on the newsman by assaulting him in public. The following interrogation reveals him to be a resident of the Communist refugee home, and the dedicated workers of the united front promptly ostracize him from their ranks due to his imprudence.

Willi's reinstatement later in the novel exemplifies the process of learning that Erpenbeck deems essential to the molding of a united front. The adventurer has benefitted by his mistakes and is now prepared to contribute to the collective effort rather than act on an individual basis. This development unfolds on a general scale as well, revealing the novel's tendentious purpose in molding disparate leftist elements into a monolithic unit. Erpenbeck's design throughout the book had been to change the Social Democratic attitude of "Abwarten" and the Communist attitude of "Abgrenzen" to one of solidarity in the common fight against capitalist oppression. He even goes so far as to include certain leftist-liberal elements in this movement as long as they serve the interests of the united front from below.

The bourgeois Social Democrats Dr. Šif and Kurt Hörschel, and the nonpartisan Czech-German Pauline Schöller ultimately prove their loyalty to a unified political program when they join with Hans and Peter on a perilous mission to intercept a courier before he falls into the clutches of border guards who had been informed of the smuggling mission.

Among the workers of the two political parties a rapprochement has also come about. Karl Damrow finally defies his leaders when they demand the eviction of the seven agitators from the refugee home. His decision to leave with them is a reversal of an earlier attitude of noninvolvement. In the Communist home Max and Inge have renounced their intolerant views and are now prepared to join forces with the Socialist camp. In light of these developments, it would appear that Erpenbeck has accomplished the task he had set for himself: he has brought about the desired schism between a united working body and the fractionalized "reactionary" factions of the Prague emigration.

Yet, if we look at the figures involved in the central event of the novel, the installation of a secret radio transmitter, it seems as though the author contradicts the strategy he had been promoting all along. With the consent of the Communist collective, Hans aligns himself with the bourgeois sympathizer of the Black Front Eugen Dormler for the purpose of exposing the insidious designs of the Nazi government. Dormler, a radio technician and announcer by profession, handles the transmission of information provided by his Communist helper.

Hans' cooperation with the bourgeois element in exile could betray a tendency on Erpenbeck's part to pave the way for the united front from above to be initiated in Moscow when the People's Front campaign was officially announced in late 1935. Such a change in ideological strategy, however, would appear inconsistent with the specific intent of the novel, for the united front from below stood in decided opposition to any kind of working agreement with the liberal groups.

A closer examination of Hans' relationship with Dormler will reveal that Erpenbeck's position in no way deviates from the dominant one he is advocating in the novel. He introduces a Communist into the ranks of the bourgeoisie in order to draw a contrast between anti-fascist undertakings which are collectively organized, and those which are destined for failure because they arise from individual motives. The exponents of the Black Front -- Eckstädt (a disguised Nazi informer), Schlözer, and Dormler -- claim to despise Hitler, but their method of denunciation smacks of a passionate nationalism that seeks restitution in tradition. Schlözer's journalistic campaign to expose Hitler typifies the attitude of the Black Front in general, which had fostered a National Socialism free of the dictatorial heads who presume to represent it: "Reichswehr, freie Gewerkschaften, vom Marxismus gereinigt, streitbarer Katholizismus -- geeinigt und verschmolzen durch uns -- die Schwarze Front! Die Deutsche Revolution!" (225).

Schlözer purports to show up the R e i c h s w e h r as a formidable opponent to the Nazi regime; in actuality it soon played into Hitler's hands. Dormler's antifascist stand is not quite so unrealistic as Schlözer's. In the messages broadcasted, he utilizes propaganda material that is seriously crippling to Hitler's position at home. His death at the hands of Nazi infiltrators (who conspire with Eckstädt to silence the transmitting station) testifies to the damaging effect of his speeches.

Nevertheless, Erpenbeck intends to show that the premise underlying Dormler's activities is fundamentally false, and hence can only work to the detriment of the anti-fascist effort. He portrays the broadcaster as a smug bourgeois who considers the inconveniences imposed on him through exile as a personal affront. Emigration has removed him from the gay, frivolous atmosphere he once enjoyed in Berlin. Accordingly, his exposure of Nazi injustice is motivated more out of the satisfaction derived from revenge than out of political conviction. He and his Communist assistant are alike only insofar as they agree on a mutual adversary. When it comes to the question of means, their positions are diametrically opposed. In the figure of Dormler, the author demonstrates why the struggle against Nazism can only be effective from below. Hans' efforts to enlighten Dormler on Communist ideology and the socialist goals it professes fail to exert an influence in light of a liberal philosophy which rejects, in principle, the subjugation of the individual to the interests of a collective body. Dormler's dissatisfaction with Marxist theory is based on the premise that questions concerning the freedom of the individual remain unanswered. Erpenbeck points out that the element of freedom for which Dormler searches in Marxist thought cannot be found because such a concept is conditioned by bourgeois experience.

The author unmasks the "decadence" of bourgeois individualism, showing in Dormler's case that it is perfectly consistent with his character that he should walk into his own death trap. One of the three Nazi agents, a woman, who had been sent to incapacitate the broadcaster and his equipment completely entangles Dormle in her web of frivolity and coquetry, qualities that he himself had been accustomed to and had always sought out in high-society women. Erpenbeck's criticism does not lie in the nature of Dormler's anti-Nazi activities, but in the politically apatheti spirit with which these functions are carried out. In Dormler, he sets out to prove the likelihood of any anti-fascist activity backfiring (e.g., the gathering at the Club House International) unless it has an ideological basis which transcends personal interests.

Erpenbeck bases his characterization of Dormler on a documentary figure to point out the disastrous results that can arise from individual opposition to the Nazi regime. Rudolf Formis (3) was beaten and shot to death in his room in the Hotel Zahoři around midnight on January 23, 1935. One of Formis' weaknesses was his flair for beautiful women, and Erpenbeck capitalizes on this episode in an attempt to widen the gap between the true and the false opposition to Nazi tyranny. The actual events surrounding the installation of the transmitter (even the name of the hotel is retained in the novel) and the intrigue which develops around it are described in great detail. Only the names of the persons involved are changed. A contrasting political perspective (Erpenbeck's own invention) is then lent to the affair in the appearance of Hans, who assumes the task of rebuilding the station after Dormler's "removal."

Throughout the novel and particularly at the end, references to the Soviet Union serve as an example to the united revolutionary front of the workers in Germany and exile. Structurally and ideologically, the emigration in Czechoslovakia acts as a connecting link between Germany, a nation experiencing the revolution, and the Soviet Union, the country that had achieved it. Peter is commissioned to return to Germany, where the active struggle is still in progress; Hans is about to leave for Moscow, where the conflict has been terminated. The idea of a united front from below embodies these two perspectives, indicating a transition from struggle to victory. Furthermore, the amalgamation of Communist and Social Democratic workers signifies the rise of the proletarian class once the revolutionary process is completed. The union of Hans, the Communist, and Ruth, the leftist Social Democratic member of the Czech student movement, points to the collective embodiment of the two previously divided parties. When Hans discovers that he has been called to Moscow, he entrusts Ruth with the responsibility of carrying on his work in Prague. Revolutionary process and its end result, the two ideas germane to the concept of a united front from below, are thus symbolized in Ruth's stay and Hans' transfer. Ruth's desire to join Hans in the Soviet Union after the struggle has ended anticipates the termination of the process of revolutionary class conflict and the ultimate rise of the workers over the forces of fascist oppression.

This overly optimistic note no doubt was induced by Erpenbeck's own transfer from Prague to Moscow. Since he completed Emigranten in the Soviet Union, it stands to reason he would create the impression that Communist exile politics could look to the leading revolutionary party as the ideological vanguard of antifascist resistance, a position which became increasingly more tenuous, however, under Stalin's dictatorship.

## CHAPTER XV

## FRIEDRICH WOLF: ZWEI AN DER GRENZE

### The Frustrated Revolutionary in Exile

Hitler's rise to power saw exiled Marxists directing their polemic against a form of government pernicious not only to their concept of a classless society but also that of a class-structured democracy. In principle, fascist ideology negated both the revolutionary aspirations of the German Communist Party as well as the nonrevolutionary ones of liberal humanism. The political exile arena of 1933 generated a potentially common ground for cooperation between these historically opposed world views. Ideologically, the Communists still regarded the Nazi regime as an outgrowth of the capitalist class system and continued to perceive it throughout the exile as an exploitative power. As far as the non-Marxist exiles were concerned, Nazi Germany was usually not assessed in such terms, but as an anti-democratic power opposed to an ideology based on the principle of liberal democracy. By late 1935, the Communist International realized that its earlier sectarian policy of a united front from below needed revision if an opposition was to be formed viable enough to make Hitler take notice. And so Moscow's pronouncement of a People's Front was designed to enlist the aid of the liberals without losing sight of the ultimate goal of a proletarian state replacing Nazi Germany's reactionary one.

Fritz Erpenbeck's E m i g r a n t e n and Friedrich Wolf's Z w e i  a n  d e r G r e n z e were produced during the Soviet enactment of the orthodox and then more "liberal" strategy of the thirties. After 1935, the united front from below embraced a larger opposition which included all German exiles who were outspokenly anti-fascist. The E i n h e i t s f r o n t of the proletariat then became the revolutionary core around which non-Marxist defiant humanists were to be rallied. For the time being, the dogmatic character of the E i n h e i t s f r o n t was to be less assertive in line with the Communists' efforts to gain the support of anti-Nazi liberals and Social Democrats in a mutually beneficial campaign. The non-Marxist literary contributions to D a s  W o r t (1936-39) illustrate, at least on the surface, this cooperative effort on an intellectual level. On a politico-military one, the literary People's Front saw its efforts actuated when anti-fascist freedom fighters of various ideologies and backgrounds banded together to assist the Spanish Republicans in their battle against fascist aggression.

Friedrich Wolf had also intended to lend his support to this cause. In early 1938 he left the Soviet Union and journeyed to Paris, from where he hoped to accompany a French resistance group to the war-torn nation. By that time, however, the nonintervention policy of France and England was in full force and Wolf found the border closed to Loyalist sympathizers attempting to cross. The expiration of his passport then prevented his return to the Soviet Union. Wolf had applied for Soviet citizenship in 1937, but the granting of this privilege was contingent upon his presence in the country. Thus he was forced to remain in France. Sanary and Paris were centers of his literary activity from January, 1938, until the outbreak of war. In 1940, the intercession of a Russian emissary aided his release from a French internment camp and he was able to return to the Soviet Union, his country of asylum throughout most of the emigration.

Zwei an der Grenze originated at a time when two critical areas -- Spain and the Sudetenland -- were experiencing the oppression of fascist tyranny. In the months leading up to his departure from the Soviet Union, Wolf had begun writing his novel dealing with the border crisis in Bohemia. The situation he describes would seem to reflect the People's Front effort in the depiction of the factory workers' struggle against the German nationalist management and in the frequent references to the plight of the Spanish people, whom the workers aid by sending clothing and money. Wolf apparently decided to put words into action when he discontinued work on the novel and embarked for Spain via France. Stranded there, he resumed his writing and completed the novel in August, 1938, just prior to the German annexation of the Sudetenland.

In Zwei an der Grenze a situation is created which opens up one of the crucial issues of exile as it pertains to the Marxist sector. It is perhaps due to the objective criteria laid down by the esthetics of social realism that so few Marxist authors gave overt expression to their real feelings about the loss of homeland. The lyricist Johannes R. Becher conspicuously stands out among those who did. His emotional affinity with Germany did not differ fundamentally from that of any uprooted exile who loved his country and its oppressed people. To say that the Soviet Union provided Communist writers with a second home is true to a degree. The ideological unity linking exiled Marxists with the foreign country receiving them allowed for an integration that was more the exception than the rule among most liberal countries of asylum. But these escapees were German emigrants, not Russian compatriots, implying that a unified political philosophy was not a reflection of national identity.

The problem of conflicting loyalties emerging from the dual concept of homeland can be demonstrated in Friedrich Wolf's case. Throughout his years in the Soviet Union he missed Germany extremely, and his life, struggle, and art were inextricably bound to the land he had so reluctantly fled. Upon arriving in Switzerland in 1933, his first impulse was to return to Germany so that the people for whom he wrote could benefit directly by the art of one who identified with the oppressed. Fortunately, Wolf was dissuaded from doing so. By that time he was a marked man in the Third Reich and his renewed presence there would have reaped little literary reward.

The issue Wolf raises in Zwei an der Grenze centers on an almost radical confrontation with the state of exile. The most revealing chapter from this standpoint --"Einsamkeit" -- affords insight into the situation of an exiled revolutionary who must choose between either obedience to party authority or duty to the German people. The events preceding this critical chapter portray the Communist machinist Hans Döll fleeing across the Bohemian border with Gestapo agents in hot pursuit. He is wounded in flight and finds refuge with the peasant girl Loni and her widowed mother. While in hiding he is nursed back to health, has a love affair with Loni, and then is directed by his party to move farther inland to evade apprehension by German border spies and Bohemian nationalist fanatics.

In the "city" (ostensibly Prague), the distasteful reality of Hans' newly acquired status as an emigrant is vividly impressed upon him while he is required to wait for weeks in a socialist refugee center for a political assignment from his party. The contrast between the inactivity Hans attributes to life in exile and the direct political involvement he had known in the homeland crystallizes in a vehement dununciation of anything remotely resembling his new condition. He lashes out bitterly at the suspicion and mistrust he sees as undermining the political emigration. The word "Misstrauen" seems to preoccupy him in particular. He hammers this point home so often that one wonders whether it is he who is lamenting conditions in Prague or whether Wolf is alluding to a state of affairs in Moscow which did, in fact, engender a sense of mistrust. Wolf never emigrated to Czechoslovakia. Thus he can hardly be narrating from direct experience. Are Hans' invectives then merely a matter of conjecture? Or do they have a basis in reality elsewhere? When Wolf began writing the novel in 1937, the Moscow purges were no longer a secret to the West, let alone to someone who was present in the Soviet Union at the time. Since the chapter in question occurs early in the novel, it could possibly belong to the Soviet period, thus accentuating the gravity of Hans' criticisms.

The tense scene is set when an office employee of the refugee center asks Hans: "Du willst also nach Deutschland zurück?" (1) Hans' reply establishes the polarity that is to reign throughout the chapter: "Kann man denn hier leben ohne euer Vertrauen, ohne Arbeit?" (31). The mistrust Hans senses is derived from the tacit suspicions of other political emigrants who are uncertain of his real motives for going into exile. Could he be a renegade Communist whose party allegiance stands to be questioned? In whose interests is he acting? It seems inconsistent with their own plight as German escapees that these comrades should ever be inclined to such suspicions. One is forced to read between the lines to arrive at a probable cause for Hans' mistrust as well as to uncover the likely target of Wolf's polemic. Little doubt exists as to the identity between author and leading character. Wolf frequently steps out of his role as detached narrator so as to confirm this relationship: "Für wen hält man ihn? Darf man einem Kameraden, der drüben an der Basis arbeitete und täglich sein Leben riskierte, mit diesem Misstrauen begegnen? Er nimmt alle Kraft zusammen, um nicht aufzuheulen in dieser bitteren Einsamkeit" (32). These words were written at a time when Wolf himself was planning to follow the example set by Moscow's promotion of a People's Front by his desire to join forces in Spain.

On other occasions as well Wolf interjects subjective commentary as an indication of his identification with the hero's predicament (e. g., "Die Furcht voreinander, das Misstrauen zwischen Mensch und Mensch macht jeden vor dem andern zum Pestkranken," 36). The severity with which the author allows Hans to attack the emigration suggests a criticism of the shallow phraseology underlying the formation of a People's Front from above (the Comintern). In principle, this movement was supposed to subdue the aggressive demands of an authoritarian ideology for the benefit of a cooperative opposition within the political emigration as a whole. In reality, just the contrary was the case. (2) The Soviet Union's hegemonic position in determining anti-Nazi strategy and the "cleansing" of all disruptive revolutionary elements in Moscow in 1936-37 not only vitiated the idea of a People's Front as far as liberal emigrants and their countries of asylum were concerned, but also shook the faith of those Communist exiles who had regarded the Soviet Union as the one nation that could make the People's Front effort an effective obstacle to Hitler's militant imperialism. (3)

With the exception of a few scenes, the chapter "Einsamkeit" functions like a miniature r o m a n à c l e f, in which Wolf takes issue with an authority that fails to put theory into practice. Hans repeatedly refers to interests that divide party organization and its followers. He desires to be committed actively, to be "eingesetzt" in a capacity instrumental to the struggle against fascist tyranny. In his dispute with Willi, the secretary of the refugee center, Hans is on the verge of open defiance to party authority. In reply to Willi's question -- "Dann haust du einfach ab, nicht wahr?" -- Hans exclaims: "Die Partei kann mir nicht helfen, sie gibt mir keine Antwort, setzt mich nicht ein, also habt mich lieb ums Morgenrot! Ich tue es selber" (55). Hans has two destinations in mind: "Wohin denn sonst? Nach Deutschland, nach Spanien, wo du dich einsetzen kannst, deinen Kopf, deine Glieder, dein Leben, verstehst du denn das nicht, Willi?!" (55).

Wolf's dilemma is a ticklish one. An open confrontation with Moscow as the controlling influence in party affairs could only mean political disaster for one who himself is a member of the Communist Party. Personal motives also come into play, considering that the author had made the Soviet Union his exiled home. By confining the conflict to Prague, it stands to reason that Wolf avoids the possibility of any direct attack on Soviet policy, thereby creating the impression that Hans' impatience with party irresoluteness is of a local nature. Any candid method of argument would certainly have jeopardized Wolf's position in the Soviet Union. Only indirectly, then, can he strike at an issue which would seem to have concerned him privately when he ceased work on the novel and left the Soviet Union with the intention of committing himself actively, just as Hans wants to do. The motif of "Misstrauen" as it pertains to party politics must be regarded in a context extending beyond the membership of the German Communist Party and having its roots in a larger organization that did engender such a feeling during the S ä u b e r u n g s a k t i o n. For obvious reasons, Wolf uses the designation "Partei" in a nonspecific context. Yet the frustrating tone of Hans' protests leaves little doubt as to the identity of the recipient: "Warum lasst ihr uns dann nicht fort?! Kann die Partei denn verlangen, dass wir hier langsam verkommen, verbittern, zu Schmarotzern werden? ... Muss uns denn nicht diese Arbeitsverweigerung, dieses dauernde Misstrauen, jawohl, dieses euer Misstrauen, dieses lungernde Warten zwischen arbeitenden Menschen, all das muss uns zwangsläufig zersetzen, degradieren, verfaulen lassen! ... Jawohl: verfaulen hab' ich gesagt! Kann die Partei das verlangen? Im Bunker unter den Stahlruten der Nazis -- ja! Im KZ -- ja! Aber hier?" (56).

In the course of his argument, Hans addresses himself particularly to the question of activity contra inactivity. It is unlikely that Wolf includes in the latter category the overall German membership of the Comintern. During the Spanish Civil War, the German units of the international brigades were comprised mainly of Communists. (4) Countless others in the G. C. P. contributed to the cause of the

Loyalists in a literary capacity. Two of these -- Willi Bredel and Erich Weinert -- arrived from the Soviet Union in the summer of 1937 to attend the International Writers' Congress in Madrid. At the close of the congress, Bredel did not return to the Soviet Union, but exchanged the literary weapon for a military one when he joined one of the battalions. (5)

In the chapter "Einsamkeit," the crux of Wolf's narrative viewpoint intimates a discontent with the usurpation of authority by certain proponents of the People's Front policy who continue to engage in political power play. His indirectness and covert polemic arises from the situation of the Marxist writer caught between conflicting loyalties: the German national struggle against fascism, of which the war in Spain is a concrete symbol, and the Soviet Union as the ideological home of the exiled Communists. Certain polarities can be established only by inference rather than open textual evidence. Wolf refrains from making any direct reference to the People's Front and to the Soviet Union which proclaimed it. Needless to say, the fascist exploitation of the Bohemian workers in the Keller textile factory and the several references to Spain point out crises that conceivably could have been minimized if the collective spirit in which the Soviet Union announced the People's Front had been determinedly carried out. The activism-passivism problem cuts through the very core of the anti-fascist People's Front issue. What the government of Moscow expressed in theory, other individuals were putting into practice on their own initiative. The lack of direct support by the Soviet Union, as well as other major powers, in matters concerning Spain and the Sudetenland attenuates the very concept of a People's Front. The nonintervention policy of France and Great Britain and the conditional material support lent to Spain by the Soviet Union, whose strategy of military noninvolvement must have clashed with the interests of German Communists participating in the struggle, historically explain the motives behind Hans' dispute over "party" policy-making.

At one point in the novel the question of international involvement in the Spanish crisis does arise after Hans, "eingesetzt" as a liaison agent, has just completed an exchange of propaganda material with his contact at a prearranged rendevous point on the border. The following passage implicitly conveys Wolf's scepticism over a "higher" organization and clearly establishes the real level of anti-fascist unity:

> Hans geht heim durch die Nacht. Fünfundachtzig Mark hat er in seiner Tasche. Jeder Groschen ist drüben vom Munde abgespart, das weiss er genau, an jedem Groschen klebt Gefahr, haftet Sympathie mit den spanischen Kämpfern. Dennoch, was können diese fünfundachtzig Mark nützen in einem Krieg, der auch den Republikanern jeden Tag Millionen kostet? Lohnen diese fünfundachtzig Mark den Aufwand an Menschen und Gefahr? Diese nächtige, indianerhafte Begegnung in der Schlucht, weil nebenan in den Dörfern die Treffs aufflogen?
>
> Das Nachrichtenmaterial aus Deutschland -- richtig, das lohnt! Auch die paar hundert Flugblätter von ihm! Aber diese fünfundachtzig Mark? Kann man diese fünfundachtzig Mark nicht viel einfacher zu einer grossen Summe schlagen, irgendeinem internationalen Komitee direkt überweisen? Nach des Stummels Auftrag aber soll auf diesen fünfundachtzig Mark daraufstehen: Von einigen deutschen Arbeitern und Arbeiterinnen in einem Betrieb

gesammelt! So soll das nach Spanien gehen, wie ein Händedruck: Kameraden, wir sind mit euch! Ihr seid nicht allein! (161-62)

The implied distinction between national and international roles parallels the difference of interests in the front movement with regard to the people, on the one hand, and the various governmental powers, on the other. Hans and his German comrades are not about to entrust these desperately needed funds to higher agencies which have advocated a hands-off policy as far as Spain is concerned. The appeasement policy of the West towards the Third Reich and the Soviet Union's detached ideological supremacy in matters concerning Communist support of the Republican cause accent the unstable political scene prevailing in Europe, and warrant Wolf's "sectarian" portrayal of a revolutionary whose motivations stand in defiance of higher authority.

In Z w e i   a n   d e r   G r e n z e one cannot help but feel that Wolf is segregating national revolutionary elements from "outside revolutionary" influence. Like Fritz Erpenbeck, he seems to be promoting an E i n h e i t s f r o n t solely from below, with the one distinction being that E m i g r a n t e n reflects a sectarian policy that coincided with Moscow's pre-1935 anti-liberal position. In the late 1930's, however, such a plan of action would run contrary to the Soviet-initiated People's Front. Whereas Erpenbeck was integrating into his novel the pre-People's Front Comintern policy of a united front from below, Wolf seems to fall back on it as a reaction to Moscow's persistently orthodox stance. In Erpenbeck's work, efforts to muster a revolutionary front out of the proletariat were made with a constant eye to the Soviet Union as the one nation that had achieved the revolution and to whom the struggling workers (also in Prague) could turn as their model. No references are made, however, to Stalinist Russia in Z w e i   a n   d e r   G r e n z e . The only indication of the existence of the Communist exiles' home base lies in the almost hymnic reverence paid to Maxim Gorki's D i e   M u t t e r . Certainly personal reasons explain Gorki's influence in the novel. Wolf had lost a respected literary mentor when this revolutionary writer died in 1936. He had always held a deep admiration for Gorki, with whom he had discussed literary topics on a number of occasions in Moscow.

But critical reasons, as well, explain the emergence of Gorki's classical work: it is a pre-Stalinist testimony to a nation in the process of revolutionary struggle. It goes without saying that one of the main motives for Stalin's ordering of the Trotsky trials lay in the eradication of the last revolutionary remnants of 1917. Wolf incorporates a literary model into his novel which portrays the pre-Bolshevic era, one demonstrating K a m p f and the collective spirit of unselfish action. Indeed, even the setting in Z w e i   a n   d e r   G r e n z e is reminiscent, in part, of an earlier period. Naive peasants and politically inexperienced workers w i t h o u t party affiliation suffer under the oppressive tactics of Nazified industrialists. D i e   M u t t e r passes from hand to hand among the ideologically unschooled as a source of inspiration and teaching aid in the methods of collective resistance. Thus the model Wolf uses to carry on the struggle is not the hegemonic Soviet Union of 1938, but the revolutionary Russian nation in its historical process of overcoming oppression. At the end of the novel Hans, whose secret assignments on the border had prevented him from directly supporting the workers' struggle and the factory strike, has indirectly won a number of Bohemian comrades over to his side through the influence of Gorki's work. The process of development from individual conflict to the collective goal of revolutionary class conflict is best illustrated in Hans' wife Loni (the "zweite" in Z w e i  a n  d e r  G r e n z e). Even though she is with child, she refuses to allow this burden to interfere with the perilous task Hans takes upon himself when he returns to Germany at the end.

In the course of the novel, the exploitation of the anti-fascist factory workers by organized fascist co-workers and leaders reveals a successful People's Front movement on the r e a c t i o n a r y  side! Whereas national and ideological differences between the democratic powers and the Soviet Union had stood in the way of a unified anti-fascist front, Germany, Austria, Italy, and the Sudetenland were demonstrating, in the meantime, the workability of their front effort. As the thirties progressed, the fascist nations manifested a solidarity of interests from above a n d below. Certain segments of the population eagerly supported the nationalist policies of their respective reactionary governments. The Spanish crisis is a case in point. The Italian and German troops aiding Franco were not volunteers, but instruments of international fascist militarism. By contrast, the democratic brigades fighting on the side of the Republicans were left on their own, struggling for a just cause while their governments appeared either to fear the threat of Communism more than Nazism (France, England, and Czechoslovakia), or sought to preserve military autonomy and internal security as a reaction to this mood (the Soviet Union).

The Sudeten border crisis shows how the reactionary People's Front had gathered in momentum by 1938. As early as 1935, an anonymous article in D a s  N e u e  T a g e b u c h forecasts the situation as it appears in Z w e i  a n  d e r  G r e n z e in its description of the tense political scene prevailing in Bohemia:

> Wie ehemals an der Saar gibt es jetzt auch in den deutschen Gebieten Böhmens keine Nazi-Partei mehr, die unter eigener Fahne anderen bürgerlichen Parteien Konkurrenz machen muss, sondern nur noch eine 'Volksfront'. Wer ausserhalb steht, ist nicht mehr bloss ein Parteigegner, sondern ein 'Volksverräter' oder 'Stammesverräter'. Und wer nicht in Treue zum Herrn Henlein hält, ist schuldig, nicht nur dem nationalsozialistischen Gauleiter -- der Henlein in Wirklichkeit ist -- den Respekt zu versagen, sondern dem 'sudetendeutschen Stammesführer', der das gesamte Deutschtum in der Tschechoslowakei repräsentiere: wodurch jeder Widerspruch eines Deutschen gegen Herrn Henlein zu einem 'Dolchstoss' in den Rücken der ganzen Nation wird. (7)

In the organization of the Keller factory, Wolf describes a representative case of an insidious "Volksfront" atmosphere pervading the Sudetenland. From top to bottom there exists among Bohemian reactionaries and racists a unity of purpose that seems almost impregnable. No ideological divergencies emerge within the class ranks of these fanatic nationalists. Party functionaries, industrial magnates, reactionary bourgeois, factory directors and foremen, T u r n b ü n d l e r and laborers all aspire to the same goal: unconditional loyalty to Nazi Germany and the eradication of all alien elements (socialists, Jews, and Slavs).

Strangely enough, Wolf places as much importance on the national heritage of the exploited workers as the fascist exploiters do on theirs. As an exiled Ger-

man who deeply missed his country, such a predilection is understandable. From
the viewpoint of international proletarian solidarity, however, which had become
virtually a slogan among Communists during the People's Front era, a solely German treatment of the class conflict intimates a reluctance on the author's part to
envision the workers' struggle as being but one aspect of a larger confrontation
between the forces of progress and reaction. At a surface glance, Wolf's depiction
of factory workers exploited by fascist racists and imperialists suggests nothing
thematically new in Marxist exile literature. Yet the indignant tone emanating
from the chapter "Einsamkeit" betrays a tendency to divorce this theme from the
exile scene, which for German Marxists necessarily implied a link to the ideological homeland of class struggle, the Soviet Union. The exploited workers in
Z w e i  a n  d e r  G r e n z e have just begun to fight. No reference is made to a
supreme party authority which might dictate policies contrary to their efforts to
organize as a monolithic body. When Hans resumes contact with comrades on the
border, the discussions invariably center on the welfare of the workers at home,
their revolutionary work and self-initiative, without any mention made of organizational interference from the top. Furthermore, Gorki's D i e  M u t t e r serves to
exemplify the collective fight of a people b e f o r e the establishment of a dictatorship of the proletariat.

An so Wolf reverts to the idea of a united front from below on a national
level (Reich and Sudeten Germans), and by so doing portrays only those proleta-
rians directly involved in the process of class struggle. By extrapolation, one
assumes that the "Misstrauen" of which Hans speaks can only refer to a proletarian
organization which has nothing better to do than maintain its own national security
by "removing" suspicious factions ("zersetzen, degradieren, verfaulen," 56). This
leitmotif has both specific and general application. "Misstrauen" exists not only
among the ideological ranks of the Soviet Union, but also between one governmental
power and the other, as well as among the more dogmatic German Marxists (e. g. ,
Erpenbeck) who are unequivocally pro-Stalin. The very phenomenon of exile
smacks of "Misstrauen," and Wolf's endeavor to obliterate the distasteful stigma
of this condition carries with it his implied discontent with the People's Front as
an effective anti-Nazi undertaking.

For this reason one hesitates to classify Z w e i  a n  d e r  G r e n z e as a
novel of exile when considered in its entirety. Hans, the sole escapee from Germany living in Bohemia, appears only at the beginning as an exile who senses the
futility of his new status. Homelessness, alienation, political uselessness, inactivity -- these are feelings seldom conveyed so bitterly by a Marxist emigrant
writer, and especially by one who had found a "home" in the Soviet Union. But by
bringing these issues to the fore, Wolf creates a situation extending beyond the
events of the novel and exposing the discrepancy between a revolution that has
attained its end (the Soviet Union) and the one currently in progress (Germany).
The activity-inactivity polarity in Wolf's work parallels the dichotomy between
Germany and exile, or, specifically, the practice of revolutionary theory at home
and on the border and the stagnant self-satisfaction of its completion in the Soviet
Union. At the point where Hans becomes a "Verbindungsmann für Material und
Freunde" (71) and resumes an active role in Germany's struggle, the stigma of
exile is erased. Even his new identity as Wenzel Langer, who marries into the

Bohemian peasant family, fails to rid him of the feeling of an alien status. The relative security of this aspect of his existence in Bohemia does not suffice to relieve his sense of isolation from his tyrannized homeland. Only when Hans is "eingesetzt" is a relationship established between ideology and nation. In this context he does make reference to a party, and in all likelihood it is directed at those Communist Party members at home who identify with and are committed to the struggle against Nazi tyranny. While contemplating suicide, Hans laments: "Wer darf Einspruch erheben, wenn du dieses tote Leben abschüttelst? Deine Arbeit? Bitte, welche Arbeit? Die Partei? Sie wird einen nutzlosen Emigranten los sein" (37). One wonders whether even the exiled G.C.P. is included here. Probably certain of its members are who recognized the urgency of direct involvement on the border or in Spain, and who did not consider the political hegemony of the Comintern to be incontestable. More important, Hans draws a distinction in this passage between emigration and party organization, implying that the latter takes on significance only when its theoretical position can be backed up by the presence of an actual revolutionary conflict. And this dialectic crystallizes in the national crisis involving Germans at home and on the Bohemian frontier. In Hans' case, party and people become one only where there is active participation in the struggle:

> Nein, man ist nicht allein! Man ist nicht vergessen! Auch hier ist man nicht zur Untätigkeit verdammt. Wellen der Liebe und Freundschaft schlagen selbst über diese höllisch bewachten Grenzen. Und auch er selbst ... ist jetzt ein festes, verwendbares Glied in dieser unsichtbaren Kette. Durch seine Hände flattern die paar hundert Flugblätter, diese Sturmvögel, hinüber nach Deutschland, durch seine Hände wandern diese Dokumente der Solidarität, diese deutschen Spaniengroschen zu den Frauen und den Kämpfern von Madrid. Ja, er ist wieder eingeschaltet in den glühenden Strom der Arbeit und der Kameradschaft. Er ist wieder mit dabei! (162)

## CHAPTER XVI

## ANNA SEGHERS: TRANSIT

A Reassessment
---

The wealth of critical analyses devoted to Anna Seghers' exile novel T r a n - s i t (1943) leads one to suspect that about every line of argument has been exhausted, and that any renewed attempt to examine the work would result in a mere reshuffling of already established opinions. Since the more important issues have repeatedly come up for discussion, Seghers scholars will no doubt wonder what constructive purpose yet another study will serve. Conflicting views over Seghers' attitude towards her subject matter, however, show that problem areas still exist which warrant further attention. For the most part, critics have concentrated on a textual analysis of T r a n s i t and have dealt only casually with the relationship of the novel to the author's own exile situation as well as to the international political atmosphere in which she was writing in 1940.

Rejecting the notion advanced by some Western critics that T r a n s i t is an untypical product of Seghers' creative method, Marxist scholars invariably take a socio-realistic approach to the work. (1) Alternatively, the existential and psychological aspects of the novel seem to draw the greatest attention among Western critics, (2) with the result that the realistic aspect of character development tends to be overlooked or, when it is acknowledged, to be restricted to Seidler's "unmotivated" change in the closing scene. (3)

Until now, critics have generally neglected to look more closely into the genesis of Seghers' novel and the personal and ideological problems related to it. In the wake of the Nazi occupation of Paris, Seghers escaped to Southern France and was stranded as a political refugee in Marseille until March, 1942, when her ship, the P a u l L e m e r l e, finally embarked for Martinique. Seghers' voyage was plagued by frustrations almost as politically traumatic as those she had experienced during her hazardous sojourn in Marseille. Alfred Kantorowicz and his wife accompanied the Seghers family on the boat, and his recollections of the trip (4) reveal a feeling of impending doom engendered by the presence of hostile ships and mines. The P a u l L e m e r l e is described as a mild form of concentration camp in which the passengers were required to sleep on planks. At the port of Oran, British officials threatened, at first, to close the passage leading through the Gibralter straits and to send the ship back to Marseille. After a period of frantic uncertainty, the vessel was allowed to pass after all. In Martinique the two families were interned by the French who controlled the island. Their release was followed by further difficulties upon arriving in Santo Domingo, where they feared immediate incarceration by the ruling fascist dictatorship. Fortunately, these officials did not appear particularly concerned about Seghers' and Kantorowicz's status as political enemies of the Third Reich.

Throughout her escape to "freedom," Seghers continued to work on T r a n s i t.

In her letters she states: "Ich fand ein Café mit einem Ventilator. Dort setzte ich mich oft hin, während wir ein geeignetes Schiff erwarteten, und schrieb an meinem Buch 'Transit', das ich schon in Marseille begonnen und unterwegs auf dem Schiff fortgesetzt hatte." (5) Recalling her confinement on the island of Martinique, Seghers mentions a series of incidents which parallel the kind of harassment marking the emigrant scene in the novel: "Als wir nach ein paar Wochen in Martinique ankamen, dem westlichsten Punkt Frankreichs, den damals noch die Vichy-Regierung verwaltete, wurden wir interniert. Es stellte sich heraus, dass es zunächst kein direktes Schiff nach Mexiko gab. Unsere Visen liefen ab. Wir suchten einen Zwischenaufenthalt, um von dort auf einem Umweg nach Mexiko zu fahren. (In meinem Roman 'Transit' steht viel über die tödliche Bürokratie in jener Zeit.) Wir beschafften uns Visen nach San Domingo." (6) The parenthetical insertion suggests that T r a n s i t is not only a comment on bureaucratic injustice in France, but away from the Continent as well, albeit the action and setting of the novel are restricted to Paris and Marseille. For Seghers, the state of exile reaches beyond the shores of Southern France; her flight to the sea is not tantamount to freedom and safety, but is an extension of the transit status of the figures in the novel. She wrote most of the work while in an actual state of transit, (7) and the artistic detachment that one might expect her to achieve as she was fleeing from the direct experience of creation is frustrated by the menacing character of the flight.

In contrast to most critical opinions of T r a n s i t , Seghers has her own views about the novel's "Zustandekommen," stating that she had never written "etwas so unmittelbar im Erlebnis Steckende [ s i c ]." (8) If one relates -- as critics have tended to do -- the experience factor in T r a n s i t only to the author's stay in Marseille, then the work becomes a b g e s c h l o s s e n in the sense that a direct correspondence arises between narrative space and time and Seghers' spatial and temporal experience of the events described. If one takes into consideration, however, that Seghers' experience of exile, during the writing process, persisted even after Marseille, then the issue of "Erlebnis" being "steckend" becomes more cogent in a critical evaluation of the novel.

In this connection it seems important to examine the author's motivation for creating, in Seidler, a figure who desires to stay in France, while she is bent on getting out. Despite the risks involved in remaining, the hero takes it for granted that his place is in Europe. Time and again he refers to the state of peril extending b e y o n d the bedlam in Marseille and threatening those who, like Seghers, have managed to obtain passage. The plight of the exiles does not terminate with the boarding of a ship; the act of departure means a perpetuation of the frustration and uncertainty that had characterized the "Horde abfahrtssüchtiger Teufel" (9) -- as Seidler sees them -- beforehand. In the K a p e l l m e i s t e r ' s advice to Seidler, "Sie müssen ... Ihr Ziel eine Zeitlang vergessen, jetzt gelten nur die Zwischenländer, sonst wird aus der Abfahrt nichts" (45), we are reminded of the interruptions that stood between Seghers and her destination as she passed through Gibralter, fascist-controlled Martinique and Santo Domingo, and finally Ellis Island where she was again interned.

The creation of a character who remains, for the most part, unaffected by the desperate desire of other emigrants to escape by sea enables Seghers to artistically relieve the burden of her own involvement. Seidler is probably the most nonautobiographical product of the author's pen; as a purely "fictional" character he assumes a role less manipulated by the dictates of empirical reality than the majority who are scrambling to acquire travel documents, the success of which is no guarantee that one has escaped the confining atmosphere of Marseille. Throughout the novel Seghers distances herself from the foreboding uncertainties of her exile environment by allowing their expression to be voiced by one who prefers the reality of French soil to the dubiosity of escape. And so Seidler can speak with total objectivity of "verjagte Menschenhaufen, die schliesslich am Meer ankamen, wo sie sich auf die Schiffe warfen, um neue Länder zu entdecken, aus denen sie wieder verjagt wurden; immer alle auf der Flucht vor dem Tod, in den Tod" (83). Furthermore, the reference to events here as already having taken place creates the impression that the author is alluding to past experiences. Actually, she is still living these experiences during the writing process. The illusion of detachment comes about through the employment of a semi-involved narrator.

The exile condition in T r a n s i t has been fittingly described as a "Bedrohung der menschlichen Ordnung." (10) In coping with this threat Seghers sets out to portray a character who cannot be classified as an exile in the irrational context in which the other figures appear. Such expressions as "Abfahrtssüchtige," "Abfahrtsbessene," "Transitärewut," and "Visumbessenheit" describe the moblike psychology of those exiles who, unlike Seidler, are driven by a single, blind impulse -- to flee. In the hero the author presents a contrasting figure to the atmosphere of havoc informing the exile scene. Her political persuasion, based on a rational order of existence, demands that her art seek a socially meaningful reality even when conditions seem adverse to it. Seidler acts as her vehicle for restoring a semblance of meaning in an environment governed by "Naziordnung" (44), which is how the K a p e l l m e i s t e r so poignantly describes the d i s o r d e r in Marseille. Seidler's sense of individual isolation -- an attitude Seghers, in another historical setting, would have been inclined to expose for ideological reasons -- is a sustaining factor which allows him to assume an ironic distance toward his own "Verwicklung" (6). As Seidler-Weidel the hero goes through the mere motions of acquiring travel documents, for the express purpose of not using them.

From the very beginning Seidler's sense of aimlessness and disorientation is accompanied by a desire to establish roots in the reality about him. The double role he plays is a game enabling him to r e m a i n in France. He perceives his freedom in terms of extensions of permits to reside. By proving to authorities that he is going through proper channels to expedite his departure, he is in fact prolonging his stay.

Seidler's gradual development towards social awareness arises from his sympathy with the simple people of France, as represented by the Binnet family. Once he relinquishes all ties with the exile scene, of which he had been a detached part in his role as Weidel, he finds himself in an environment where his earlier search for meaning can now become a reality. The nonexile side of life in Southern France provides Seidler with a new existence, much as Anna Seghers found a new home in Mexico following her release from an irrational exile milieu that had extended beyond the shores of Southern France, rendering impossible any sort of purposeful human contact. In this connection it is certainly worth noting that the conclusion of the novel, showing Seidler's integration into the French rural community, was not written en route to Mexico, but after Seghers had reached her destination. (11)

To further elucidate the genesis of T r a n s i t , the personal involvement of the author with the setting must be expanded to include the international political scene in which she was writing. From an ideological standpoint, the maelstrom from which T r a n s i t emerged was hardly appropriate to the creation of antifascist forces -- certainly not in France, the final haven for Communist exiles, other than the Soviet Union, after Czechoslovakia's capitulation. With the absence of epoch-making social forces among exiles in any Western European front, Seghers could revert to the only source of material remaining at her disposal -- the chaos of reality itself. The Republican cause in Spain had failed; the Moscow trials had precipitated ideological panic among rank and file Communist exiles; Hitler's militant territorial expansion had engulfed Austria and Czechoslovakia; the Hitler-Stalin nonaggression pact had prepared the demise of the People's Front campaign; and now a wartime condition was prevailing in most of Western Europe.

At one point in the novel the subject of the Soviet Union does come up for discussion, the brevity of which ostensibly accounts for its nontreatment by critics. Yet the tenor of the episode unmistakably establishes the Soviet Union as a nation that had betrayed the hopes of those who had regarded it as a counterforce to Nazi imperialism: "Die Hälfte der Binnets behauptete, Russland denke bloss an sich selbst, es habe uns im Stich gelassen. Die andere Hälfte der Binnets behauptete, die hiesigen und die deutschen Herren hätten ausgemacht, sie sollten ihr Heer zuerst auf die Russen werfen statt auf den Westen, das eben habe Russland vereitelt" (14). Any further discussion of this sensitive issue is promptly dropped with Seidler's laconic remark to his fictitious audience: "Bitte verzeihen Sie diese Abschweifung!" (14). Such a reaction suggests two things: first, the fact that Seidler regards this rather crucial political debate as mere digression vitiates the significance of any leftist argument envisaging him as a seminal revolutionary hero; second, it stands to reason that Seghers, as a member of the Party, would eschew any extended polemic against the ideological homeland of the Communist exiles. Thus it would seem that the isolationism of the Soviet Union and its pact with Nazi Germany, both of which are discernible in this scene, account in part for the author's treatment of a theme devoid of revolutionary struggle.

If Seghers had countered the pandemonium in Marseille with an anti-fascist resistance guided by the ideology of class struggle and revolution, she would have satisfied certain artistic tenets of socialist realism, (12) but not those elicited by historical reality. The disruptive nature of the exile milieu precludes her employing a method of art postulating a dialectic process in social conflict. In her debate with Georg Lukács (1938-39) concerning the writer's creative method, Seghers establishes the theoretical tenor of that which was to become a reality for her in 1940-41. Throughout her correspondence such expressions as "Bewusstmachung von Wirklichkeit," "Splitterchen," and "Bruchteil" (13) appear regularly, characterizing both her artistic concept of reality and her relationship to it. All that was needed to actualize esthetic principle was the raw material, and this was provided the author in late 1940 when empirical reality had lost all semblance of normality in Nazi-occupied France. In her letters to Lukács, Seghers discloses her position on artistic creation for the first time -- in the late emigration, a period in which the uncertainties of a socialist reality modelled after that of the Soviet Union were already beginning to surface. Thus the emigration prompted Seghers not only to outline her esthetic postulates; it in turn brought about the expression of a creative posture quite appropriate to the situation at hand. In other words, Seghers lays down in her letters, however unsystematically, a kind of esthetics of uprootedness that was to be incorporated in her novel T r a n s i t about a year later.

On yet another occasion, after she had settled in the German Democratic Republic, Seghers attempts to elucidate her views on literary creation as they pertain to the novel. In a letter she states: "Ich glaube, die Frage 'Mit Abstand schreiben oder sofort' wird meistens falsch gestellt. Der Roman 'Transit' wurde beinahe in der Zeit geschrieben, in der sich seine Handlung abgespielt hat. Die Schriftsteller stellen manchen Eindruck sofort dar und manchmal den gleichen nach Jahrzehnten. Als junger Mensch beschrieb Tolstoi, was er im Kaukasus erlebte, und im hohen Alter entstand aus denselben Erfahrungen H a d s c h i  M u r a t." (14) Since this observation was made as late as 1963, any personal dilemma Seghers may have experienced in connection with the writing of T r a n s i t would hardly be a matter of importance to a citizen of the GDR -- at least outwardly. Actually, there is an obvious difference in narrative attitude between an author who creates initially out of "Abstand" and one who approaches his subject matter "sofort" by virtue of his own individual involvement. In the GDR it is understandable that Seghers would prefer not to elaborate on any personal dilemma or momentary ideological disorientation that may have directly influenced the creative process back in 1940. The noncommittal tenor of her statement explains the undifferentiated emphasis placed on "Abstand" and "sofort." One wonders, though, whether she really would have written the same T r a n s i t in 1963 as she had in 1940-41, a view she seems to hold in her reference to Tolstoy. Certainly an author who creates "sofort" in an effort to achieve "Abstand," as Seghers does in T r a n s i t in her portrayal of a hero who is both involved and detached, evinces an attitude quite different from that of the writer who approaches his material after the impact of experience has dulled with time. In the act of writing, the creation of a first-person narrator, who tells the story in retrospect, enabled Seghers to free herself from the trauma of exile to which she was directly exposed at the time.

Most Marxist scholars interpret in the hero's devolopment -- that is, in his "socialistic" identification with the people of France who lead "ein gewöhnliches Leben " (42) -- a corresponding ideological renunciation of his past life. Seidler's earlier individual inclinations are seen as typical manifestations of bourgeois society's incapacity for human contact, and his evolving sense of solidarity with the Binnet family and Marcel on the farm in turn signifies a collective commitment in political terms. Seidler's "comrade" Heinz is usually cited as the main source of inspiration because he is a Communist, (15) although this cannot be born out by textual evidence. Finally, the hero's readiness to take up arms against a reactionary enemy is supposed to reflect a leftist political alignment on his part.

This amalgamation of ideology and art appears somewhat tenuous in light of the novel's genesis ("Zustandekommen"). The episode dealing with the Soviet Union, noted earlier, suggests that the author was not operating on a very sound ideological basis at the time of T r a n s i t's inception. It is not surprising, then, that certain passages reveal a symbolism which, if considered in leftist-ideological terms, strikes one as being more regressive than progressive. Seidler's "socialistic" awakening fails to embrace even the most fundamental precondition for a revolutionary W e l t a n s c h a u u n g, namely, that of the conflict of classes seen in the opposition of reaction (Nazism) to progress (Communism). By having Seidler join Marcel on the farm, the author in fact insures he engages in an occupation that does not engender a political class consciousness. In the closing scene the hero emerges in the role of a peasant whose sense of human solidarity, however prepared it might be to actively resist the invaders, derives not from leftist-political motives, but from the preindustrial simplicity of a nonalienating nature setting: "Es kommt mir vor, ich kennte das Land zu gut, seine Arbeit und seine Menschen, seine Berge und seine Pfirsiche und seine Trauben. Wenn man auf einem vertrauten Boden verblutet, wächst etwas dort von einem weiter wie von den Sträuchern und Bäumen, die man zu roden versucht" (262). Rather than remain with the laborer George Binnet in a capacity more suitable to his own profession as a M o n t e u r in an industrial society, Seidler retreats to a more unproblematic way of life in the country, one which admittedly frees him from the oppressing exile scene in Marseille, but also from the political causes ("Naziordnung") underlying this oppression.

Our discussion of the influence of historical backdrops on the creation of T r a n s i t (the political impotence of the People's Front effort in the late thirties and Seghers' continued plight beyond Marseille) does not presume to negate existing approaches to the novel, but to provide them with a possible tool for future reinterpretation. The purpose of the present discussion is to show that structure and content receive an added critical dimension if elucidated in the broader framework of the novel's genesis.

Until now, most of the literature on T r a n s i t has rendered a fractionalized and often conflicting impression of the author's intent. In Marxist circles, for example, critics seem divided on the issue of historical continuity. Some place the novel in a context dialectically related to Seghers' works as a whole, rejecting the argument (which we advance here) that the conditions under which she was writing at the time may have inspired a creative method which had the effect of obscuring the revolutionary mission of the working class (Seidler's ambiguous role at the end). Paul Rilla and Frank Wagner are perhaps the most intransigent proponents of this view. Both establish their case by envisaging Heinz and Seidler as historical figures who embody the idea of a new social order emerging from the chaos of a "bourgeois"-fascist reality. Rilla contends that it is "der historische Prozess, den die Bücher der Anna Seghers nachzeichnen," (16) and interprets T r a n s i t as a functional link in the artistic illustration of this process. In his opinion, the "Gedanken der grossen Veränderung" (17) lend an epoch-making quality to the novel which points out its revolutionary significance in the development of the author's total oeuvre.

Wagner, in turn, refers to the "Transitwelt im Zeichen der Zeitenwende" (18) and sees the epochal nature of the work exemplified in the "Uebergang vom Kapitalismus zum Sozialismus." (19) He disagrees with those Marxist critics who take too narrow a view of Seidler's "Schlussentscheidung." (20) Rather, the hero's "collective" commitment at the end must be seen in the larger context of an "Epochenentscheidung. " (21) Seidler's "individuelle Veränderung" then becomes a "Teilnahme am kollektiven Vorgang der Veränderung. " (22)

Other GDR critics are less prepared to view the novel in such optimistic terms. Heinz Neugebauer assumes a somewhat ambivalent position when he, at first, affirms and then questions the development of the hero in the context of a historical process. Like Wagner, he too interprets the novel's title as meaning a transition from the old to the new: "Es bedeutet nicht nur die Erlaubnis, ein Land durchfahren zu können, es bedeutet zugleich den Uebergang eines Menschen zu einer neuen Station in seinem Leben. Dieser Prozess vollzieht sich in dem Helden des Romans, dem deutschen Monteur Seidler. " (23) But then the quasi-existential milieu created by the author apparently raises some doubt in this critic's mind about the certainty of the process embodied in the hero. He speaks of the "verworrenen Situationen, in denen er [Seidler] sich selbst nicht zurechtfinden kann. " (24) The "Uebergang" and "Prozess" which were to be symbolized in Seidler's development suddenly emerge outside the realm of his actions in Neugebauer's following remark: "Im Roman nehmen die persönlichen Erlebnisse des Helden, seine Gedanken und Empfindungen, die vielfach widerliche Alltäglichkeit des Emigrantendaseins breiten Raum ein; sie überdecken oft die grossen historischen Ereignisse. " (25) It would be interesting to discover how Neugebauer relates these "great historical events" to the text during a period in which Nazi domination had scattered left-wing exiles in all directions.

Matthias Wegner has correctly pointed out Seidler's unique situation as an outsider who defies the absurd world manipulating the destinies of the other emigrants. (26) In this respect he shares the view advanced by Marxist critics who see in the hero a potential for development and change. Wegner is also correct, however, in deemphasizing the revolutionary significance Marxists place on this development. Referring to the closing scene, he states: "Er [Seidler] schliesst sich den einfachen Bauern des Landes an, um mit ihrer Hilfe zu retten, was zu retten ist. Nur von diesem entscheidenden Punkt des Romans her kann eine Beziehung zur kommunistischen Ideologie festgestellt werden, obgleich diese Beziehung viel zu indirekt, viel zu individualistisch dargestellt ist, als dass sie von den kommunistischen Ideologen widerspruchslos hätte akzeptiert werden können. " (27) One need only recall Seidler's own admission of nonpartisanship (18) to realize that his "social" consciousness at the end was not a result of left-wing sympathies.

In Jörg Bernhard Bilke's analysis of T r a n s i t , the highly relevant concept of S o n d e r s t e l l u n g is introduced which places the novel in a special relationship to Seghers' other works, thereby conflicting with those interpretations which approach it as an integral part of an artistic continuum. "Alle ihre [Seghers'] Gestalten, " states Bilke, "agieren nicht nur als sich selbst genügende Individuen, sondern stellvertretend für ganze Schichten und Klassen des Volkes. ... Dieses Urteil gilt jedoch nicht mehr für den Roman T r a n s i t , der eine Sonderstellung einnimmt. ... Es geht hier um das Schicksal von deutschen Flüchtlingen in Marseille, die sich vergeblich um Transitvisa bemühen. Die Sinngebung dieser Schicksale durch kommunistische Heilserwartung ist aus diesem Buch völlig verdrängt. " (28)

Needless to say, the effectiveness of this remark is eclipsed by Bilke's desire to restore Seghers' ideology to her art. To make his point, he refers to that scene which depicts the impact of Weidel's manuscript on the disoriented Seidler: "Diese Textstelle, eine der ergreifendsten in diesem Buch, zeigt, wie Anna Seghers Literatur verstanden wissen wollte: als Lebenshilfe für das nach Orientierungen suchende Proletariat. Die Entsprechung: der Schriftsteller als Erzieher der Massen, war mit den Losungen der Partei identisch." (29) Yet the facts of Seghers' novel would seem to indicate otherwise. Weidel's fragmentary work does not orient Seidler to reality; rather, it enables him momentarily to e s c a p e the reality of his existence. Even critics in the East have observed in this scene the problematical relationship between art and reality and have applied it to Seghers' own situation during a period of general disorientation. Kurt Batt notes in this regard: "In der Isolation, der Verlassenheit entsteht keine Literatur, jedenfalls keine, wie Anna Seghers sie beabsichtigt; solche Literatur müsste zwangsläufig ... Fragment bleiben -- wie das Leben selbst, dem sie zugehört." (30) Once again, the "Sonderstellung" of Seghers' work comes ineluctably to the fore. For the sake of critical objectivity, then, one ought to look more closely into the historical conditions that influenced the novel's inception. As we have attempted to show, such an approach reveals new problems and assumptions with regard to the nature of reality and its relationship to the creative process. That which by Seghers' own admission is "steckend" in the work really invites criticism to uncover further possibilities of interpretation.

# FOOTNOTES

## Introduction

1) <u>Die humanistische Front: Einführung in die deutsche Emigranten-Literatur</u> (Zürich: Europa, 1946), I, 108.

2) "Emigrantenliteratur 1933-47," in <u>Reallexikon der deutschen Literaturge-schichte</u>, ed. Paul Merker and Wolfgang Mohr, 2nd ed. (Berlin: DeGruyter, 1958), p. 338.

3) <u>Exil und Literatur</u>, 2nd ed. (Frankfurt am Main: Athenaeum, 1968), p. 175.

4) "Die deutsche Emigration der Hitlerzeit," <u>Neue Politische Literatur</u>, 6 (1960), 466.

5) See Hans-Albert Walter, "Die Helfer im Hintergrund: Zur Situation der deutschen Exilverlage 1933-1945," <u>Frankfurter Hefte</u>, 20 (1965), 126. Walter quotes Wieland Herzfelde's conclusions regarding the causes that adversely affected the German exile book market. One of these reads: "Ein erheblicher Teil der in Frage kommenden Leser lebt in Oesterreich, in der Tschechoslowakei und in der Schweiz. In der Tschechoslowakei sind ebenso wie in Oesterreich grosse Teile des deutschen Publikums und noch grössere der deutschen Buchhändler Bewunderer des Dritten Reiches. In der Schweiz sind Anzeichen einer ähnlichen Entwicklung vorhanden."

6) <u>Exil und Literatur</u>, pp. 173-223.

7) "Konfrontation der Inneren und Aeusseren Emigration: Erinnerung und Deu-tung," in <u>Exil und Innere Emigration</u>, ed. Reinhold Grimm and Jost Hermand, Third Wisconsin Workshop (Frankfurt am Main: Athenäum, 1972), pp. 75-87.

8) "Der Reisepass," <u>Das Neue Tagebuch</u>, 23 (1937), 547-48.

9) "An der Grenze," <u>Das Wort</u>, 2 (1939), 119-22.

10) "Fünf Blicke auf Deutschland," <u>Das Wort</u>, 7 (1937), 84-86.

11) "Zwei an der Grenze," <u>Die Neue Weltbühne</u>, 52 (1938), 1639-40.

12) A. M. F. , "Klaus Mann: <u>Der Vulkan</u>," <u>Mass und Wert</u>, 3 (1940), pp. 407-09. Writing as if he were in dire need of consolation, the reviewer suppresses the "earthshaking" implications of Mann's volcano imagery by retitling <u>Der Vulkan</u> as "<u>Lehrjahre</u> oder <u>Wahrheit und Dichtung</u>." In the same breath he admits that the novel is "chaotisch" and then justifies his schizophrenia by saying: "Denn woher sollte die Distanz rühren zu einem Geschehen, in das wir aufs engste verstrickt sind?" This tone would appear to reflect the psychology of many liberal intellectuals around this time (1940). They were not inclined to criti-cal analysis. It seems rather that they preferred to identify with the situa-tions an author was describing, finding satisfaction in the knowledge that the writer was the true spokesman of their plight. Fritz Erpenbeck's article, "Manchmal habe ich Heimweh," <u>Das Wort</u>, 3 (1939), 127-30, treats Keun's novel along politically tendentious lines that betray the reviewer's position as an orthodox Marxist. Erpenbeck undertakes to impose an ideological bias on <u>Kind aller Länder</u> which would win the novel over to the cause of the anti-fascist People's Front. Needless to say, decidedly different issues stand in the forefront of the work.

13) Erich Maria Remarque's exile novels are an exception. Liebe deinen Nächsten and Arc de Triomphe received immediate attention in a flood of American journals, magazines, and newspapers after they appeared in translation. Since only native critics conducted these reviews, however, the question of "Wirkungsästhetik" within the exiled body no longer comes into play. Furthermore, that the exile scene in Remarque's novels is transferred to the European Continent would also explain the absence of any influence among Americans who might otherwise have discussed these works from a less superficial point of view had the novels confronted the problems of exile in the United States.

14) See note 1.

15) Ein Abriss der deutschen Literatur im Exil 1933-1947 (Berlin: Dietz, 1948).

16) (Heidelberg: Schneider, 1962).

17) (Frankfurt am Main: Deutsche Bibliothek, 1965).

18) Exil und Literatur, pp. 12-13.

19) Ibid., p. 13.

20) Ibid.

21) Ibid., p. 174.

22) Some critics will argue that Bruno Frank's Der Reisepass is just as much a novel about Nazi Germany as it is of exile in light of the equal emphasis lent to both settings. We place priority on the second category because the hero's experiences in Germany constitute a historical prelude to his actual state at the end.

23) Drei über die Grenze: Ein Abenteuer unter deutschen Emigranten (Geneva: Editions Union, 1937), p. 105.

24) "Konfrontation der Inneren und Aeusseren Emigration: Erinnerung und Deutung," pp. 75-87.

25) Ibid., p. 77.

26) Ibid., p. 79.

27) Ibid., p. 77.

28) Ibid.

29) Ibid., p. 78.

30) Ibid., p. 79.

31) Ibid., p. 78.

32) Gisela Berglund's Deutsche Opposition gegen Hitler in Presse und Roman des Exils: Eine Darstellung und ein Vergleich mit der historischen Wirklichkeit, Stockholmer Germanistische Forschungen, 11 (Stockholm: Almqvist & Wiksell, 1972) gives the source, historical setting, and detailed plot summaries of a few of the novels treating the exile experience. Berglund, like Wegner, also recognizes this novel as a distinct type of prose narrative. Her heavily documented work provides a wealth of information for scholars embarking on a variety of research paths in exile literature. Unlike Wegner and Mayer, however, her approach to the material, being primarily historical, disregards the problems of critical analysis which are the main concern of the present study.

1) With Erika Mann (Boston: Houghton Mifflin Co. , 1939), pp. 13-14.

2) This is not to suggest that Mann had been politically indifferent prior to going into exile. See Wilfried Dirschauer, Klaus Mann und das Exil, Deutsches Exil 1933-1945: Eine Schriftenreihe, 2, ed. Georg Heintz (Worms: [n.p. ], 1973), p. 31.

3) The Turning Point (New York: L. B. Fischer, 1942), p. 283.

4) See Hans-Albert Walter, "Klaus Mann und Die Sammlung: Porträt einer Literaturzeitschrift im Exil," Frankfurter Hefte, 22 (1967), 49-58.

5) The Turning Point, p. 265.

6) Ibid. , p. 266.

7) See Mann's "Brief an Gottfried Benn," in Klaus Mann: Die Heimsuchung des europäischen Geistes, ed. Martin Gregor-Dellin (München: Deutscher Taschenbuch Verlag, 1973), pp. 12-14. Written May 9, 1933, this letter antedates Mann's work on Flucht in den Norden by about a year. At first glance there seems to be little connection between the two documents. In the one, Mann is antipathetic to Marxism; in the other, he is sympathetic. Yet his aversion to materialistic literature carries with it a certain scepticism about literature that is nonmaterialistic. In his polemic against Benn, Mann is particularly disturbed by this writer's propensity for the irrational in art. He sees in Benn's contempt for literary leftists a corresponding tendency to preserve an artistic form that favors reaction. When one considers that the irrational as an esthetic principle had always played a role in Mann's own creative process, one can understand the problem he was faced with in writing his anti-fascist novel.

8) Mann addresses himself to the issue of a "breiter Einheitsfront" in "Die Schriftsteller in Paris: Der Internationale Schriftsteller-Kongress zur Verteidigung der Kultur," Die Sammlung, II (1934-35), 724-25.

9) Flucht in den Norden (Amsterdam: Querido, 1934), pp. 42, 45. Subsequent references appear parenthetically in the text by page number.

10) See Hans-Helmuth Knütter, "Zur Vorgeschichte der Exilsituation," in Die deutsche Exilliteratur 1933-1945, ed. Manfred Durzak (Stuttgart: Reclam, 1973), p. 32.

11) See Dirschauer, pp. 17-18.

12) Mann's portrayal of a "bourgeois communist" anticipates the mixed feelings about the function of literature which he experienced at the writers' convention. In "Notizen in Moskau," Die Sammlung, II (1934-35), 82, 83, he states: "Ist der nichtmaterialistische Schriftsteller wirklich schon reaktionär und arbeitet, ohne es zu wissen, im Dienst des Fascismus? -- Es gibt heute keine andre Frage, die mich so tief beunruhigt wie diese"; "die grossen Eindrücke bewegen mein Herz und meine Gedanken. In meinem Herzen und in meinen Gedanken wechseln Ergriffenheit und Widerspruch miteinander ab. "

## Chapter II

1) <u>Die Sammlung</u>, II (1934-35), 83. See also note 12 in Chapter I.

2) <u>The Turning Point</u> (New York: L.B. Fischer, 1942), p. 287.

3) Ibid.

4) See Matthias Wegner, <u>Exil und Literatur</u>, 2nd ed. (Frankfurt am Main: Athenäum, 1968), p. 190.

5) Erika and Klaus Mann, <u>Escape to Life</u> (Boston: Houghton Mifflin Co., 1939), p. 13.

6) In <u>Klaus Mann: Prüfungen</u>, ed. Martin Gregor-Dellin (München: Nymphenburger Verlagshandlung, 1968), p. 152.

7) <u>Exil und Literatur</u>, p. 191.

8) <u>Der Vulkan: Roman unter Emigranten</u> (München: Nymphenburger Verlagshandlung, 1968), pp. 340-41. Subsequent references appear parenthetically in the text by page number.

9) <u>Exil und Literatur</u>, p. 191.

10) Which, of course, was the case in <u>Flucht in den Norden</u>.

11) See Martin Gregor-Dellin, "Klaus Manns Exilromane," in <u>Die deutsche Exilliteratur 1933-1945</u>, ed. Manfred Durzak (Stuttgart: Reclam, 1973), p. 461: "Es ist jedoch die ephemerste und morbideste Figur, Kikjou, die über die Handlung des Romans hinausweist. Dieser kaum noch der Wirklichkeit angehörende, fromm-verderbte, zerrissene, empfindsame, aber zur Hoffnung entschlossene junge Mann erfährt seine entscheidenden Eindrücke und Wandlungen unter der Führung eines Engels."

12) See p. 256 of the novel where Kikjou avoids the debate over the "Einheitsfront"; see also p. 259 where he defends God against politics.

13) See Wilfried Dirschauer, <u>Klaus Mann und das Exil</u>, Deutsches Exil 1933-1945: Eine Schriftenreihe, 2, ed. Georg Heintz (Worms: [n.p.], 1973), p. 78.

14) See Richard Christ, "Das unausweichliche Entweder-Oder!" <u>Neue Deutsche Literatur</u>, 18 (1970), 171.

15) I speak here of Marion in her role as an apocalyptic seer, not as a polemic artist, although the latter function has an indirect bearing on the former. Her visions of Nazi terror venting its wrath unchallenged emerge, in part, as a result of her unsuccessful attempts to inspire the public to defiance.

16) <u>The Turning Point</u>, p. 228.

17) In <u>The Turning Point</u>, pp. 226-27, Mann describes Jesus Christ as "the Son of Man [who] is friendly and experienced, intimately versed in all our sorrows, pleasures, and endeavors: there is no quest or adventure he did not pass through, no emotion he could not share." The irrational comes into play as well when the Son of Man is linked to Dionysus, whom Mann defines as the "preincarnation of the Messiah himself."

18) In this connection Dirschauer, p. 79, raises the question "ob in politisch so gefährlich bewegter Zeit eine metaphysische Ueberhöhung der Exilsituation eine Hilfe für die Bewältigung der aktuellen Probleme sein konnte, ob also der Roman nicht unzeitgemäss und von zweifelhaftem Wert für die Zeitgenossen war. Es wird hier ja schliesslich darauf verzichtet, die Möglichkeiten der Literatur als geistige Waffe im politischen Kampf voll auszuschöpfen."

19) "Die Wirkung Frankreichs," p. 150.

20) Ibid., p. 152. See Klaus Mann, "Thomas de Quincey," Die Sammlung, I (1934), 488-98, for the probable source used in the creation of Martin. Mann's sympathy for the sensitive artist suffering under the disparity between dream and reality is strongly evidenced in this essay. Like Martin, de Quincey sought to alleviate this problem through the intoxicating effect of opium. The Marxist surrealist Marcel bears a close resemblance to the French writer René Crevel. For an analysis of this relationship see Klaus Mann, "In Memoriam René Crevel," in Prüfungen, pp. 36-41. See also "Die Wirkung Frankreichs," pp. 141-52, for a more exhaustive list of possible literary influences. Crevel is discussed again at some length as well as Julian Green, who could have provided Mann with the source for the angel.

21) Ibid.

22) See Hans Mayer, "Konfrontation der Inneren und Aeusseren Emigration: Erinnerung und Deutung," in Exil und Innere Emigration, ed. Reinhold Grimm and Jost Hermand (Frankfurt am Main: Athenäum, 1972), p. 78.

## Chapter III

1) Merz states in a personal letter dated August 13, 1972: "Die Friedhöfe vom Krieg. Ostberlin. Kein Haus, wo er gewohnt hatte, war noch Haus. Nur das letzte stand noch da. Es sprach nicht mehr mit ihm. Die Erinnerung ist eine Lügnerin, sogar unsre Fotos noch sind Lügner. Die Zeit vor Hitler ist der Zeit nach Hitler entnommen."

2) Ein Mensch fällt aus Deutschland (Amsterdam: Querido, 1936), p. 13. Subsequent references appear parenthetically in the text by page number.

3) "Vorläufige Gedanken zu einer Typologie der Exilliteratur," Akzente, 15 (1968), 570-71.

4) Ibid., 572.

5) Ibid., 574.

## Chapter IV

1) All My Sins, trans. E. Osers (London: George G. Harrap & Co., 1957), p. 207.

2) Ibid., p. 221.

3) Ibid., p. 222.

4) Drei über die Grenze: Ein Abenteuer unter deutschen Emigranten (Genève: Editions Union, 1937), p. 103. Subsequent references appear parenthetically in the text by page number.

5) All My Sins, p. 221.

6)   Ibid., p. 122.
7)   Ibid., p. 207.


Chapter V
_____

1)   <u>Exil</u> (Amsterdam: Querido, 1940), VIII, 986. Subsequent page references
     are to this edition and appear in the text.
2)   See Wolfgang Berndt, "The Trilogy <u>Der Wartesaal</u>," in <u>Lion Feuchtwanger:</u>
     <u>The Man, His Ideas, His Work</u>, Univ. of Southern California Studies in Comp.
     Lit., Vol. 3, ed. John M. Spalek (Los Angeles: Hennessey & Ingalls, Inc.,
     1972), p. 149.
3)   Lion Feuchtwanger, <u>Moskau 1937</u> (Amsterdam: Querido, 1937), 152.
4)   Horst Hartmann, "Die Antithetik 'Macht-Geist' im Werk Lion Feuchtwangers,"
     <u>Weimarer Beiträge</u>, 4 (1961), 685.
5)   Ibid., 685-86.
6)   Matthias Wegner, <u>Exil und Literatur: Deutsche Schriftsteller im Ausland</u>
     <u>1933-1945</u>, 2nd ed. (Frankfurt am Main: Athenäum, 1968), p. 207.
7)   <u>Moskau 1937</u>, p. 145.
8)   In L. F., <u>Centum Opuscula</u> (Rudolstadt: Greifenverlag, 1956), pp. 535-36.
9)   "Brief an den Kongress," <u>Das Wort,</u> 10 (1937), 63.
10)  See Hartmann, p. 667 ff. and Berndt, p. 131 ff.
11)  Hans Mayer, "Lion Feuchtwanger oder die Folgen des Exils," <u>Die Neue</u>
     <u>Rundschau</u>, 1 (1965), 127.
12)  In addition to note 10, see also Jürgen Rühle, <u>Literatur und Revolution: Die</u>
     <u>Schriftsteller und der Kommunismus</u> (München, Zürich: Knaur, 1963),
     p. 162 ff.
13)  Cf. Feuchtwanger's vitriolic article "Der Aesthet in der Sowjetunion (1937),"
     in <u>Centum Opuscula</u>, pp. 519-22, where these same sentiments are uttered
     against Gide. The contrast between the two writers is noteworthy. Both
     leftist intellectuals had the privilege of being granted entrance to the Soviet
     Union. Where this experience did not solve the problem of individualism and
     collectivism in Gide's case, it apparently did in Feuchtwanger's. This
     impression is conveyed not only by the supercilious tone emanating from
     the polemic, but also through the characterization of Tüverlin.
14)  Dieter Faulseit, "Die Darstellung der Figuren (speziell Figurentechnik) in
     den beiden Romantrilogien Lion Feuchtwangers (Wartesaal-Trilogie und
     Josephus-Trilogie)," Diss. Leipzig 1961, p. 67.
15)  Ibid., p. 68.
16)  A scandal linking a newspaper publisher with a Nazi collaborator did take
     place in Paris, but not until 1936. The editor of the <u>Pariser Tageblatt,</u>
     Georg Bernhard, and other members of his staff had falsely accused their
     publisher of selling out to the Nazis in Paris. Wladimir Poljakow, the
     publisher named in the scandal, was finally exonerated. It is reasonable to
     assume that Feuchtwanger did initially base his source on the Nazification
     of the Saar newspaper <u>Westland</u> in 1935, but then drew subsequently on the

controversial affair that broke out in Paris a year later. In the preface to Exil his outright denial of this affair as a material source was necessitated in response to objections raised in Das Wort, 2 (1939), 139, which saw in the novel a direct connection to real persons and events. These objections are not surprising when one considers that Feuchtwanger draws a most despicable portrait of the "fictitious" publisher Gingold, whose dealings with the Nazis recall the alleged ones of Poljakow. Furthermore, the founding of the Pariser Deutsche Post by the staff of the Pariser Nachrichten parallels the actual chain of events in 1936 when the members of the Pariser Tageblatt created the Pariser Tageszeitung. (See in this regard Konrad Heiden, "Der Prüfungsfall der Emigration," Das Neue Tagebuch, 12 (1937), 276-80.) Feuchtwanger refutes almost too emphatically any direct reference to the real episode. Needless to say, the similarities to persons and events are too compelling to be just coincidental. Heilbrun, for example, the back-biting editor of the Pariser Nachrichten, takes great delight in digging up dirt about Wiesener's intimate relationship with the Jewess Lea. This vendetta bears strong resemblance to the underhandedness of Bernhard. Feuchtwanger's preface should therefore be read with some caution. As a historical writer whose main concern is objectivity (the intent of which is not artistically born out in the novel), it is understandable that he would be quick to repudiate any statements accusing him of personal exposure.

17) See note 2.
18) See Marcel Reich-Ranicki, "Lion Feuchtwanger oder Der Weltruhm des Emigranten," in Die deutsche Exilliteratur 1933-1945, ed. Manfred Durzak (Stuttgart: Reclam, 1973), p. 449.
19) "Grösse und Erbärmlichkeit des Exils," Das Wort, 6 (1938), 3-6.
20) Mayer, 126.
21) Klaus Jarmatz, Literatur im Exil (Berlin: Dietz, 1966), p. 81.
22) Ibid., p. 80.
23) Ibid.


Chapter VI
-------

1) Mrs. Liesl Frank-Lustig believes this character might have been modelled after the Prince of Hessen who had studied art history in Munich (personal letter dated October 19, 1972). As we shall see, Frank's penchant for drawing portraiture has a functional value in the novel.
2) "Fünf Blicke auf Deutschland," Das Wort, 7 (1937), 84-85.
3) "Der Reisepass," Das Neue Tagebuch, 23 (1937), 547.
4) Der Reisepass (Amsterdam: Querido, 1937), p. 107. Subsequent references appear parenthetically in the text by page number.
5) "Der Reisepass," 547.
6) "Fünf Blicke auf Deutschland," 85.
7) This chapter originally appeared as an article carrying the same title in Monatshefte, Volume LXVII, Number 1 (c 1975 by the Regents of the Uni-

versity of Wisconsin), pp. 37-47. The publisher has kindly granted permission to have the article reprinted. Only slight stylistic revisions have been made.

## Chapter VII

1) See Hans Wagener, "Erich Maria Remarque" (unpub. art., Univ. of California Los Angeles), pp. 7-8.

2) Nor did he seem to take seriously his status as a literary emigrant, a position that explains the silent treatment afforded him by most exiled writers. The novelist and former exile Robert Neumann states in "Dass er uns so genau kannte ...," Der Spiegel, 14 June 1971, p. 126: "Immer lebte er am Rand der Filmwelt, bis zu seinem Ende war er eine Film-Figur, nicht eigentlich eine Literatur-Figur, als Schriftsteller nahmen die emigrierten Schriftsteller ... im Elend der Fremde ihn nicht sehr ernst. Und den in Millionen und immer neuen Millionen Schwimmenden als einen Mit-Emigranten, als einen der ihren zu betrachten, fiel ihnen nicht ein."

3) Deutsche Literatur in West und Ost (München: Piper & Co., 1963), p. 255.

4) Ibid.

5) "Helden in der Krise: Zu Erich Maria Remarques Emigrationsromanen," Német Filológiai Tanulmányok II. (Arbeiten zur deutschen Philologie II.), 2 (1966), 92-93.

6) Ibid., 91.

7) The hopeful outlook envisioned in the couple's voyage to Mexico -- away from the real exile scene -- is a possible allusion to Remarque's already secure existence in the United States when he wrote Liebe deinen Nächsten. (The English version, Flotsam, first appeared in the summer of 1939 as a serial in Collier's.) If one can speak at all of a personal tone pointing to the author's own exile situation, it would have to be at the close of the novel where Remarque implicitly contrasts a disruptive exile condition in Europe with a favorable one (as he experienced it) in an overseas country. See in this regard Wagener's comment in "Erich Maria Remarque," p. 5, which describes Remarque's view of America as a deterrent ("Friedenshoffnung") to the threat of total war.

8) Liebe deinen Nächsten (München: Kurt Desch, 1953), p. 19. Subsequent references appear in the text parenthetically by page number.

9) "Helden in der Krise," 86.

10) See Lewis J. Edinger, German Exile Politics (Berkeley: Univ. of California Press, 1956), pp. 198-204.

11) See Erich Stern, Die Emigration als psychologisches Problem (Boulogne-sur-Seine: Selbstverlag, 1937). The complexity of types that Stern points out in this study lends credence to Remarque's representative portrayal.

## Chapter VIII

1) See Hans Wagener, "Erich Maria Remarque" (unpub. art., Univ. of California Los Angeles), p. 5.
2) See Orville Prescott's review of Arc de Triomphe in the New York Times, 21 Jan. 1946, p. 21. Prescott mentions the motif of "forgetfulness," induced through such pastimes as sex and drink. He is right in interpreting this as a reaction to the sense of doom which has befallen Europe.
3) Arc de Triomphe (Zürich: Micha 1946), p. 264. Subsequent references are to this edition and appear in the text.
4) "Helden in der Krise: Zu Erich Maria Remarques Emigrationsromanen," Német Filológiai Tanulmányok II. (Arbeiten zur deutschen Philologie II.), 2 (1966), 88.
5) "Dass er uns so genau kannte ...," Der Spiegel, 14 June 1971, pp. 126-27.
6) Ibid., p. 126.
7) See Wagener, "Erich Maria Remarque," pp. 4-5.


## Chapter IX

1) See Deutsche Literatur im Exil: Briefe Europäischer Autoren 1933-1949, ed. Hermann Kesten (Wien: Kurt Desch, 1964), p. 127.
2) See Exil-Literatur 1933-1945: Katalog zur Ausstellung der Deutschen Bibliothek, comp. Werner Berthold, 3rd ed. (Frankfurt am Main: Deutsche Bibliothek, 1967), p. 200.
3) See Hermann Kesten, "Irmgard Keun," in Meine Freunde die Poeten, by Hermann Kesten (Wien: Donau, 1953), p. 241.
4) See Hans-Albert Walter, "Das Bild Deutschlands im Exilroman," Die Neue Rundschau, 3 (1966), 446.
5) Originally a speech delivered in the United States in 1943. Retitled "Schrift-steller im Exil," in Centum Opuscula (Rudolstadt: Greifenverlag, 1956), pp. 547-552.
6) "Die Helfer im Hintergrund: Zur Situation der deutschen Exilverlage 1933-1945," Frankfurter Hefte, 20 (1965), 127.
7) "Manchmal habe ich Heimweh," Das Wort, 3 (1939), 130.
8) "Irmgard Keun," Meine Freunde die Poeten, p. 247.
9) "Manchmal habe ich Heimweh," 130.
10) Kind aller Länder (Amsterdam: Querido, 1938), p. 229. Subsequent references appear in the text parenthetically by page number.
11) "Manchmal habe ich Heimweh," 130.
12) Ibid., 129.
13) "Irmgard Keun," Meine Freunde die Poeten, p. 247.
14) See Deutsche Literatur im Exil, ed. Hermann Kesten, p. 127.

## Chapter X

1) <u>Niemandsland</u> (Zürich: Oprecht, 1940), p. 9. Subsequent references appear in the text parenthetically by page number.
2) (New York: Willard Publishing Co. , 1944), pp. 51-52.

## Chapter XI

1) Kurt Pinthus, ed. , <u>Walter Hasenclever: Gedichte, Dramen, Prosa</u> (Reinbek bei Hamburg: Rowohlt, 1963), p. 59.
2) Ibid. , p. 8.
3) See Alfred Hölzel, "Walter Hasenclever's Political Satire," <u>Monatshefte</u>, 61 (1969), 35-36.
4) <u>Die Rechtlosen</u>, rpt. in Pinthus, <u>Walter Hasenclever</u>, p. 439. Subsequent references are to this anthology and appear in the text parenthetically by page number.
5) "Zeit und Dichtung: Ein Dialog zwischen Rudolf Leonhard und Walter Hasenclever. Zuerst gesprochen über den Sender Köln am 8. Dezember 1929," <u>Sinn und Form</u>, 16 (1964), 355-67.
6) Pinthus, <u>Walter Hasenclever</u>, p. 59.
7) Ibid. , p. 60.
8) Wegner, <u>Exil und Literatur</u>, 2nd ed. (Frankfurt am Main: Athenäum, 1968), p. 185.
9) See Miriam Raggam, <u>Walter Hasenclever: Leben und Werk</u> (Hildesheim: Gerstenberg, 1973), pp. 269-71.

## Chapter XII

1) <u>Flugsand: Dokumentarischer Roman eines Heimatlosen</u> (Zürich: Pan-Verlag, 1945), pp. 5-6. Subsequent references appear in the text parenthetically by page number.

## Chapter XIII

1) See <u>Lexikon Sozialistischer Deutscher Literatur</u>, ed. Inge Diersen et al. (Halle: Sprache und Literatur, 1963), pp. 149-50.
2) See Frank Trommler, "Emigration und Nachkriegsliteratur," in <u>Exil und Innere Emigration</u>, ed. Reinhold Grimm and Jost Hermand, Third Wisconsin Workshop (Frankfurt am Main: Athenäum, 1972), pp. 178-79. Trommler dis-

cusses the literary journal Die Kolonne, which was established in 1929 by a group of nature lyricists and carried the undertitle "Junge Gruppe Dresden." The esthetic program set forth in the first issue -- "Noch immer leben wir von Acker und Meer, und die Himmel, sie reichen auch über die Stadt" (quoted after Trommler) -- evokes an imagery bearing a certain resemblance to the dominant theme in Groetzsch's novel. Groetzsch probably had no direct association with the younger writers grouped around Die Kolonne, but his residence in Dresden at the time could mean he was at least familiar with the journal. The mere designation of Herkner's proletarian following as "Kolonne" would not justify a direct link to this literary organ. Such a description could conceivably carry a political meaning with regard to a group of defiant workers. Groetzsch's Rousseauistic characterization of the "Kolonne," however, calls to mind the literary goal set by the journal. The artist is to sense a union with elemental nature. Politics and ideology play no role in the poeticizing of the subject. The idyllic, pastoral scenes emerging in Wir suchen ein Land and describing the "Kolonne's" relationship to nature would seem to point to a source whose idential name is more than fortuitous.

3) Wir suchen ein Land: Roman einer Emigration (Bratislava: Eugen Prager, 1936), p. 15. Subsequent references appear in the text parenthetically by page number.

4) (Zürich: Europa, 1936), p. 160.

5) Ibid. , pp. 162, 182.

6) Ibid. , p. 160.

7) Ibid. , p. 161.

## Chapter XIV

1) Emigranten (Berlin: Volk und Welt, 1955), pp. 134-35. Subsequent references appear parenthetically in the text by page numer.

2) This omission is strategically conceived and does not indicate a relaxation of Erpenbeck's basic orthodoxy. Occasional references to the Soviet Union as the model for revolutionary struggle suggest a Kunstpolitik that is very much party-directed. Thus Erpenbeck's left-sectarianism should not be interpreted to mean a departure from Comintern policy in favor of revolutionary objectives on a national scale.

3) See Kurt R. Grossman, Emigration: Geschichte der Hitler-Flüchtlinge 1933-1945 (Frankfurt am Main: Europäische Verlagsanstalt, 1969), pp. 95-97.

## Chapter XV

1) Zwei an der Grenze (Berlin: Aufbau, 1951), V, 31. Subsequent references to this edition appear parenthetically in the text by page number.

2)    See Hans-Albert Walter, "Internationale Literatur/Deutsche Blätter (I): Eine Exilzeitschrift in der Sowjet-Union," Frankfurter Hefte, 24 (1969), 588-90; see also Matthias Wegner, Exil und Literatur, 2nd ed. (Frankfurt: Athenäum, 1968), pp. 61-62, 65.

3)    See Walter, "No pasarán!: Deutsche Exilschriftsteller im Spanischen Bürgerkrieg," Kürbiskern, 1 (1967), 10.

4)    Ibid., 7-8.

5)    Ibid., 13.

6)    Ibid., 7. Walter points out: "Hilfe erhielt das republikanische Spanien nur aus Mexiko und aus der Sowjetunion. Indes war Mexiko ein kleines Land, seine Unterstützung eher symbolisch, und die der Sowjetunion musste nicht nur mit den gesamten spanischen Goldreserven erkauft werden ..., sie war auch an politische Forderungen geknüpft, und blieb, als diese nicht erfüllt wurden, in entscheidenden Situationen aus."

7)    "Henleins Ernte," Das Neue Tagebuch, 44 (1935), 1039.

## Chapter XVI

1)    Kurt Batt, Anna Seghers: Versuch über Entwicklung und Werke (Frankfurt a. M.: Röderberg, 1973),pp. 152-64, and "Variationen über Unmittelbarkeit: Zur ästhetischen Position der Anna Seghers," Sinn und Form, 21 (1969), 943-62; Heinz Neugebauer, Anna Seghers, Schriftsteller der Gegenwart, 4 (Berlin: Volk und Wissen, 1959); Paul Rilla, Die Erzählerin Anna Seghers, Schriftenreihe der Deutschen Akademie der Künste, 1 (Berlin: Deutsche Akademie der Künste, 1950); Frank Wagner, "Transit-Lektüre im Jahre 1969," Weimarer Beiträge, Sonderheft, 15 (1969), 149-67.

2)    Jörg Bernhard Bilke, "Anna Seghers: Von der Klassenkampf- zur Staatsliteratur," Deutsche Studien, 8 (1970), 357-75, and "Sturz aus der Geschichte? Anna Seghers' Roman Transit," in Die deutsche Exilliteratur 1933-1945, ed. Manfred Durzak (Stuttgart: Reclam, 1973), pp. 312-25; Werner Merklin, "Zwischenspiel im exemplarischen Realismus," Frankfurter Hefte, 7 (1952), 146-51; Helena Szépe, "The Problem of Identity in Anna Seghers' Transit," Orbis Litterarum, 27 (1972), 145-52; Matthias Wegner, Exil und Literatur: Deutsche Schriftsteller im Ausland 1933-1945, 2nd ed. (Frankfurt a. M.: Athenäum, 1968), pp. 212-23.

3)    Marcel Reich-Ranicki, Deutsche Literatur in West und Ost (Reinbek bei Hamburg: Rowohlt, 1970), pp. 236-38.

4)    Exil in Frankreich (Bremen: Schünemann, 1971), pp. 236-43.

5)    Briefe an Leser (Berlin and Weimar: Aufbau, 1970), p. 68.

6)    Ibid., pp. 65-66.

7)    Only the conclusion was written in Mexico. See Briefe, p. 44.

8)    Ibid.

9)    Transit (Berlin: Aufbau, 1951), V, 60. Subsequent references are to this edition and appear parenthetically in the text by page number.

10)   Wegner, p. 212.

11)   See note 7.

12)   In her <u>Briefe</u>, p. 25, Seghers states: "Ich wusste über manches (durchaus nicht über alles) ganz gut Bescheid. Ueber eins wusste ich damals absolut nicht Bescheid: über den sozialistischen Realismus."

13)   "Ein Briefwechsel zwischen Anna Seghers und Georg Lukács," in Georg Lukács, <u>Probleme des Realismus</u> (Berlin: Aufbau, 1955), pp. 246, 259.

14)   <u>Briefe</u>, pp. 68-69.

15)   Batt, <u>Anna Seghers</u>, p. 158, although he admits this characterization is only "flüchtig gezeichnet."

16)   Rilla, p. 12.

17)   Ibid., p. 40.

18)   Wagner, 152.

19)   Ibid., 160.

20)   Ibid., 167.

21)   Ibid., 160.

22)   Ibid.

23)   Neugebauer, p. 69.

24)   Ibid., p. 70.

25)   Ibid., p. 71.

26)   Wegner, p. 214.

27)   Ibid., p. 223.

28)   Bilke, "Anna Seghers: Von der Klassenkampf- zur Staatsliteratur," 364.

29)   Ibid., 366.

30)   Batt, "Variationen über Unmittelbarkeit ...," 943. Reich-Ranicki, p. 236, is of a similar opinion in his remark: "Da die Partei in dem Chaos nach dem Zusammenbruch Frankreichs andere Sorgen hatte als Literatur, war Anna Seghers in dieser Zeit, was ihre berufliche Arbeit betrifft, sich selbst überlassen."

Albrechtová, Gertruda, "Zur Frage der deutschen antifaschistischen Emigrations-literatur im tschechoslowakischen Asyl." Historica, 8 (1964), 177-233.

Batt, Kurt. "Variationen über Unmittelbarkeit: Zur ästhetischen Position der Anna Seghers." Sinn und Form, 21 (1969), 943-62.

Berendsohn, Walter A. "Emigranten-Literatur 1933-47." Reallexikon der deutschen Literaturgeschichte. Ed. Werner Kohlschmidt and Wolfgang Mohr. 2nd ed. Berlin: DeGruyter, 1958, pp. 336-43.

_____. Die humanistische Front: Einführung in die deutsche Emigranten-Literatur. Vol. I. Zürich: Europa, 1946.

Berglund, Gisela. Deutsche Opposition gegen Hitler in Presse und Roman des Exils: Eine Darstellung und ein Vergleich mit der historischen Wirklichkeit. Stockholmer Germanistische Forschungen, 11. Stockholm: Almqvist & Wiksell, 1972.

Bermann-Fischer, Gottfried. Bedroht-Bewahrt: Der Weg eines Verlegers. Frankfurt am Main: Fischer Bücherei, 1971.

Bilke, Jörg Bernhard. "Anna Seghers: Von der Klassenkampf- zur Staatsliteratur." Deutsche Studien, 8 (1970), 357-75.

Brand, Renée. Niemandsland. Zürich: Oprecht, 1940.

Brenner, Hildegard. "Deutsche Literatur im Exil 1933-1947." Handbuch der deutschen Gegenwartsliteratur. Ed. Hermann Kunisch. Munich: Nymphenburger, 1965, pp. 677-94.

Cazden, Robert E. German Exile Literature in America 1933-1950. Chicago: American Library Assn., 1970.

Christ, Richard. "Das unausweichliche Entweder-Oder!" Neue Deutsche Literatur, 18 (1970), 167-72.

Davie, Maurice R. Refugees in America: Report of the Committee for the Study of the Recent Immigration from Europe. New York: Harper & Bros., 1947.

Deutsche Exil-Literatur 1933-1945: Eine Bio-Bibliographie. Ed. Wilhelm Sternfeld and Eva Tiedemann. Heidelberg: Schneider, 1962.

Deutsche Literatur im Exil: Briefe europäischer Autoren 1933-1949. Ed. Hermann Kesten. Vienna: Kurt Desch, 1964.

Dickson, Paul. "Das Amerikabild in der deutschen Emigrantenliteratur seit 1933." Diss. Univ. of Munich, 1951.

Die deutsche Exilliteratur 1933-1945. Ed. Manfred Durzak. Stuttgart: Reclam, 1973.

Dirschauer, Wilfried. Klaus Mann und das Exil. Deutsches Exil 1933-1945: Eine Schriftenreihe, 2. Ed. Georg Heintz. Worms: [n.p.], 1973.

Döblin, Alfred. Aufsätze zur Literatur. Olten und Freiburg im Breisgau: Walter, 1963.

_____. Flucht und Sammlung des Judenvolks. Amsterdam: Querido, 1935.

Drews, Richard and Alfred Kantorowicz. Verboten und Verbrannt: Deutsche
Literatur zwölf Jahre unterdrückt. Munich: Ullstein, Kindler, 1947.
Dreyfus, P. and Jacob Berthold. "In Sachen Bernhard und Genossen." Das Neue
Tagebuch, 10 (1937), 232-33.


Eckert, Horst. "Die Beiträge der deutschen emigrierten Schriftsteller in der
'Neuen Weltbühne' von 1933-1939: Ein Beitrag zur Untersuchung der Bezie-
hungen zwischen Volksfrontpolitik und Literatur." Diss. Univ. of Humboldt,
1962.
Edinger, Lewis J. German Exile Politics. Berkeley: Univ. of California Press,
1956.
Erpenbeck, Fritz. Emigranten. Berlin: Volk und Welt, 1955.
_____. "Manchmal habe ich Heimweh." Das Wort, 3 (1939), 127-30.
Exil-Literatur 1933-1945: Katalog zur Ausstellung der Deutschen Bibliothek. Comp.
Werner Berthold. 3rd ed. Frankfurt am Main: Deutsche Bibliothek, 1967.


F., A.M. "Klaus Mann: Der Vulkan." Mass und Wert, 3 (1940), 407-09.
Faulseit, Dieter. "Die Darstellung der Figuren (speziell Figurentechnik) in den
beiden Romantrilogien Lion Feuchtwangers (Wartesaal-Trilogie und Josephus-
Trilogie)." Diss. Univ. of Leipzig, 1961.
Feuchtwanger, Lion. "Brief an den Kongress." Das Wort, 10 (1937), 63.
_____. Centum Opuscula. Rudolstadt: Greifenverlag, 1956.
_____. Exil. Vol. VIII. Amsterdam: Querido, 1940.
_____. Moskau 1937. Amsterdam: Querido, 1937.
_____. Unholdes Frankreich. Mexico: El libro libre, 1942.
_____. "Zwei an der Grenze." Die Neue Weltbühne, 52 (1938), 1639-40.
F., W. "Kleine deutsche Chronik -- Paris." (Includes a brief commentary on Lion
Feuchtwanger's Exil). Das Wort, 2 (1939), 139.
Franck, Wolf. Führer durch die deutsche Emigration. Phönix Bücher, 4. Paris:
Editions du Phénix, 1935.
Frank, Bruno. Der Reisepass. Amsterdam: Querido, 1937.
Frei, Bruno. "Die deutsche antifaschistische literarische Emigration in Prag
1933-1936." Weltfreunde: Konferenz über die Prager deutsche Literatur.
Ed. Eduard Goldstücker. Prague: Academia, 1967, pp. 361-71.


Graf, Oskar Maria. An manchen Tagen. Frankfurt am Main: Nest, 1961.
Gregor-Dellin, Martin. "Klaus Mann und seine Generation." Neue Deutsche Hefte,
12, No. 2 (1969), 46-64.
Groetzsch, Robert. Wir suchen ein Land: Roman einer Emigration. Bratislava:
Eugen Prager, 1936.
Grossmann, Kurt R. Emigration: Geschichte der Hitler-Flüchtlinge 1933-1945.
Frankfurt am Main: Europäische Verlagsanstalt, 1969.
_____. "Das Leben der deutschen jüdischen Flüchtlinge in den Vereinigten Staaten."
Frankfurter Hefte, 8 (1953), 60-64.
Gumpert, Martin. First Papers. New York: Duell, Sloan & Pearce, 1941.

Habe, Hans. All My Sins. Trans. E. Osers. London: Harrap & Co., 1957.
_____. Drei über die Grenze: Ein Abenteuer unter deutschen Emigranten. Geneva: Editions Union, 1937.
Hartmann, Horst. "Die Antithetik 'Macht-Geist' im Werk Lion Feuchtwangers." Weimarer Beiträge, 4 (1961), 667-93.
Hasenclever, Walter. Irrtum und Leidenschaft. Berlin: Universitas, 1969.
_____. Gedichte, Dramen, Prosa. Ed. Kurt Pinthus. Hamburg: Rowohlt, 1963.
Heiden, Konrad. "Der Prüfungsfall der Emigration." Das Neue Tagebuch, 12 (1937), 276-80.
"Henleins Ernte." Das Neue Tagebuch, 44 (1935), 1039-40.
Hölzel, Alfred, "Walter Hasenclever's Political Satire." Monatshefte, 61 (1969), 30-40.
_____. "Walter Hasenclever's Satiric Treatment of Religion." German Quarterly, 41 (1968), 59-70.

Jarmatz, Klaus. Literatur im Exil. Berlin: Dietz, 1966.
Jehser, Werner. Friedrich Wolf: Leben und Werk. Schriftsteller der Gegenwart, 17. Berlin: Volk und Wissen, 1965.

Kantorowicz, Alfred. Exil in Frankreich. Bremen: Schünemann, 1971.
Kesten, Hermann. Der Geist der Unruhe. Cologne: Kiepenheuer, Witsch, 1959.
_____. Meine Freunde die Poeten. Vienna: Donau, 1953.
Keun, Irmgard, Kind aller Länder. Amsterdam: Querido, 1938.

Leonhard, Rudolf and Walter Hasenclever. "Zeit und Dichtung: Ein Dialog zwischen Rudolf Leonhard und Walter Hasenclever. Zuerst gesprochen über den Sender Köln am 8. Dezember 1929." Sinn und Form, 16 (1964), 355-67.
Lexikon sozialistischer deutscher Literatur. Ed. Inge Diersen et. al. Halle (Saale): Sprache und Literatur, 1963.
Lindt, Peter M. Schriftsteller im Exil: Zwei Jahre deutsche literarische Sendung am Rundfunk in New York. New York: Willard, 1944.
Lukács, Georg. Probleme des Realismus. Berlin: Aufbau, 1955.

Mann, Erika and Klaus Mann. Escape to Life. Boston: Houghton Mifflin Co., 1939.
Mann, Golo. "Deutsche Literatur im Exil: Rede." Die Neue Rundschau, 79 (1968), 38-49.
Mann, Klaus. Flucht in den Norden. Amsterdam: Querido, 1934.
_____. Die Heimsuchung des europäischen Geistes. Ed. Martin Gregor-Dellin. München: Deutscher Taschenbuch Verlag, 1973.
_____. "In Memoriam René Crevel." Klaus Mann: Prüfungen. Ed. Martin Gregor-Dellin. Munich: Nymphenburger, 1968, pp. 36-41.
_____. "Notizen in Moskau." Die Sammlung, II (1934-35), 72-83.
_____. "Der Reisepass." Das Neue Tagebuch, 23 (1937), 547-48.
_____. "Die Schriftsteller in Paris: Der Internationale Schriftsteller-Kongress zur Verteidigung der Kultur." Die Sammlung, II (1934-35), 724-25.
_____. "Thomas de Quincey." Die Sammlung, I (1934), 488-98.
_____. The Turning Point. New York: L. B. Fischer, 1942.

_____. Der Vulkan: Roman unter Emigranten. Munich: Nymphenburger, 1968.

_____. "Die Wirkung Frankreichs." Klaus Mann: Prüfungen. Ed. Martin Gregor-Dellin. Munich: Nymphenburger, 1968, pp. 141-52.

Marcuse, Ludwig. "Fünf Blicke auf Deutschland." Das Wort, 7 (1937), 84-86.

Mayer, Hans and Stephan Hermlin. Ansichten über einige Bücher und Schriftsteller. Wiesbaden: Limes, 1947.

_____. "Konfrontation der Inneren und Aeusseren Emigration: Erinnerung und Deutung." Exil und Innere Emigration. Ed. Reinhold Grimm and Jost Hermand. Third Wisconsin Workshop. Frankfurt am Main: Athenäum, 1972, pp. 75-87.

_____. "Lion Feuchtwanger oder die Folgen des Exils." Die Neue Rundschau, 1 (1965), 120-29.

Merklin, Werner. "Zwischenspiel im exemplarischen Realismus." Frankfurter Hefte, 7 (1952), 149-51.

Merz, Konrad. Ein Mensch fällt aus Deutschland. Amsterdam: Querido, 1936.

_____. (Personal letter dated 13 Aug. 1972).

Natonek, Hans. In Search of Myself. Trans. Barthold Fles. New York: G. P. Putnam's Sons, 1943.

Neubach, Ernst. Flugsand: Dokumentarischer Roman eines Heimatlosen. Zürich: Pan, 1945.

Neugebauer, Heinz. Anna Seghers. Schriftsteller der Gegenwart, 4. Berlin: Volk und Wissen, 1959.

Neumann, Robert. "Dass er uns so genau kannte ..." Der Spiegel, 14 June 1971, pp. 126-27.

Osterle, Heinz D. "Die Deutschen im Spiegel des sozialkritischen Romans der Emigration 1933-50." Diss. Brown Univ., 1964.

_____. "The Other Germany: Resistance to the Third Reich in German Literature." German Quarterly, 41 (1968), 1-22.

Paetel, Karl O. "Die deutsche Emigration der Hitlerzeit." Neue Politische Literatur 6 (1960), 465-82.

Pfeiler, William K. German Literature in Exile: The Concern of the Poets. Univ. of Nebraska Studies, NS 16. Lincoln: Univ. of Nebraska Press, 1957.

Pollatschek, Walther. Friedrich Wolf: Eine Biographie. Berlin: Aufbau, 1963.

Prescott, Orville. (Review of Arch of Triumph). New York Times, 21 Jan. 1946, p. 21.

Pross, Helge. Die deutsche akademische Emigration nach den Vereinigten Staaten 1933-1941. Berlin: Duncker & Humboldt, 1955.

Raggam, Miriam. Walter Hasenclever: Leben und Werk. Hildesheim: Gerstenberg, 1973.

Reich-Ranicki, Marcel. Deutsche Literatur in West und Ost. Munich: Piper & Co., 1963.

Remarque, Erich Maria. Arc de Triomphe. Zürich: Micha, 1946.

_____. Liebe deinen Nächsten. Munich: Kurt Desch, 1953.

Rilla, Paul. Die Erzählerin Anna Seghers. Schriftenreihe der Deutschen Akademie der Künste, 1. Berlin: Deutsche Akademie der Künste, 1950.

Rudolf, Helmut. "Helden in der Krise: Zu Erich Maria Remarques Emigrations-romanen." Német Filológiai Tanulmányok II (Arbeiten zur deutschen Philologie·II), 2 (1966), 83-93.

Rühle, Jürgen. Literatur und Revolution: Die Schriftsteller und der Kommunismus. Cologne: Kiepenheuer, 1960.

Seger, Gerhart. Reisetagebuch eines deutschen Emigranten. Zürich: Europa, 1936.

Seghers, Anna. Briefe an Leser. Berlin, Weimar: Aufbau, 1970.

_____. Transit. Vol. V. Berlin: Aufbau, 1951.

Stern, Erich. Die Emigration als psychologisches Problem. Boulogne-sur-Seine: Selbstverlag, 1937.

Ter Braak, Menno. "Emigranten-Literatur." Das Neue Tagebuch, 52 (1934), 1244-45.

Trommler, Frank. "Emigration und Nachkriegsliteratur." Exil und Innere Emigration. Ed. Reinhold Grimm and Jost Hermand. Third Wisconsin Workshop. Frankfurt am Main: Athenäum, 1972, pp. 173-97.

Verbannung: Aufzeichnungen deutscher Schriftsteller im Exil. Ed. Egon Schwarz and Matthias Wegner. Hamburg: Christian Wegner, 1964.

Vordtriede, Werner. "Vorläufige Gedanken zu einer Typologie der Exilliteratur." Akzente, 15 (1968), 556-75.

Wagener, Hans. "Erich Maria Remarque." Unpub. art. Univ. of California Los Angeles.

Wagner, Frank. "Transit-Lektüre im Jahre 1969." Weimarer Beiträge, Sonder-heft, 15 (1969), 149-67.

Walter, Hans-Albert. "Das Bild Deutschlands im Exilroman." Die Neue Rundschau, 3 (1966), 437-58.

_____. "Deutsche Literatur im Exil." Merkur, 273 (1971), 77-84.

_____. "Die Helfer im Hintergrund: Zur Situation der deutschen Exilverlage 1933-1945." Frankfurter Hefte, 20 (1965), 121-32.

_____. "Internationale Literatur/Deutsche Blätter (I): Eine Exilzeitschrift in der Sowjet-Union." Frankfurter Hefte, 24 (1969), 580-93.

_____. "Internationale Literatur/Deutsche Blätter (II): Eine Exilzeitschrift in der Sowjet-Union." Frankfurter Hefte, 24 (1969), 648-58.

_____. "Klaus Mann und Die Sammlung: Porträt einer Literaturzeitschrift im Exil (II)." Frankfurter Hefte, 22 (1967), 49-58.

_____. "Leopold Schwarzschild und das Neue Tage-Buch." Frankfurter Hefte, 21 (1966), 549-58.

_____. "No pasarán!: Deutsche Exilschriftsteller im Spanischen Bürgerkrieg." Kürbiskern, 1 (1967), 5-27.

_____ "Der Streit um Die Sammlung: Porträt einer Literaturzeitschrift im Exil (I)." Frankfurter Hefte, 21 (1966), 850-60.

Weiskopf, F.C. Unter fremden Himmeln: Ein Abriss der deutschen Literatur im Exil 1933-1947. Berlin: Dietz, 1948.

Werth, Heinrich. "An der Grenze." Das Wort, 2 (1939), 119-22.

Wolf, Friedrich. Zwei an der Grenze. Vol. V. Berlin: Aufbau, 1951.

EUROPÄISCHE HOCHSCHULSCHRIFTEN

Reihe I   Deutsche Literatur und Germanistik

Nr. 1   Henning Boetius, Frankfurt a.M.: Utopie und Verwesung. Zur Struktur von Hans Henny Jahnns Roman "Fluss ohne Ufer". 174 S. 1967.

Nr. 2   Gerhard Trapp, Frankfurt a.M.: Die Prosa Johannes Urzidils. 235 S. 1967.

Nr. 3   Bernhard Gajek, Frankfurt a.M.: Sprache beim jungen Hamann. 113 S. 1967. (Neudruck)

Nr. 4   Henri Paucker, Zürich: Heinrich Heine: Mensch und Dichter zwischen Deutschland und Frankreich. 95 S. 1967. (Neudruck)

Nr. 5   Fritz Hackert, Stuttgart: Kulturpessimismus und Erzählform. Studien zu Joseph Roths Leben und Werk. 220 S. 1967.

Nr. 6   Michael Böhler, Zürich: Formen und Wandlungen des Schönen. Untersuchungen zum Schönheitsbegriff Adalbert Stifters. 100 S. 1967. (Neudruck)

Nr. 7   Rudolf Schäfer, Wiesbaden: Hugo von Hofmannsthals "Arabella". Wege zum Verständnis des Werkes und seines gattungsgeschichtlichen Ortes. 332 S. 1968.

Nr. 8   Leslie MacEwen, Washington: The Narren-motifs in the Works of Georg Büchner. 52 p. 1968.

Nr. 9   Emil Wismer, Neuenburg: Der Einfluss des deutschen Romantikers Zacharias Werner in Frankreich (Die Beziehungen des Dichters zu Madame de Staël). 98 S. 1968. (Neudruck)

Nr. 10   Franz Hagmann, Freiburg: Aspekte der Wirklichkeit im Werke Robert Musils. 204 S. 1969.

Nr. 11   Ilpo Tapani Piirainen, Helsinki: Textbezogene Untersuchungen über "Katz und Maus" und "Hundejahre" von Günter Grass. 84 S. 1968.

Nr. 12   Georg Alexander Nowak, Wheeling, West Virginia, USA: Abhandlungen zur Germanistik. 80 S. 3 Karten. 1969.

Nr. 13   Gawaina D. Luster, Washington: Untersuchungen zum Stabreimstil in der Eneide Heinrichs von Veldeke. 112 S. 4 Tafeln. 1969.

Nr. 14   Kaspar Schnetzler, Zürich: Der Fall Maurizius. Jakob Wassermanns Kunst des Erzählens. 120 S. 1968.

Nr. 15   Dorothea W. Dauer, White Plains/USA: Schopenhauer as Transmitter of Buddhist Ideas. 40 p. 1969.

Nr. 16   Hermann Bitzer, Zürich: Goethe über den Dilettantismus. 124 S. 1969.

Nr. 17   Urs Strässle, Zürich: Geschichte, geschichtliches Verstehen und Geschichtsschreibung im Verständnis Johann Georg Hamanns. 166 S. 1970.

Nr. 18   Stefan F. L. Grunwald, Norfolk, Va./USA: A Biography of Johann Michael Moscherosch (1601–1669). 96 p. Illustrated. 1970.

Nr. 19   Philipp H. Zoldester, Charlottesville, Va./USA: Adalbert Stifters Weltanschauung. 186 S. 1969.

Nr. 20   Karl-Jürgen Ringel, Düsseldorf: Wilhelm Raabes Roman "Hastenbeck". 192 S. 1970.

Nr. 21   Elisabeth Kläui, Zürich: Gestaltung und Formen der Zeit im Werk Adalbert Stifters. 112 S. 1969.

Nr. 22   Hildegund Kunz, Baldegg: Bildersprache als Daseinserschliessung. Metaphorik in Gotthelfs "Geld und Geist" und in "Anne Bäbi Jowäger". 164 S. 1969.

Nr. 23   Martin Kraft, Zürich: Studien zur Thematik von Max Frischs Roman "Mein Name sei Gantenbein". 84 S. 1970.

Nr. 24   Wilhelm Resenhöfft, Kiel: Existenzerhellung des Hexentums in Goethes "Faust". (Mephistos Masken, Walpurgis) Grundlinien axiomatisch-psychologischer Deutung. 128 S. 1970.

Nr. 25   Wolfgang W. Moelleken, Davis/USA: "Der Stricker: Von übelen wiben". 68 S. 1970.

Nr. 26    Vera Debluë, Zürich: Anima naturaliter ironica – Die Ironie in Wesen und Werk Heinrich Heines. 100 S. 1970.

Nr. 27    Hans-Wilhelm Kelling, Stanford/USA: The Idolatry of Poetic Genius in German Goethe Criticism. 200 p. 1970.

Nr. 28    Armin Schlienger, Zürich: Das Komische in den Komödien des Andreas Gryphius. Ein Beitrag zu Ernst und Scherz im Barocktheater. 316 S. 1970.

Nr. 29    Marianne Frey, Bern: Der Künstler und sein Werk bei W. H. Wackenroder und E. T. A. Hoffmann. Vergleichende Studien zur romantischen Kunstanschauung. 216 S. 1970.

Nr. 30    C. A. M. Noble, Belfast: Krankheit, Verbrechen und künstlerisches Schaffen bei Thomas Mann. 268 S. 1970.

Nr. 31    Eberhard Frey, Waltham/USA: Franz Kafkas Erzählstil. Eine Demonstration neuer stilanalytischer Methoden an Kafkas Erzählung "Ein Hungerkünstler". 382 S. 1974 (2. Auflage).

Nr. 32    Raymond Lauener, Neuchâtel: Robert Walser ou la Primauté du Jeu. 532 p. 1970.

Nr. 33    Samuel Berr, New York: An Etymological Glossary to the Old Saxon Heliand. 480 p. 1970.

Nr. 34    Erwin Frank Ritter, Wisconsin: Johann Baptist von Alxinger and the Austrian Enlightenment. 176 p. 1970.

Nr. 35    Felix Thurner, Fribourg: Albert Paris Gütersloh – Studien zu seinem Romanwerk. 220 S. 1970.

Nr. 36    Klaus Wille, Tübingen: Die Signatur der Melancholie im Werk Clemens Brentanos. 208 S. 1970.

Nr. 37    Andreas Oplatka, Zürich: Aufbauform und Stilwandel in den Dramen Grillparzers. 104 S. 1970.

Nr. 38    Hans-Dieter Brückner, Claremont: Heldengestaltung im Prosawerk Conrad Ferdinand Meyers. 102 S. 1970.

Nr. 39    Josef Helbling, Zürich: Albrecht von Haller als Dichter. 164 S. 1970.

Nr. 40    Lothar Georg Seeger, Washington: The "Unwed Mother" as a Symbol of Social Consciousness in the Writings of J. G. Schlosser, Justus Möser, and J. H. Pestalozzi. 36 p. 1970.

Nr. 41    Eduard Mäder, Freiburg: Der Streit der "Töchter Gottes" – Zur Geschichte eines allegorischen Motivs. 136 S. 1971.

Nr. 42    Christian Ruosch, Freiburg: Die phantastisch-surreale Welt im Werke Paul Scheerbarts. 136 S. 1970.

Nr. 43    Maria Pospischil Alter, Maryland/USA: The Concept of Physician in the Writings of Hans Carossa and Arthur Schnitzler. 104 p. 1971.

Nr. 44    Vereni Fässler, Zürich: Hell-Dunkel in der barocken Dichtung – Studien zum Hell-Dunkel bei Johann Klaj, Andreas Gryphius und Catharina Regina von Greiffenberg. 96 S. 1971.

Nr. 45    Charlotte W. Ghurye, Terre Haute, Indiana/USA: The Movement Toward a New Social and Political Consciousness in Postwar German Prose. 128 p. 1971.

Nr. 46    Manfred A. Poitzsch, Minneapolis, Minnesota/USA: Zeitgenössische Persiflagen auf C. M. Wieland und seine Schriften. 220 S. 1972.

Nr. 47    Michael Imboden, Freiburg: Die surreale Komponente im erzählenden Werk Arthur Schnitzlers. 132 S. 1971.

Nr. 48    Wolfgang Dieter Elfe, Massachusetts/USA: Stiltendenzen im Werk von Ernst Weiss, unter besonderer Berücksichtigung seines expressionistischen Stils (Ein Vergleich der drei Druckfassungen des Romans "Tiere in Ketten"). 80 S. 1971.

Nr. 49    Alba Schwarz, Zürich: "Der teutsch-redende treue Schäfer". Guarinis "Pastor Fido" und die Übersetzungen von Eilger Mannlich 1619, Statius Ackermann 1636, Hofmann von Hofmannswaldau 1652, Assman von Abschatz 1672. 284 S. 1972.

Nr. 50   Martin Kraft, Zürich: "Schweizerhaus" – Das Haus-Motiv im Deutsch-schweizer Roman des 20. Jahrhunderts. 72 S. 1971.

Nr. 51   Hansjörg Büchler, Zürich: Studien zu Grimmelshausens Landstörtzerin Courasche (Vorlagen/Struktur und Sprache/Moral). 116 S. 1971.

Nr. 52   Robert Van Dusen, Hamilton, Canada: The Literary Ambitions and Achievements of Alexander von Humboldt. 68 p. 1971.

Nr. 53   Thomas Feitknecht, Bern: Die sozialistische Heimat. Zum Selbstverständnis neuerer DDR-Romane. 104 S. 1971.

Nr. 54   Margareta Gasser-Mühlheim, Bern: Soziale Aufwertungstendenzen in der deutschen Gegenwartssprache. 112 S. 1972.

Nr. 55   Wolfgang von Wangenheim, Genf: Das Basler Fragment einer mitteldeutsch-niederdeutschen Liederhandschrift und sein Spruchdichter-Repertoire (Kelin, Fegfeuer). 326 S. 1972.

Nr. 56   Volker Zimmermann, Heidelberg: Die Entwicklung des Judeneids. Untersuchungen und Texte zur rechtlichen und sozialen Stellung der Juden im Mittelalter. 286 S. 1973.

Nr. 57   Jürg Kielholz, Zürich: Wilhelm Heinrich Wackenroder, Schriften über die Musik. Musik- und literaturgeschichtlicher Ursprung und Bedeutung in der romantischen Literatur. 136 S. 1972.

Nr. 58   Hermann Gelhaus, unter Mitarbeit von Roger Frey und Otfried Heyne, Basel: Vorstudien zu einer kontrastiven Beschreibung der schweizerdeutschen Schriftsprache der Gegenwart. Die Rektion der Präpositionen trotz, während und wegen. 124 S. 1972.

Nr. 59   Silvia Weimar-Kluser, Zürich: Die höfische Dichtung Georg Rudolf Weckherlins. 128 S. 1971.

Nr. 60   Eva Acquistapace, Bochum: Person und Weltdeutung. Zur Form des Essayistischen im Blick auf das literarische Selbstverständnis Rudolf Kassners. 164 S. 1971.

Nr. 61   Dieter Helle, Klaus-Peter Klein, Rainer Kuttert, Christel Schulte, Uwe-Dieter Steppuhn, Heinz-Burkhard Strüwer, Bochum: Zur Entstehung des Neuhochdeutschen. Sprachgeographische und -soziologische Ansätze. Herausgegeben von Ilpo Tapani Piirainen. 156 S. 1972.

Nr. 62   Wilhelm Resenhöfft, Kiel: Goethes Rätseldichtung im "Faust" (mit Hexenküche und Hexen-Einmal-Eins) in soziologischer Deutung. 178 S. 1972.

Nr. 63   Christoph Mühlemann, Zürich: Fischarts "Geschichtklitterung" als manieristisches Kunstwerk. Verwirrtes Muster einer verwirrten Zeit. 176 S. 1972.

Nr. 64   Marcel Roger, Syracuse: "Hiermit erhebte sich ein abscheulich Gelächter" – Untersuchungen zur Komik in den Romanen von Johann Beer. 132 S. 1973.

Nr. 65   Charles Whitney Carpenter, Bloomsburg/Pennsylvania: The Systematic Exploitation of the Verbal Calque in German. 132 p. 1973.

Nr. 66   Artur Rümmler, Mainz: Die Entwicklung der Metaphorik in der Lyrik Karl Krolows (1942–1962). Die Beziehung zu deutschen, französischen und spanischen Lyrikern. 285 S. 1972.

Nr. 67   Wilhelm Resenhöfft, Kiel: Nietzsches Zarathustra-Wahn. Deutung und Dokumentation zur Apokalypse des Übermenschen. 140 S. 1972.

Nr. 68   Keith L. Roos, Provo, Utah/USA: The Devil in 16th Century German Literature: The Teufelsbücher. 132 p. 1972.

Nr. 69   Herbert Schütz, Toronto: Hermann Kasack: The Role of the Critical Intellect in the Creative Writer's Work. 146 p. 1972.

Nr. 70   Wolfgang Mieder, East Lansing, Michigan/USA: Das Sprichwort im Werke Jeremias Gotthelfs. Eine volkskundlich-literarische Untersuchung. 168 S. 1972.

Nr. 71   Jürg Aggeler, Zürich: Der Weg von Kleists Alkmene. 164 S. 1972.

Nr. 72    Hermann Gelhaus, Basel: Synchronie und Diachronie. Zwei Vorträge über Probleme der nebensatzeinleitenden Konjunktionen und der Consecutio temporum. 52 S. 1972.

Nr. 73    Xaver Kronig, Freiburg: Ludwig Hohl. Seine Erzählprosa mit einer Einführung in das Gesamtwerk. 188 S. 1972.

Nr. 74    Christine Merian, Basel: Die Gestalt des Künstlers im Werk Conrad Ferdinand Meyers. 116 S. 1973.

Nr. 75    Veronica C. Richel, Vermont: Luise Gottsched. A Reconsideration. 120 p. 1973.

Nr. 76    Theo Bungarten, Bonn: Sprache und Sprachanalyse des Deutschen. Vier Beiträge zur Methode und Theorie. 152 S. 1973.

Nr. 77    Wolfgang Köhler, Frankfurt a.M.: Hugo von Hofmannsthal und "Tausendundeine Nacht". Untersuchungen zur Rezeption im epischen und essayistischen Werk. Mit einem einleitenden Überblick über den Einfluss von "Tausendundeine Nacht" auf die deutsche Literatur. 180 S. 1972.

Nr. 78    Thomas Alfred Gehring, Zürich: Johanne Charlotte Unzer-Ziegler 1725–1782. 148 S. 1973.

Nr. 79    Alfons-M. Bischoff, Freiburg: Elias Canetti – Stationen zum Werk. 184 S. 1973.

Nr. 80    Roger C. Norton, Endicott: Hermann Hesse's Futuristic Idealism / *The Glass Bead Game* and its Predecessors. 150 p. 1973.

Nr. 81    Günther Schneider, Freiburg: Untersuchungen zum dramatischen Werk Robert Musils. 292 S. 1973.

Nr. 82    Gerhard Dünnhaupt, Washington: Diederich von dem Werder / Versuch einer Neuwertung seiner Hauptwerke. 148 S. 1973.

Nr. 83    Walter Gorgé, Bern: Auftreten und Richtung des Dekadenzmotivs im Werk Georg Trakls. 322 S. 1973.

Nr. 84    Alan B. Galt, Washington: Sound and Sense in the Poetry of Theodor Storm: A phonological-statistical study. 138 p. 1973.

Nr. 85    Heinz Eugen Greter, Freiburg: Fontanes Poetik. 202 S. 1973.

Nr. 86    Marcel Roland Mattes, Zürich: Das Bild des Menschen im Werk Otto F. Walters. 130 S. 1973.

Nr. 87    Michael Hadley, Victoria: The German Novel in 1790. A Descriptive Account and Critical Bibliography. 306 p. 1973.

Nr. 88    Gerhard Doerfer, Göttingen: Anatomie der Syntax. 257 S. 1973.

Nr. 89    Marie Theres Nölle, Zürich: Formen der Darstellung in Hartmanns 'Iwein'. 76 S. 1974.

Nr. 90    Bärbel Becker-Cantarino, Austin. Aloys Blumauer and the Literature of Austrian Enlightenment. 132 p. 1973.

Nr. 91    Ursula Gray, Heidelberg: Das Bild des Kindes im Spiegel der altdeutschen Dichtung. 382 S. 1974.

Nr. 92    Jules Grand, Basel: Projektionen in Alfred Döblins Roman "Hamlet oder Die lange Nacht nimmt ein Ende". 204 S. 1974.

Nr. 93    Gisela Wünsche Hale, Detroit: Carossas Weg zur Schulderlösung. 84 S. 1974.

Nr. 94    Markus Diebold, Zürich: Das Sagelied/Die aktuelle deutsche Heldendichtung der Nachvölkerwanderungszeit. 120 S. 1974.

Nr. 95    Claus Süssenberger, Frankfurt/M.: Rousseau im Urteil der deutschen Publizistik bis zum Ende der Französischen Revolution. Ein Beitrag zur Rezeptionsgeschichte. 354 S. 1974.

Nr. 96    Victor Sialm-Bossard, Freiburg: Sprachliche Untersuchungen zu den Chemiefaser-Namen. Ein Beitrag zur Beschreibung der deutschen Gegenwartssprache. 348 S. 1975.

Nr. 97    John McCarthy, Philadelphia: Fantasy and Reality – An Epistemological Approach to Wieland. 166 p. 1974.

Nr. 98   Alfred Fritsche, Bern: Dekadenz im Werk Arthur Schnitzlers. 280 S. 1974.

Nr. 99   Hans-Joachim Lange, Bonn: Aemulatio Veterum sive de optimo genere dicendi. Die Entstehung des Barockstils im XVI. Jahrhundert durch eine Geschmacksverschiebung in Richtung der Stile des manieristischen Typs. 286 S. 1974.

Nr. 100  Annemarie Schnetzler-Suter, Zürich: Max Frisch – Dramaturgische Fragen. 152 S. 1974.

Nr. 101  Roy L. Ackermann, Louisville: "Bildung" and "Verbildung" in the Prose Fiction Works of Otto Julius Bierbaum. 95 p. 1974.

Nr. 102  Siegmar Tyroff, Salzburg: Namen bei Thomas Mann in den Erzählungen und den Romanen Buddenbrooks, Königliche Hoheit, Der Zauberberg.

Nr. 103  Sara Ann Malsch-Wilkinson, Amherst: The Image of Martin Luther in the Writings of Novalis and Friedrich Schlegel. 162 p. 1974.

Nr. 104  Heinz B. Heller, Kassel: Untersuchungen zur Theorie und Praxis des dialektischen Theaters. Brecht und Adamov. 213 S. 1975.

Nr. 105  Volker Wendland, Tübingen: Ostergelächter und Ostermärchen.

Nr. 106  Gernot Heide, Hamburg: Graphematisch-phonomatische Untersuchungen zum Altjiddischen. Der Vokalismus. 450 S. 1974.

Nr. 107  Manfred Misch, Berlin: APIS EST ANIMAL – APIS EST ECCLESIA. Ein Beitrag zum Verhältnis von Naturkunde und Theologie in spätantiker und mittelalterlicher Literatur. 220 S. 1974.

Nr. 108  Karl-Bernhard Bödeker, Würzburg: Frau und Familie im erzählerischen Werk Franz Kafkas. 180 S. 1974.

Nr. 109  Roland Richter, Tucson/USA: Georg Rollenhagens Froschmeuseler: Ein rhetorisches Meisterstück. 140 S. 1975.

Nr. 110  Jakob Spälti, Zürich: Interpretationen zu Heinrich von Kleists Verhältnis zur Sprache. 106 S. 1975.

Nr. 111  Markus Werner, Zürich: Bilder des Endgültigen – Entwürfe des Möglichen. Zum Werk Max Frischs. 90 S. 1975.

Nr. 112  Peter Bürgel, Frankfurt/M.: Die Briefe des frühen Gutzkow 1830–48. Pathographie einer Epoche. 428 S. 1975.

Nr. 113  Johann Christoph Bürgel, Bern: Goethe und Hafis. 80 S. 1975.

Nr. 114  Peter Ochsenbein, Basel: Studien zum Anticlaudianus des Alanus ab Insulis. 204 S. 1975.

Nr. 115  Elke Ukena, Berlin: Die deutschen Mirakelspiele des Spätmittelalters. Studien und Texte. 2 Bände. 973 S. 1975.

Nr. 116  Eberhard Frey, Waltham/USA: Stil und Leser. Theoretische und praktische Ansätze zur wissenschaftlichen Stilanalyse. 150 S. 1975.

Nr. 117  Wilhelm Johannes Schwarz, Québec, Canada: War and the Mind of Germany. 90 p. 1975.

Nr. 118  Ingeborg Springer-Strand, Cincinnati/USA: Barockroman und Erbauungsliteratur. Studien zum Herkulesroman von Andreas Heinrich Bucholtz.

Nr. 119  Gabriel Imboden, Bern: Gottfried Kellers Ästhetik auf der Grundlage der Entwicklung seiner Naturvorstellung. Studie zur Begründung der geometrischen Struktur in der Novellistik. 187 S. 1975.

Nr. 120  Georg Alexander Nowak, Wheeling/USA: Das Bild des Lehrers bei den Brüdern Mann. 148 S. 1975.

Nr. 121  Colin H. Good, Norwich/GB: Die deutsche Sprache und die kommunistische Ideologie. 225 S. 1975.

Nr. 122  Daniel Schönbächler, Zürich: Erfahrung der Ambivalenz. Das Bild der Wirklichkeit im Werk Josef Vital Kopps. 162 S. 1975.

Nr. 123  Irmela Schneider, Frankfurt/M.: Kritische Rezeption. "Die Blechtrommel" als Modell.